AŚOKA

AŚOKA

D.R. BHANDARKAR

MANOHAR
2026

Due to the academic and scholarly importance of this volume, we are reprinting/republishing it from the original source without any modifications or changes. Therefore, some misprints and errors may occur.

First published 1925
Reprinted 2026
First eBook edition 2025

ISBN 978-93-6080-185-4 (hardbound)
ISBN 978-93-6080-190-8 (eBook)

Published by
Ajay Kumar Jain *for*
Manohar Publishers & Distributors
4753/23 Ansari Road, Daryaganj
New Delhi 110 002

Printed and bound in India

To

The Shared Memory

of

Sir Asutosh Mookerjee, Sarasvati

PREFACE TO THE FIRST EDITION

So much has been said and written about Aśoka that some of those who happen to see this book may perhaps wonder what new things yet remain to be said about that Indian monarch. It must not, however, be forgotten that the records which Aśoka has left in stone are a literature by themselves, and it will take many years yet for scholars to understand clearly all that he has said. A student of Indian Epigraphy need not be told that there are passages, by no means few, in these records, which are yet far from clear, and every day new and better interpretations are being proposed by scholars. There is, again, such a thing as piecing together the various items of information supplied by these inscriptions so as to give a vivid picture of the royal missionary. I am afraid, this work of piecing together is by no means complete yet and must continue for some more years to come. There is no section of Indian epigraphy, so interesting and I should say so edifying, as that represented by the records of Aśoka. And as I have participated not only in the work of interpretation but also of collation and unification of his records, I hope I stand in no need of explanation for bringing out this book which sets forth my views about the Buddhist monarch.

My study of the inscriptions of Aśoka began as early as 1898. There were before me translations and notes on these records not only by Prinsep, Wilson and Burnouf, but also by Prof. Kern, M. Senart and Prof. Bühler. I devoured the contents of all these books. But none interested and benefited me so much as "The Inscriptions of Piyadasi" by M. Senart which had appeared in English garb in the pages of the *Indian Antiquary*. I could at once detect in the French savant not only an epigraphist, not only a scholar of Sanskrit, Pali, and Prakrit, but also a historian whose aim was to piece together the different scraps of information supplied by the epigraphic and literary records so as to form one connected whole. Chapter IV of his book thus sets forth not only the chronological position of Aśoka or his inscriptions but also the extent of his empire, his administrative system, his independent neighbours, his connection with the Grecian world, his conversion to Buddhism, the nature of his Dhaṃma and so forth. It was M. Senart who first showed the way how to construct the history of Aśoka from a systematic study of his records.

It will thus be seen that it is nearly a quarter of a century that I have studied the inscriptions of Aśoka with a view to find out what light they throw upon the history of India. What real advance, if any, I have made can be best told by scholars and historians. Eager to know, however, how far my attempt has become successful, I sent to the French savant the page proofs of the first seven chapters of this book as soon as they were available, with a request that he might tell me unreservedly what he thought about it. But for a long time no reply was received, and just as this Preface was being put in type, the long expected letter came to hand. "You will forgive a delay," it begins, "due to the somewhat shaken health of an old colleague. I would have wished to thank you sooner for having sent me the good pages of your Aśoka. You kindly remembered the studies which I devoted years ago to the religious king and his precious inscriptions. How should I not be impressed by the testimony of such an enlightened judge as yourself? You can imagine that these researches of my youth are always dear and present to me. Your book leads me back to them once more. I am very grateful to it. I am grateful because it has brought me a brilliant example of the ingenious and passionate skill with which Modern India endeavours to reconstruct its past."

M. Senart is frank enough in this letter to tell me in what points he differs from me. All of these represent minor differences of opinion except one. This last is in regard to the responsibility I have thrown upon Aśoka (which in his opinion the monarch little deserved) for his change of foreign policy, "for the mansuetude of his pitiful reflections," which rendered easy the success of foreign invasions, Greek and Turanian, that infested the country after him. "It is quite possible," says he, "that Buddhist Pacifism in the long run has tended to weaken certain people, whom it did not render more gentle except by making them less fit for action[1]. . . . I prefer to recognise in him simply a spirit of idealism and of

[1] In justice to myself I may state that this idea also had occurred to me, but I had to discard it as the interval was too short between Aśoka and the Greek invasion after him. Aśoka is taken to have died about 236 B.C.; and the death of Euthydemus, the first Bactrian

deep religiousness which we know well, for it animates the whole remote past of India and it has perhaps stood for a greater spiritual honour than it has deprived India of realisations of external successes, for which it is doubtful whether its genius ever had made it fit." When, therefore, he has favoured me with such frank criticism, one feels inclined to believe, as a sincere expression of his opinion the following that he has given to show what he thinks about my work as a whole: "It was not so much your purpose to establish a critical history of Aśoka by a general examination of the traditions more or less in keeping with the epigraph information, but you intended to show by analysis of the inscriptions what information hitherto unexpected they can yield to a sagacious and penetrating explorer. You have been prepared for this task as nobody else by your extended familiarity with literature. It is a marvel of a singular power that by throwing light on the monuments with the help of books you have enlivened your picture."

There are many questions connected with Aśoka, which are still of a complicated nature. One of these is the effect of his foreign policy on India.

Greek invader, is supposed to have taken place about 190 B.C. There is thus scarcely an interval of fifty years, during which, again, Antiochus the Great is reported to have carried out a successful expedition into the north-west frontiers of the Mauryan Empire (*The Cambridge History of India*, pp. 442 and 444). The Greek invasion thus came off almost immediately on the death of Aśoka. Does it give enough time to Buddhism to spread and make the people, above all, the Magadha army, as gentle and pacific as to render them unfit for militarism—just that army which Alexander's men were afraid to encounter and which repulsed the forces of Seleucus after him?

How far or whether Buddhism had spread over Western Asia through his missionary efforts is another such question. It is not possible to reach any final conclusions unless they are freely and fearlessly discussed. I have expressed my views for what they are worth, and it would now be interesting to see what different views are expressed by scholars and, above all, historians. The more diverse these opinions are, the more are the view-points from which the questions may be looked at and the greater is consequently the likelihood of arriving at early solutions of them.

It is true that history, and not epigraphy, is the main object of this book. Nevertheless, time has not yet come, and perhaps may never come, so far as Ancient India is concerned, to separate History altogether from Epigraphy, Archaeology, or Sanskrit and Sanskritic literature. There are still some words and passages in the Aśokan inscriptions which require to be properly interpreted or understood though Dr. F. W. Thomas has done a yeoman's service in this field recently. I have, therefore, by no means neglected this source of our ancient history. That I have given sufficient attention to it may be seen especially from Chapter VIII which contains translation and annotation of Aśoka's Edicts.

I have said that the Aśokan inscriptions have engrossed my attention for a quarter of a century. But I cannot help adding that much progress in this respect I was able to achieve only when I came to Calcutta to occupy the Chair of the Carmichael Professor of Ancient Indian History and Culture and breathe in the pure intellectual atmosphere of the Calcutta University, which is the unique creation of the monumental genius of the late Sir Asutosh Mookerjee, Sarasvati, whose guidance, I should say, providence, in the development of the post graduate studies is now for ever lost to us. He was especially interested in the publication of this book. And it will for ever be a matter of extreme regret to me that he was not spared just a little longer to see this book which has now come to light after being two years in the press.

The Index of this volume is the work of Mr. Girindramohan Sarkar, who was my pupil some time ago. As regards proof-reading and general help, I am highly indebted to Mr. Jitendranath Banerjea and Mr. Nanigopal Majumdar, Lecturers of the Calcutta University, and also to my pupils Mr. Rakhohari Chatterji and Mr. Chintaharan Chakravarty. And I cannot better conclude this Preface than with the words with which the French savant concludes his letter: "To this famous ancestor you, true to the beautiful traditions, familiar to solid knowledge, wanted to render the tribute of your researches and the inspirations of your patriotism. If I cannot, in order to do you full justice, enter into a detail which would compel me to exceed the limits of a letter, allow me at least to address to you my hearty felicitations. I like to place this fertile union of sympathy and work—in which the piety of India and the respectful curiosity of the West should join—under the patronage of our hero in common."

D. R. B.

PREFACE TO THE SECOND EDITION

It was in September, 1928, that I was informed by the Assistant Registrar, Calcutta University, that the stock of my book on Aśoka was practically sold out and that a second edition of the same would be necessary. But to prepare the book for the second edition was a matter of no small difficulty. In the first place, I had to give my careful attention to what the critics of my book had said. Secondly, there were many scholars who had written about Aśoka or his inscriptions after the first edition was out. Thirdly, in the course of my studies and preparation for lectures to the Post-graduate classes, I had myself lighted upon many new interpretations and angles of vision. All these scattered rays had to be brought to a focus. This meant time. Besides, I myself was keeping anything but good health for a long time. This is the reason why so much delay has occurred in bringing out this second edition.

As regards the reviews that were published of my book, some contained nothing but praise about me and my work. I will make no mention of them. There was however one review which was a condemnation of my book, from beginning to end. It was published in JBORS., Vol. XI, pp. 402-3, and I request scholars to read it at least once, and find out who wrote it and how it came to be published. That will surely conduce much, if not to their scholarship, certainly to their psychological research. That will also convince them that Patna has been correctly identified with Pāṭaliputra where Kauṭilya and Rākshasa as well as Aśoka and Chandragupta-Vikramāditya flourished.

Of the remaining reviews of my book there are only four which are worth noticing. The first of these was written by Dr. Jarl Charpentier in JRAS., 1925, p. 805 ff.; the second by Dr. S. K. Belvalkar in ABORI., Vol. VII, p. 166 ff.; the third by the late Mr. S. M. Edwardes in IA., 1926, p. 239; and the fourth by Truman Michelson in JAOS., Vol. 46, p. 256 ff. Edwardes winds up his review with the following remarks: "I have said enough to indicate that Dr. Bhandarkar's book is full of information as one would expect from a scholar of his reputation, and contains suggestions of much interest to all who ponder over the problems of India's past history." Dr. Belvalkar expresses his opinion of the book in this manner: "It is perhaps hardly necessary to enumerate in this fashion all the points in which Prof. D. R. Bhandarkar has made a distinctive contribution to Aśokan scholarship. A careful perusal of the book enables one to visualise the pious Monarch and his manifold religious and administrative activities to a much better extent than had been hitherto possible with the Aśokan literature already in the field. To build up out of the dead lithic records of this mighty emperor such a living, speaking likeness of Aśoka the man with all his frailties and his noble aspirations is certainly an achievement of which any scholar might well be proud." The first of these critics was an Editor of the *Indian Antiquary* and was the scholar who revised and practically overhauled the Fourth Edition of the 'Early History of India' by V. A. Smith. The second is Professor of Sanskrit in the Deccan College, Poona, and Editor of the 'Government Oriental Series,' Bombay. Both the critics have spared no pains to point out the blemishes of my 'Aśoka,' and when they express the opinion they have done of the book as a whole, it cannot be doubted that their opinion is impartial and carries some weight. See now what Dr. Charpentier has said about it. "Professor Bhandarkar's name," says he, "holds a high rank within the scholarly world of India, and the present writer therefore feels it somewhat painful to admit that his latest book is a heavy disillusion...The author has on the whole very little new to add to the results of his predecessors, and where he tries to supply us with some hitherto undiscovered facts we generally feel inclined to disagree with him." This is in direct contradiction with what the late Mr. Edwardes and Dr. Belvalkar had thought, namely, that my book was full of information and suggestions and enabled one to visualise Aśoka much better. Not long after, appeared the review of the American scholar, Dr. Truman Michelson, containing a more detailed criticism of my book. Edwardes was a historian, not an epigraphist or a philologist; Prof. Belvalkar is both a Sanskritist and an historian though not an epigraphist. Naturally therefore their criticism was concerned with the history portion of my book. Dr. Michelson on the other hand is a philologist, not an historian. His criticism was therefore directed against that part of my book, which comprised the Notes and Translation of Aśoka Inscriptions. And if anybody peruses this review carefully, he cannot but be convinced that Dr. Michelson has not at all feared to differ from me in many places. And yet in this review he says: "In this connection it may be observed that the notes on the translations are ordinarily very full, so that even the publication of the new edition of C. I. I. will not render this part of Bhandarkar's work superfluous; and it cannot be denied that occasionally he has made real contributions in the interpretation (*e.g.*, the sense of *samāja*)." Evidently by 'C. I. I.' he means the *Inscriptions of Asoka* brought out by E. Hultzsch. This itself will show what the American scholar thinks of my book. The contributions made by Michelson to Aśokan studies are too well-known to require any mention and are equalled only by those of Senart, Bühler and Lüders. When therefore the above remarks of Dr. Michelson acquired publicity, everybody in India began to wonder how that Professor of Upsala saw no good whatever in my book.

The truth of the matter is that Dr. Charpentier does not seem to have read any part of the book other than Chapter VII, which deals with "Asoka's place in History." Whatever real criticism is contained in his review is centred upon this chapter and this chapter only. If any proof is needed, it is furnished by the following remark that he makes: 'But to Professor Bhandarkar it seems perfectly clear that Buddhism has deeply influenced Christianity—unfortunately, he does not tell us on which points, except by the somewhat vague expression "brotherhood of man"...' Prof. Charpentier is evidently referring to p. 223 of the first edition [1] of my book. Unfortunately he exposes his own ignorance. For pages 162-5 of the last edition do set forth on *which* points, according to Max Müller and myself, Buddhism has influenced Christianity. If he had at all read these pages, he would never have indulged in the sweeping remark that I have not told on *which* points Buddhism has influenced Christianity. It seems that he never read Chapter V of my book which treats of "Aśoka as a Missionary," and, in fact, there is no indication whatever that he read any chapter or part of it except Chapter VII about which alone he has passed what may be called criticism. As a matter of fact, if he had gone carefully over the other chapters as was done by the late Mr. Edwardes, Dr. Belvalkar and Dr. Michelson who certainly were not inferior to him in scholarship and the last of whom is decidedly superior to him in Aśokan studies, I am sure he would have practically come to the same opinion that was expressed by these scholars. His aspersion therefore that my book is 'a heavy disillusion' is itself a fantasm of *kha-pushpa* held up by an Avidyā-putra. How can better work be expected of a critic who had a large number of books to review for the Journal of the Royal Asiatic Society, and who could not be expected to have any leisure to go through every one of these carefully? But what is most inexplicable is why he, if he is a real Sarasvatīputra, should indulge in aspersions

[1] See p. 167 ff. of this edition.

against a book which he had not the time or patience to wade through. And it is really painful how critical scholarship sinks in his case into a pious brief for Christianity or for 'our religion' as he calls it. He has thereby made a laughing-stock of himself. See, for example the criticism levelled against him in *Ind. Hist. Quart.*, 1925, p. 784, by N. C. G., who, I am told, is a Quaker himself.

So far, however, as Dr. Charpentier's criticism of Chapter VII of the book is concerned, I welcome it wholeheartedly. It is not possible to see eye to eye with him in most respects. Nevertheless, it is a criticism made after reading the chapter at least once and does not indulge in mere sweeping comments.

My reply to the various points of his criticism will be found in the same chapter of this edition. But I cannot help thinking that he has rushed even to this criticism without carefully and patiently reading what I have stated while comparing Aśoka with Marcus Aurelius, Alexander and Caesar. He has forgotten what I have remarked on p. 229 (first Ed.)[1] where I say that these monarchs "were probably greater warriors and greater administrators than Aśoka even" but were not great men as compared to him if we have to judge by "the standard whether they rendered the world any way happier and better." In fact, this is the point on which I have expatiated on the pages following it. Curiously enough this is just the conclusion with

[1] See p. 244 of this edition,

which Prof. Charpentier's review ends, for he says that "Aśoka ... was as a man, by far better than both Alexander and Caesar; it is just as obvious that as a ruler of man he cannot stand up for comparison with either of them." One wonders why so many pages of the *Jour. R. As. Soc.* were wasted on a point where we substantially agreed.

The case is however different in regard to the review of Dr. Truman Michelson. As I have already remarked, he deals principally with the Translation and Notes portion of my book. It is true that he is merciless in his criticism of my views, but who can deny that he has read very carefully what he is criticising? It is also true that sometimes his philological enthusiasm overshoots the mark. Nevertheless, it cannot be gainsaid that almost the whole of his criticism is sound and thought-provoking. And he has set it forth in such a detailed and thorough fashion that one feels that it is Bühler or Senart that is speaking through him. I confess I have profited much by his comments, and if the second part of this edition has made any advance over the first the credit is chiefly due to this American savant. If a copy of this book is again sent to the Royal Asiatic Society for review, as I hope it will, and if Prof. Charpentier is again entrusted with the work, he will do well to tread in the worthy footsteps of Dr. Michelson and furnish us with constructive criticism which will enable me to improve this book still further if it ever runs into a third edition. He need not use the polite language of the late S. M. Edwardes, but let his criticism be based upon a careful perusal of the whole book. His language may be rugged and brusque like that of Aśoka, but let there be sincerity and thoroughness behind it as it was behind the work of that Buddhist Emperor.[1]

Some of my friends were urging me to recast this work of mine into a convenient text book for the students who offered Aśoka as a subject of study for M.A. This however means that the University students even in the M.A. stage should not develop the library-going habit and should not form first-hand acquaintance with the works of Senart, Bühler, Michelson and Lüders, or for the matter of that, with any such learned periodicals as the IA., JRAS., and so forth. In other words, it means that even the M.A. students should not learn how to cook their own dish, but should be served with ready-made food just as the undergraduate students are, when they are supplied with the annotated editions of Scott's 'Lady of the Lake' or Burke's 'French Revolution.' If my work had been similarly converted into a cram book of Aśoka's Inscriptoins, that would have doubtless brought more money to the Calcutta University but also perhaps cast a slur upon the noble edifice of Post-graduate studies which was built up by the transcendent genius of the late Sir Asutosh Mookerjee and to which I have the honour to belong. No University Professor who has a capacity or passion for research work, ought ever to stoop to

1 Unfortunately, however, Prof. Charpentier is of the opinion that "it is exceedingly questionable whether Aśoka has laid open to us ir has concealed the greater part of his own personality" (see below, p. 262 ff.).

bring out a copiously annotated edition of any book or text he is lecturing upon to the M.A. students.

The Index of this book is the work of Messrs. Dinesh Chandra Sircar and Charu Chandra Dasgupta, who up till recently were my pupils. The first of these again gave me occasional help in the laborious task of proof-reading. In conclusion, I am exceedingly thankful to Mr. J. C. Chakravorti, the Assistant Registrar, and Mr. A. C. Ghatak, Press Superintendent, without whose help and forbearance it would not have been possible for me to bring out this edition in the present state of my health.

D. R. B.

LIST OF ABBREVIATIONS

ABORI—Annals of the Bhandarkar Oriental Research Institute.

AR-ASEC—Annual Report, Archaeological Survey, Eastern Circle.

ASI-AR—Archaeological Survey of India—Annual Report.

ASSI—Archaeological Survey of Southern India.

ASWI—Archaeological Survey of Western India.

CASR—Cunningham's Archaeological Survey Reports.

CCII—Cunningham—Corpus Inscriptionum Indicarum.

CHI—Cambridge History of India.

CII—Corpus Inscriptionum Indicarum.

CL—Carmichael Lectures.

DDMV—Dr. Modi Memorial Volume

EB—Encyclopaedia Britannica.

EC—Epigraphia Carnatica.

EHI—Early History of India.

EI—Epigraphia Indica.

ERE—Encyclopaedia of Religion and Ethics.

EZ—Epigraphia Zeylanica.

GI—Gupta Inscriptions.

HAS—Hyderabad Archaeological Survey.

HASL—History of Ancient Sanskrit Literature.

HIEA—History of Indian and Eastern Architecture.

IA—Indian Antiquary.

IHQ—Indian Historical Quarterly.

JAOS—Journal of the American Oriental Society.

JASB—Journal of the Asiatic Society of Bengal.

Jat—Jatakas.

JBBRAS—Journal of the Bombay Branch of the Royal Asiatic Society.

JBORS—Journal of the Bihar Orissa Research Society.

JDL—Journal of the Department of Letters (Calcutta University).

JPTS—Journal of the Pali Text Society.

JRAS (NS)—Journal of the Royal Asiatic Society (New Series).

MASB—Memoirs of the Asiatic Society of Bengal.

MASI—Memoirs of the Archaeological Survey of India.

MCNL—Manindra Chandra Nandy Lectures, 1925, (Delivered by D. R. Bhandarkar before the Benares Hindu University).

PR-ASNWFP—Progress Report of the Archaeological Survey of North-Western Frontier Province.

PR-ASWI—Progress Report of the Archaeological Survey of Western India.

PTFOC—Proceedings and Transactions of the First Oriental Conference, Poona.

PTS—Pali Text Society.

SAMSJV—Sir Asutosh Mookerjee Silver Jubilee Volume.

SBB—Sacred Books of the Buddhists.

SBE—Sacred Books of the East.

SSPS—Sanskrit Sahitya Parishat Series, Calcutta.

VOJ—Vienna Oriental Journal.

VP—Vishṇu-Purāṇa.

ZDMG—Zeitschrift der Deutschen Morgenlandischen Gesellschaft.

CONTENTS

D—1849 B.

CHAPTER I

Aśoka and His Early Life

There is hardly any educated person in India who has not heard of Aśoka and his stone inscriptions. Aśoka, he knows, was a prince of the Maurya dynasty and grandson of Chandragupta, the Sandrakottos of the Greek writers and, for some time, a contemporary of Alexander the Great. The inscriptions of this monarch, he again knows, have been found all over India. But he may not be aware of their contents and may not know what account they furnish of that Maurya king. There are, no doubt, some Buddhist works, which set forth his life and work, but their trustworthy character has been rightly called in question. They mention many stories, which represent him to have been Kālāśoka or Black Aśoka before, and Dharmāśoka or Pious Aśoka after, his conversion to Buddhism. As the one aim of these works is to eulogize Buddhism by showing how it transformed Aśoka the Ogre into Aśoka the Pious, a suspicion naturally crosses our mind in regard to the correctness of their account. Such is not, however, the case with his epigraphic monuments, which being contemporary records and engraved by his orders, are of undoubted veracity. Nay, as we go through them, we feel as if his voice is still speaking to us and confiding what is passing in the innermost recesses of his mind. The story of Aśoka that is being narrated is based almost entirely on these monuments, and we can be pretty certain that our account is not fiction, but history.

What kind of records has Aśoka left behind him? Are they sufficiently numerous and important in details? A full account of his epigraphic monuments at this stage is sure to be irksome, and has, therefore, been reserved for a future chapter. But some idea of the nature of these records must be given here, in order that the contents of this and the following chapters may be properly understood. These records, as we know, are all engraved on stone. They have been inscribed either on rocks or pillars or in caves. His rock inscriptions, again, are of two kinds: namely, (1) the Fourteen Rock Edicts, and (2) the Minor Rock Edicts. The former are called Fourteen Rock Edicts, because they together form a set of fourteen different inscriptions following a serial order, and have been found in seven different localities,—all on the confines of India, at any rate, of his empire. The Minor Rock Edicts consist of two different records. They are inscribed together only in the three copies found in Mysore; in all other places, which are no less than four, Edict I only has been engraved. Aśoka's Pillar Inscriptions also may be distinguished into two classes: (1) Seven Pillar Edicts, and (2) the Minor Pillar Inscriptions. The former of these constitute a group, but the latter are four different epigraphs. The Cave Inscriptions of Aśoka are, of course, those engraved in caves in the Barābar Hills of Bihār. These are altogether no less than thirty-three different inscriptions, and, as we shall see in the course of our narrative, they throw light on a number of points connected with Aśoka, his administration, his religious faith, his missionary operations, and so on. A careful comparison of these records is just what is needed in order to obtain the maximum that is knowable and historically acceptable about Aśoka.

Those who have studied these epigraphs know full well that they profess to have emanated from a king who calls himself Piyadasi, that is, Priyadarsin. When they were first being deciphered, now about three-quarters of a century ago, by James Prinsep to whom must go the credit of having unravelled the mystery of the Brāhmī *lipi*, he was very much puzzled by the name Priyadarśin. He did not know who this Priyadarśin was, to what dynasty he belonged, and in what age he flourished. Soon thereafter, however, Turnour, who belonged to the Ceylon Civil Service, and was himself a great Pāli scholar, identified Priyadarśin with Aśoka. He pointed out that the Sinhalese chronicle, the Dīpavaṁsa, gave Piyadassi or Piyadassana as but another name of Aśoka, grandson of Chandragupta, the founder of the Maurya dynasty. This identification, it is true, has not since then been called in question, but it was definitively demonstrated only nine years ago when the sixth copy of Minor Rock Edict I was discovered at Maski in the Raichur District, Nizam's Dominions. For this inscription mentions the name of Aśoka clearly and in the very first line. It is not therefore possible now to doubt that Priyadarśin and Aśoka are one and the same person, and that the author of these inscriptions is really the grandson of Chandragupta, who founded the Maurya empire.

We thus see that the author of our epigraphic records was known both as Aśoka and Priyadarśin. It was customary for the kings of ancient India to have more than one name, of which one was their proper individual name and the others epithets or *birudas* as they are called. One of these two appellations must have been the personal name of the king, and the other his epithet. And it appears that Priyadarśin was his epithet, for we know that Aśoka's grandfather, Chandragupta, has also been styled Piyadassana like him in one of the Ceylonese chronicles. Nobody can doubt that Chandragupta was his individual name. Priyadarśana or Priyadarśin must, therefore, be taken to be the *biruda* or secondary name. We know that this epithet in the case of Aśoka was Priyadarśin, and it is quite possible that Priyadarśin and not Priyadarśana was the *biruda* of his grandfather also. For in later times we find grandfather and grandson belonging to the same dynasty adopting the same *biruda*. The Ceylonese chronicles style Aśoka not only Priyadarśin but also Priyadarśana, taking the two words apparently in one and the same sense. And as from Aśoka's inscriptions we find that he was known really as Priyadarśin and not Priyadarśana, it is natural to presume that his grandfather also was Priyadarśin, not Priyadarśana. It is curious that this records call him Aśoka, only once, and Priyadarśin, in all other places. But instances are not wanting of kings being known almost invariably by their epithets. Thus the son of Govinda III of the Rāshṭrakūṭa family of Mānyakheṭa is known to us from all the documents so far only by his epithet, Amoghavarsha. We are somewhat better in regard to the author of our inscriptions. For one record at least gives his personal name, Aśoka.

In most of his inscriptions Aśoka styles himself Devānāṁ-priya Priyadarśī Rājā. This is the fullest appellation of the king. But sometimes the formula is abbreviated by the omission of one or two of these components. Thus we find Aśoka designated also Devānāṁ-priya Priyadarśī, Priyadarśī Rājā, Devānāṁ-priya Rājā, or even Devānāṁ-priya merely.[1] The second component of Aśoka's full name is Priyadarśin, which we have just considered. Literally it means 'one of amiable look,' and may be freely rendered by 'one who is of gracious mien.' When and why he adopted this epithet we do not know, but certain it is that he used it almost as his personal name. We had better not, therefore, translate it, but leave it as it is. It is worthy of note that although Aśoka was a supreme ruler, he designates himself simply Rājā. The

[1] JRAS., 1908, 482-3.

grandiloquent titles, Mahārāja and Rājādhirāja, employed singly or conjointly, had not come into use in Aśoka's time. What is more worthy of note is that he calls himself Devānāṁ-priya, and one can well understand how the modern students of Grammar (*vyākaraṇa*) may feel inclined to laugh at it. For do not Bhaṭṭoji Dīkshita, author of the *Siddhāntakaumudī*, and Hemachandra, author of the *Abhidhānachintāmaṇi*, tell us that Devānāṁ-priya means 'a fool' or 'dunce'? They are, therefore, apt to wonder what Aśoka means by calling himself Devānāṁ-priya. But it is to be noted that though this word has now a derogatory sense, it was not so originally, and especially in the time of Aśoka. Patañjali, we know, associates this word with *bhavat*, *dīrghāyus*, *and āyushmat*. This shows that like these honorific terms Devānāṁ-priya was employed as an auspicious mode of address or characterisation. Now, if we turn to Rock Edict VIII of Aśoka, we shall find that for *Devānāṁ-priya* of some versions we have *rājāno* of others. This means that Devānāṁ-priya was an auspicious mode of address used with reference to kings. And, as a matter of fact, the Dīpavaṁsa[1] applies the appellation Devānāṁ-priya to Tissa, the ruler of Ceylon and contemporary of Aśoka, and often employs it alone to denote that king. Epigraphic records also point to the same conclusion. Thus in the Nāgārjunī Hill Cave inscriptions,[2] the term

[1] XI. 14, 19, 20, 25, &c.
[2] IA., XX, 364 & ff.

Devānāṁ-priya is used to designate a king called Daśaratha, who has been taken to be the grandson of Aśoka. Similarly, an epigraph from Ceylon gives this epithet among other kings to Vaṅkanāsika-Tissa, Gajabāhuka-gāminī, and Mahallaka-Nāga.[1] Devānāṁ-priya was thus an auspicious mode of address or honorific characterisation, before the Christian era, confined to the kings only, and was so used probably to indicate the belief that the rulers were under the protection of the gods (*devas*).[2] The term had therefore be better translated by "dear unto the gods," or "beloved of the gods." Aśoka's full royal style was thus "king Priyadarśin, beloved of the gods."

Many of Aśoka's inscriptions commence with the formula: *Devānaṁ-priyo Piyadasī Rājā evaṁ āha*, "thus saith king Priyadarśin, beloved of the gods." This has been rightly compared by Senart[3] with the phrase with which the proclamations of the Achaemenides, from Darius to Artaxerxes Ochus, begin. One such instance is *thātiy Dārayavaush kshayāthiya*, "thus saith the king Darius." In both cases the form of address commences with a phrase in the third person, and what is further worth noticing is that this phrase is immediately followed by the use of the first person. Of course, nobody can now maintain that this formula was imitated by Aśoka directly from Persia, for, as a matter of

1 EZ., I. 60 f.
2 MCNL., 142.3 & 145.
3 IA., XX. 255-6.

fact, we know that this was one of the protocols of the royal chancery noticed by Kauṭilya in his Arthaśāstra and consequently prevalent before the time of Aśoka.[1] But nothing precludes us from holding with the French savant that the Indians adopted the Persian protocol and that this adoption was due to the Achaemenian conquest and administration of north-west India.

Wherever in his records Aśoka gives any dates, he counts the years from the time of his coronation. This has led scholars to believe the Sinhalese tradition that Aśoka was crowned four years after his accession to the throne. But this tradition also tells us that after the death of his father, Aśoka seized the throne by massacring ninety-nine of his brothers, and spared only one, the youngest, namely Tishya. This story is, however, refuted by his inscriptions which speak, not of one brother, but of several, living and staying again not only in Pāṭaliputra, his capital, but also in various towns of his empire. And if this is found to be a fiction, it is not intelligible why we should hold fast to that part of the tradition which places his coronation four years after his seizing the throne. In fact, it is not at all clear how his dating certain events of his reign from his coronation is evidence of there having been an interval between his coronation and accession to the throne. Again, in the Nāgārjunī Hill caves

[1] *Ibid.*, XLVII. 51-2.

there are at least three inscriptions which are dated immediately after the coronation of Daśaratha, grandson of Aśoka. Are we to suppose here also that because these records, in their dating, refer to Daśaratha's coronation, this event did not coincide with his coming to the throne and that some period must have elapsed between them? There is therefore no good reason to think that any long interval such as that of four years elapsed between Aśoka's coronation and his assumption of the reins of government.

It appears that Aśoka was in the habit of celebrating the anniversary of his coronation by the release of prisoners. This is inferrible from what he says at the end of Pillar Edict V. "By me, who am consecrated twenty-six years up till now," says he there, "twenty-five jail deliveries have been effected just in that period." As prisoners were released twenty-five times in the space of twenty-six years, it means that the twenty-sixth year of his reign had not elapsed but was running on when the Pillar Edict was promulgated. It thus seems that the dates which he specifies for the incidents of his life are current regnal years, and not expired, as has been taken by scholars.

Kauṭilya in his Arthaśāstra lays down that the king shall prohibit castration and destruction of animal fœtus on certain days. Among these he includes the days of the *nakshatra* of the king and the country. In Pillar Edict V, Aśoka speaks of castration and branding of animals, and specifies on what days he has prohibited them.

Curiously enough, most of these days agree with those mentioned by Kauṭilya.[1] And what is noteworthy is that here he specifies only two *nakshatra* days, namely, Tishya and Punarvasu. One of these is most probably the *nakshatra* of the king and the other of the country. And the question must arise: which *nakshatra* is of the king and which of the country? It is worthy of note that the Tishya *nakshatra* has been mentioned also in the two separate Edicts of Dhauli and Jaugaḍā. These edicts, we know, were intended by Aśoka solely for the exhortation and guidance of the officials of the newly conquered province of Kaliṅga, and he issues the order that they shall be recited every Tishya day for their benefit. Evidently, of the two *nakshatras* greater importance has thus been assigned to Tishya than to Punarvasu. This may be seen also from the fact that although in the usual list of the *nakshatras* Tishya comes after Punarvasu, it is placed prior to the latter, not once but twice, in Pillar Edict V. It is difficult to avoid the conclusion that as so much importance has been given to Tishya, that must be the *nakshatra* of the king. If this inference is correct, Punarvasu becomes the *nakshatra* of the country, by which, we suppose, we have to understand the country of Magadha.

The edicts of Aśoka are concerned with his Dhaṁma and the means he adopted to disseminate it. They naturally, therefore, throw a flood of

[1] *Arthaśāstra*, p. 407.

light on his life and career after he became a Buddhist. But let us here try and see what little these records tell us about his earlier life, both in his private and public capacity. We have already seen that he had several brothers and sisters living till the thirteenth year of his reign, and that they were residing not only in Pātaliputra but also in the mofussil towns. Of course, Aśoka had his *avarodhana* or closed female apartments. How many queens he actually had we do not know. But he had at least two, for there is reference to his second queen in one of his inscriptions. And the very fact that she had been designated Second Queen shows that the relative rank of the queens had in his day been fixed. The name of this Second Queen was Kāruvākī, and his son from her was Tīvara. The object of the inscription is to ensure for this queen the merit of any donation she might be pleased to make. In Pillar Edict VII Aśoka speaks of his having commissioned some of his officers to induce the members of his royal household to make gifts and to see to their proper organisation. It is interesting to note what members of his family he mentions in this connection. Of course, he first speaks of himself and his queens. But immediately after his queens he makes reference to his *avarodhana* and tells us that its inmates were living not only at his capital but also in the provinces. Anybody who reads the passage carefully cannot but think that his queens were not the only members of his *avarodhana*. Who could then be the other members? They cannot be the wives of his male relatives, for they cannot with propriety be called his *avarodhana*. Were they his left-handed wives? His *avarodhana* would thus comprise not only the queens but also other *Purdah* ladies of lower status. This no doubt reminds us of the Sinhalese tradition that when Aśoka during his father's life-time was viceroy at Ujjain, he formed connection with a lady of the Seṭṭhi caste, who resided at Vedisagiri, modern Besnagar near Bhilsā, and continued to reside there even when Aśoka seized the throne and his children by her accompanied him to his capital. This legend clearly confirms the inference deducible from the Pillar Edict that Aśoka had women other than queens and that his *avarodhana* was not all in Pāṭaliputra, but that some of its members stayed in the mofussil. In the same Pillar Edict and in continuation of the same subject, namely, the distribution of the charities of the Royal Household, Aśoka speaks of his own sons and other *devīkumāras*. The sons of Aśoka are thus distinguished from the latter. Who could the 'other *devīkumāras*' be? Most probably, Aśoka is here referring to the sons not of his own Devīs or queens but the queens of his father and consequently to his non-co-uterine brothers. Again, how many sons Aśoka had we do not know. But he must have had at least four sons. In ancient times it was customary for a king to appoint his sons, as far as possible, as viceroys of the outlying provinces. And four such princes we find mentioned in his epigraphic records, as being in charge of the four viceroyalties of Takshaśilā, Ujjayinī, Suvarṇagiri, and Tosalī. To what modern provinces these viceroyalties corresponded we will see in the next chapter. But what we have here to notice is that Aśoka had at least four sons. To sum up, Aśoka had a very large family. He had several brothers and sisters staying not only at Pāṭaliputra but also outside in the empire. Some of them were certainly his co-uterine brothers, but there were also some, sprung, no doubt, from his father, but by different mothers. Aśoka had also his *avarodhana* or closed female apartments, not only in his capital but also in the provinces. They were occupied not only by his queens but also other women with whom he had connection. He had at least two queens, one of whom was named Kāruvākī, and at least four sons. But whether Tīvara, son of Kāruvākī, was one of them it is not possible to determine.

We know very little of Aśoka's private life. His records shed very little light upon it. There is, however, one passage in Rock Edict VI which is interesting. This edict describes how often and at what different places he dispatched the business of his people. Here he tells us that he has arranged to dispose of it at all places and at all times so that no king prior to him ever did it. Naturally, therefore, he specifies the places where he formerly whiled away his time but where now he attends to their affairs. "This therefore, I have done," says he, "namely that at all hours and in all places—whether I am eating or I am in the closed female apartments, in the inner chamber (*garbhāgāra*), with the stud (*vraja*), on horse-back (*vinīta*) or in pleasure orchards, the Reporters may report people's business to me.'' Evidently, therefore, when Aśoka had no business to dispose of and, of course, was not asleep, he was to be found at his capital either regaling in the dining hall, engaged with the inmates of his harem, chatting in his retiring cabin, or inspecting the royal stud, enjoying a horse ride, or beguiling his time in the orchards. What special tastes and fascinations he had developed or evinced in these matters we do not know, but we do know what articles of food gratified his palate. Even when he was rigorously carrying out his programme of stopping the slaughter and injury to living beings, he made certain reservations in regard to his royal table. "But even now when this document of Dhaṁma was written,'' says he in Rock Edict I, "only three animals were killed for curry, namely, two peacocks and only one deer, but even that deer not regularly. Even these three animals will not afterwards be killed.'' Aśoka here admits that although he has stopped the butchering of all other animals, he has allowed the killing of peacocks and deer to serve him with meat. Evidently, he was fond of the flesh of these animals. And as he says that the animal that was regularly butchered for his table was not the deer, but the peacock, it appears that he was inordinately fond of the pea-fowl. In this connection what Buddhaghosha says in his commentary on the *Saṁyutta-*

nikāya is worth noting. "To the people of the frontier provinces, *gaṇḍu-ppādas* are delicious, but they are abominable to those of the Middle Country. To the latter the flesh of a pea-fowl is delicious. It is, however, abominable to others."[1] It is, therefore, no wonder if Aśoka, who was a native of the Middle Country, could not for a long time give up the eating of the pea-fowl flesh. We need not, however, harbour any doubt as to his having ultimately eschewed it, as promised in his edict, and thus turned a staunch vegeterian.

In another inscription Aśoka gives us another glimpse into his private life. Rock Edict VIII informs us that for a long time past kings were in the habit of going out on *vihāra-yātrās* or pleasure tours, where they enjoyed chase and other similar diversions but that he has replaced these by *Dhaṁma-yātrās* or tours for Dhaṁma since the tenth year of his reign when he visited Saṁbodhi, that is, the place where Buddha obtained enlightenment. What Aśoka gives us here to understand is that until the tenth year he, like all other kings, used to go out on pleasure excursions, where he indulged in manifold diversions, the most pre-eminent of which, however, was hunting. We cannot have any clear idea of this *vihāra-yātrā*, as Aśoka gives us no details and as no account of it is also forthcoming from any work of literature. The Āśramavāsika Parvan of the Mahābhārata, no

[1] *Sāratthappakāsinī* of Buddhaghosha, published by Thera Vimalabuddhi in Ceylon in 1898, p. 105 ff.

doubt, contains a reference to the *vihāra-yātrās* which Yudhishṭhira organised for enabling Dhṛitarāshṭra to forget the grief caused by the death of his hundred sons. But only one verse it gives to show what items constituted these *vihāra-yātrās.* "There," we are told, "the *āralikas* (jugglers?), chefs, and singers of *rāgas* and *shāḍavas* waited on king Dhṛitarāshṭra as in town." [1] The programme of Dhṛitarāshṭra's pleasure trip thus consisted of music, dainties, and conjurer's tricks. There is no mention of chase here, because an old and blind man like Dhṛitarāshṭra cannot be expected to take delight in chase. But as Aśoka speaks of chase only and tells us nothing of the other diversions when he adverts to *vihāra-yātrās*, it appears that hunting formed the most important feature of a pleasure excursion in his time. In fact, hunting was so much indulged in by the kings that it was considered by some ancient writers on Hindu polity to be a vice which they were exhorted to avoid. Piśuna, for instance, condemns chase, because danger from robbers, enemies, wild animals, forest conflagration, fear of stumbling, inability to distinguish the cardinal points, and so on, are the evils associated with it.[2] Kauṭilya, on the other hand, strongly recommends it, because according to him exercise, reduction of fat and bile, skill in aiming at stationary and moving bodies, knowledge of the minds of animals and of their ever-changing movements when they are enraged are the good points of chase. Some of these good points, we

[1] I. 18.
[2] *Kauṭilīya Arthaśāstra*, p. 327.

know, are mentioned by Kālidāsa when Dushyanta in Act II of the Śākuntala is made to praise hunt ing. The poet also portrays a good scene of hunting in the first two acts of the drama. The description of royal hunting has also been preserved for us by Megasthenes, who was almost contemporaneous with Aśoka. One purpose for which the king leaves his palace, says he, "is to go to the chase, for which he departs in bacchanalian fashion. Crowds of women surround him, and outside of this circle spearmen are ranged. The road is marked off with ropes, and it is death, for man and woman alike, to pass within the ropes. Men with drums and gongs lead the procession. The king hunts in the enclosures and shoots arrows from a platform. At his side stand two or three armed women. If he hunts in the open grounds, he shoots from the back of an elephant. Of the women, some are in chariots, some on horses, and some even on elephants, and they are equipped with weapons of every kind, as if they were going on a campaign."[1] The Śākuntala also, no doubt, describes the chase of Dushyanta as something like an expedition and even represents the king as being attended by Yavana women with bows in hand. One can very well imagine Aśoka as revelling in such sports in the earlier part of his life like his contemporary or previous kings, but the sanctity of animal life which made an indelible impression on his mind afterwards made his soul recoil from such enjoyment, and he gave up all sports and diversions which

[1] IA., VI. 132.

involved any kind of brutality or butchery to life.

We shall now try to see what Aśoka was like in his capacity as king before he became a staunch missionary of Buddhism. Very little about him even in this capacity is known, and what little we know is from Rock Edict I. From it it appears that like all other kings Aśoka was in the habit of feasting and amusing his subjects,—probably a diplomatic move to keep his people pleased and satisfied. One mode of public entertainment that he practised was the celebration of the *samāja*. The *samāja* was of two kinds. In one the people were treated to dainty dishes in which meat played the most important part. In the other they were treated to dancing, music, wrestling, and other performances. The former was obviously a convivial meleé. The latter was intended for the amusement of the people, and in this sense the *samāja* was synonymous with *raṅga* or *prekshāgāra*, that is, the amphitheatre, and sometimes denoted 'the concourse of the people,' assembled there. All the instances of the *samāja* described in the Brahmanical and the Buddhist literature show that they were intended to feast the palate or the eye and the ear of the people. There can be no doubt that the ancient kings of India were in the habit of holding *samājas*. Thus in the celebrated Hāthigumphā inscription we are told that Khāravela, king of Kaliṅga, amused his capital-town by celebrating *utsavas* and *samājas*. Precisely the same thing is reported in a Nāsik cave inscription to have been done by Gautamīputra Śātakarṇi, a king of the Dekkan. And, in fact, Kauṭilya himself lays down that a king " shall imitate (the people's) attachment to the *samāja*, *utsava*, and *vihāṛa* of their country or divinity." [1] Both the kinds of the *samājas* seem to have been celebrated by Aśoka. But when he began to preach Dhaṁma, he naturally tabooed those where animals were slain to serve meat, as we may infer from Rock Edict I. As there was nothing in the other *samājas* for him to object to, he retained them, but slightly changed the character of the exhibition of the public spectacles. He no doubt must have provided such spectacles as would not only cause amusement to his subjects but also generate, develop and disseminate Dhaṁma amongst them. What these scenes were we will see in a future chapter.

Reasons of state may also have dictated his taking another step in the same direction. In the same record Aśoka tells us that the slaughter of hundreds of thousands of animals was daily going on in the royal kitchen before the edict was promulgated. The case is precisely like that narrated in the Vanaparvan of the Mahābhārata where we are informed that two thousand cattle and two thousand kine were slain every day in the kitchen of a king called Rantideva and that by doling out meat to his people he attained to incomparable fame. And, in fact, the practice of daily doling out food to hundreds of people is still found in the Native States of India. Like Rantideva, Aśoka must have

[1] *Arthaśāstra*, p. 407.

been in the habit of distributing meat among his subjects, and that his object in doing so must have been precisely the same, namely, that of making himself popular. But he put a stop to this terrible animal carnage, the moment his conscience was aroused and he commenced teaching Dhamma.

We thus see what Aśoka was as a private individual and also as a king till he embraced Buddhism. The picture we have here is certainly not as lucid and full as we may desire, but we do obtain something which is reliable and not based on mere legend. We see what sort of family he had, what individual tastes and likings he possessed, and in what pursuits he engaged himself when he was free from his routine work as a ruler. We also know what titles he assumed as king, how he began his royal career, and what measures he adopted to entertain his people and enlist their attachment. He also regularly celebrated the anniversary of his coronation by releasing prisoners from jails. This is all we know of him as ruler before he became a Buddhist, that is, till after the eighth year of his reign when he subjugated Kaliṅga. Whether the earlier part of his reign was uneventful or whether he had made similar conquests or not we do not know. The earliest event of his reign that we find referred to in inscriptions is his conquest of Kaliṅga, which roughly corresponds to the tract of land on the coast of the Bay of Bengal between the Vaitaraṇī and Languliya rivers. He vividly describes the horrors and miseries of this war. "1,50,000," says he, "were carried away (as captives); 1,00,000 were slain, and many times as many died." These are the figures for Kaliṅga only, and do not include the casualties in the king's army. We thus have to note that even in such a small province as Kaliṅga, as many as 1,00,000 were killed on the battle-field, many times as many died as the result of burning and sacking, and, what is more, no less than 1,50,000 were seized as slaves. Surely, these are appalling figures for a tiny district like Kaliṅga, and indicate the extreme horrors of a war even in that ancient period when the weapons of destruction were not so diabolical and deadly as now. Soon after this war Aśoka was converted to Buddhism and began to preach Dhaṁma. And the remembrance of this war struck him with extreme and genuine remorse. When an unconquered province, says he, is being conquered slaughter, death and captivity must occur. This is regrettable enough. But what is still more regrettable is that among those who die, are slaughtered or are taken captive, there must be many who are devoted to Dhaṁma and that such contingencies to these men, again, must spell disaster and affliction to their friends, acquaintances, and relatives, who, though they themselves are safe, yet feel undiminished affection for them. "This is the lot of all men and is considered regrettable by the Beloved of the gods." The language is instinct with personal feeling, and the rocks still echo across the ages the wail of a penitent soul. There can be no doubt that this was genuine remorse. For, when the edict was proclaimed, he had already commenced in that country a zealous protection, longing and teaching of Dhamma. When a territory is newly subjugated and is in an unsettled condition, the officers who are charged with proper administration and maintenance of peace there are apt to transgress the bounds of justice and mercy. Such transgressions did actually occur on the part of his officers, and we know from one of his inscriptions how severely he chastised them and what steps he took to prevent such excesses in the future. Nay, the inhuman and iniquitous nature of the war so much haunted his mind that he was even ashamed of engraving this edict in the Kaliṅga country. There are two places in Kaliṅga where his Rock Edicts have been inscribed. But while the edict which describes his conquest of this province has been incised along with other Rock Edicts at all other places this alone has been omitted from the copies coming from Kaliṅga. Surely, remorse and sense of shame cannot further go.

We may be pretty certain that Aśoka made no further conquests. But why he conquered and annexed Kaliṅga to his empire, which was already very extensive, is not quite clear. It seems, however, that Kaliṅga was a thorn in the body politic of his dominions. From Rock Edict XIII we know that the provinces of Andhra and Pārimda were included in his kingdom. Of these Andhra denoted roughly the country comprising the Kistnā and Godāvarī Districts. As the capital of his Empire was Pāṭaliputra, it is not unreasonable to suppose that it included the greater portion of modern Bengal. And this receives confirmation if my suggestion is true that Pārimda was somewhere on the eastern outskirts of the Mauryan Empire, possibly in Bengal. Kaliṅga was thus a sort of wedge driven into the body politic and might at any time conspire with the foreign Choḍa kingdoms which were to the south. For the safety and consolidation of his state it was thus absolutely necessary to conquer Kaliṅga and make his empire one compact mass ; and this he did.

A year after his conquest of Kaliṅga he became a Buddhist. For one year he was lukewarm, but thereafter he became very strenuous in his exertions for the Dhaṁma, and the idea of becoming a Chakravartī Dhārmika Dharmarāja haunted his mind. What this appellation exactly is we will see in Chapter VII, but, suffice it to say here, that it denoted the supreme ruler of the earth, not through conquest, but through righteousness. This ideal stimulated him to promote the temporal and spiritual good not only of his people but of the subjects of his independent neighbours, and not only of the human race, but of the whole animate world. We will take note of all his manifold activities, but shall first see what he did for his people as a ruler. For this, however, it is necessary to find out what the extent of his empire was. Both these points we will tackle in the next chapter.

CHAPTER II

Aśoka's Empire and Administration

In this chapter we shall attempt to trace, as far as possible, the limits of Aśoka's dominions and find out over what area his sway extended. And thereafter we shall also discuss how he ruled his kingdom and what innovations, if any, he introduced in the administration. In both these enquiries we shall allow ourselves to be guided mainly by his inscriptions. In regard to the first of these queries, that is, the one relating to the extent of his empire, we have both internal and external evidence to take into account. The external evidence is, of course, that furnished by the find-spots of his monuments. Of these his Rock Edicts are of the highest importance to us, as we find that they have been discovered on the borders of his empire. We will begin with the east, and move westwards. Two copies of his Fourteen Rock Edicts were found in the south-eastern part of his dominions, near the Bay of Bengal. Of these the northern copy is engraved near a village called Dhauli, about seven miles to the south of Bhuvaneśvar, in the Purī District of Oṛissā. The southern copy is inscribed in the town of Jaugaḍā, in the Ganjām District of the Madras Presidency. Both these versions of the Rock Edicts were put up in the newly conquered province of Kaliṅga, which, being in the south-easternmost part of India, must have also formed the south-easternmost boundary of Aśoka's empire. Turning northwards we find that a third copy of Aśoka's Rock Edicts has been engraved on a rock near the village of Kālsī, in the Dehrā Dun District. Proceeding westwards, we have to notice two versions, both found in the North-West Frontier Province. One of these has been inscribed at Manserā in the Hazārā District, fifteen miles to the north of Abbottābād, and the other at Shāhbāzgaṛhī in the Peshāwar District, forty miles to the north-east of Peshāwar. Proceeding from here to the south and coming to the western coast, we have to note one copy that was discovered near Junāgarh in Kāṭhiāwār, and another at Sopārā, in the Ṭhāṇā District, about thirty-seven miles north of Bombay. Only recently, one set of these Fourteen Rock Edicts has been found on the southern confines of Aśoka's dominions, namely, at Yerraguḍi in the Kurnool District of the Madras Presidency. Side by side with these has been traced Minor Rock Edicts I & II also. In 1903, however, thanks to Mr. Lewis Rice, three copies of the Minor Rock Edicts were discovered in three localities, all close to one another, in the Chitaldrug District of Northern Mysore. All these Rock Edicts, the find-spots of which have just been indicated, give us a fairly accurate idea of the wide expanse of Aśoka's territory.

We shall now see what the actual contents of these records have to tell us as regards the extent of his empire. In other words, let us see how far the internal evidence corresponds to the external.

In no less than two edicts (RE. II and XIII) Aśoka speaks of contemporary kings. Of these, those who were ruling outside India were, the Yavana king Aṃtiyoka, and, on the farther side, the four kings, Turumāya, Aṃtekina, Maga, and Alikasuṃdara. To the south of Aśoka's empire but in India and beyond were the Choḍas, Pāṃḍiyas, Keralaputra, Sātiyaputra, and Taṃbapaṃṇī. Again, it is worthy of note that in two places (RE. V and XIII) Aśoka refers to the outlying provinces of his kingdom. They are the Yonas, Kaṃbojas, Gaṃdhāras, Rāsṭika-Petenikas, Bhoja-Petenikas, Nābhaka-Nābhapaṃtis, Aṃdhras, and Pāriṃdas. Through the misreading and misinterpretation of one phrase in Rock Edict XIII, they had all for a long time been regarded as *Hida-rājas* or the feudatory chieftains in Aśoka's dominions. But the recovery of a lost portion of the Girnār version of this Edict repudiates the interpretation. And we have to take these names as those of subject peoples, occupying some of the frontier districts of Aśoka's empire. It is highly essential to fix the boundaries of these districts first, and afterwards, of the territories held by his independent neighbours in India.

Who were the Yonas? They were, of course the Greeks. But where are they to be placed? It deserves to be noticed here that they formed part of Aśoka's empire and had therefore nothing to do with the dominions of his Greek neighbours. This Yona province, which was subject to Aśoka's power, has not yet been satisfactorily identified.

But I have elsewhere shown[1] that there was a Greek colony of the pre-Alexandrian period on the north-west confines of India and that it was established between the rivers Kophen and the Indus. I still cling to that view. In Rock Edict XIII, Aśoka tells us that there is no country in his empire except that of the Yavanas, where are not found the two congregations,—the Brāhmaṇas and the Śramaṇas. This means that the Yavana province was the only country where the Hindu Aryan civilisation had not spread. How can this be possible in a neighbouring district of India except on the supposition that it was colonised by the Yavanas and had therefore the Hellenic civilization only prevalent there? Again, if the Greeks had for the first time been known to the Indians in the time of Alexander the Great, they would have been known by another name, but certainly not by 'Yavana' (Ionian), because the Greeks who accompanied Alexander were not Ionians. It was in Ionia that the commercial development of the Greeks was the earliest and greatest. In the most distant regions, the Ionian was first in the field.[2] Whether the Ionian had actually planted any colony on the north-west borders of India is doubtful. But there can be no doubt that it was on account of the enterprising spirit displayed by the Ionians that the Persians coined the word *Yauna* as a generic name for all Greeks. And the Greek colony on the north-west frontiers of India, whether it was established by Ionians or other Greeks, may,

1 CL., 1921, pp. 25 & ff.

2 EB., XII. 445; XIV. 730.

for that reason, have been designated Yauna by the Indians, the neighbours of the Persians. Yavana is, of course, the Sanskrit, and Yona the Pāli, equivalent, of Yauna. But even the form Yauna is, by no means, unknown to Sanskrit literature, and what is curious is that it is mentioned along with Kaṃboja and Gandhāra at least once in the Mahābhārata[1] exactly in the order in which they occur in Rock Edict V of Aśoka. If my view that the Yonas are to be located between the Kophen and the Indus is correct, the ancient place whose ruins are found near Shāhbāzgaṛhī, where one version of Aśoka's Rock Edicts has been found, and which is called *Po-lu-sha* by Hiuen Tsang, becomes the headquarters of the outlying province of Aśoka's dominions. And Kaṃboja will have to be placed somewhere near this Yona province. In the Mahābhārata the Kaṃbojas are mentioned side by side with the Yavanas as (north-western) peoples famous as fighters. And in the Droṇaparvan[2] their capital Rājapura, is also mentioned. If this Rājapura is the same as *Ho-lo-she-pu-lo* mentioned by Hiuen Tsang[3] and if the latter has been correctly identified by Cunningham[4] with Rajaori to the south of Kāshmīr, we can locate the Kaṃbojas with pretty certainty. It must have been the province round about Rajaori, including the

[1] XII. 207.43; attention to this was first drawn by Dr. H. C. Raychaudhuri, in his *Early History of the Vaishṇava Sect*, p. 17.

[2] 4.5; H. C. Raychaudhuri's *Political History of Ancient India* (2nd Ed.), p. 94.

[3] Beal, I. 163; Watters, I. 284.

[4] *Ancient Geography of India*, p. 129.

Hazārā District of the North-West Frontier Province and with perhaps the headquarters of a subdivision not far from Mānserā (Mansahra) where was discovered one copy of Aśoka's Fourteen Rock Edicts. The province of Kaṃboja would thus be contiguous with that of Yona, and both with Gandhāra whose capital in Aśoka's time was Takshaśilā, the seat of a Kumāra viceroyalty, as we shall see further on.

Senart seems to be right in supposing that the outlying provinces have been enumerated in Rock Edict XIII in a definite order. The Nābhapaṃtis of Nābhaka must therefore be looked for somewhere between the Yona-Kaṃbojas on the one hand and the Bhoja-Petenikas on the other, that is, somewhere between the North-West Frontier Province and the Western Coast of India. This weakens Bühler's suggestion [1] that the Nābhaka of Aśoka's edict must be Nābhikapura placed by the Brahmavaivartapurāṇa in the Uttarakuru or some trans-Himalayan region. And no other scholar has yet come forward with a new identification. Turning southwards, Rock Edict XIII mentions the Bhoja-Petenikas, corresponding to which Rock Edict V has Rāsṭika-Petenikas. Scholars have so long separated Petenika from both Rāsṭika and Bhoja, and regarded it as standing for a separate people, namely, those of Paiṭhaṇ. But this is a mistake. Of course, it is possible to derive such a word as Peṭhanika from Pratishṭhāna (Paiṭhaṇ). But the

[1] *Beiträge zur Erklärung der Aśoka-Inschriften*, p. 118.

word can mean "the inhabitants of Paiṭhaṇ", and not denote a tribal people like the Kaṃbojas or Gandhāras. Besides, Peṭhanika has a lingual *th*, and Petenika a dental *t*. The latter cannot thus stand for the former, as was first correctly pointed out by Bühler. Again, as I have elsewhere shown [1], the phrase *Raṭṭhika Pettanika* occurs in the Aṅguttara-Nikāya as denoting a ruler of the second rank, next only to the king, and the word *pettanika* has been explained by the commentator to mean 'one who enjoys hereditary property'. Rāsṭika-Petenika of Aśoka's inscription must therefore be taken as one word and as denoting 'one who is the hereditary ruler of a *rāshṭra* or province,' though originally his ancestor may have been a governor appointed by some king. There must have been many such rulers in ancient India. But those of Rock Edict V have to be located somewhere on the Western Coast, as they have been there classed under Aparāntas, 'peoples of the western coast'. They have naturally therefore to be identified with the Mahāraṭhis of Western India Cave Inscriptions, who seem to have been petty rulers, holding the Poona and neighbouring districts

[1] IA., 1919, p. 80. Prof. Barua criticises my view, by relying upon the passage of the *Aṅg. N.*, p. 300 (*Old Brahmi Inscriptions in the Udayagiri and Khaṇḍagiri Caves*, pp. xix and xx). If this passage had been the only one of its kind, it would have been possible as much to separate *pettanikassa* from *Raṭṭhikassa* as to take them together as I have done. But he knows that there are two more passages of this kind on pp. 76 and 78 where *pettanikassa* has been conjoined to *raṭṭhikassa* so as to form one designation which is thereafter distinguished from a number of others which occur also in the first passage. When such is the case, the logical course would be to take them together as one title on p. 300 also.

of Mahārāshṭra. These inscriptions speak also of Mahābhojas as minor rulers and as holding the present Ṭhāṇā and Kolābā districts of the Bombay Presidency. They must, of course, be the same as the Bhoja-Petenikas of Rock Edict XIII and were another people of Aparānta impliedly referred to in Rock Edict V. The capital of Aparānta in ancient times was Śurpāraka, the modern Sopārā, in the Ṭhāṇā district, were also one version of the Fourteen Rock Edicts was brought to light.

The region between the Kistnā and the Godāvarī Districts is at present known as the Andhra-deśa, that is, the country of the Andhras. But whether this was the original home of the people is not clear. One Buddhist Jātaka adverts to a place called Andhapura or the Capital town of the Andhras and locates it on the Telavāhā river. I have elsewhere thrown out the suggestion that Telavāhā is either the modern Tel or Telingiri, both flowing not far from each other and on the common confines of Madras and the Central Provinces.[1] This rather shows that the country of Andhra must have at the early period comprised Jaipur and part of Vizāgapaṭam District of the Madras Presidency along with some conterminous districts of the Central Provinces. And it is not at all impossible that it may have also included the southern parts of the Nizam's Dominions, and the Kistnā and Godāvarī Districts corresponding to modern Telingānā. Megasthenes gives us the

[1] IA., 1918, p. 71.

numerical and military strength of the Andhra territory when it was yet unsubdued by the Maurya Dynasty. This account gives us the impression, as V. A. Smith [1] rightly says, that the Andhra nation "was reputed to possess a military force second only to that at the command of the king of Prasii, Chandragupta Maurya". This clearly shows that the Andhra country must have been a pretty extensive territory and must have spread as far south as the mouth of the Kistnā. This also agrees, as we shall see further on, with the most likely northern limits of the independent Choḷa kingdom. We have now to localise the Pārimdas. The name Pārimda is quite clear in the Girnār version, and the readings P[ā]lade[sh]u and *Palideshu* of Kālsī and Shāhbāzgaṛhī, can easily conform to Pārimda. What is noteworthy about this name is that the first letter, *pā*, is clear in the Girnār and Kālsī copies and that nowhere it is *pu*. Secondly, there can be no doubt as to there being *ra* in the second letter. This *ra* may, owing to the Magadha court language became *la*, but this is clear that if the second letter of the original is really *la*, it cannot become *ra* in any version. The name tacked on to Aṃdhra cannot thus be Pulimda as has been taken by Prof. Mookerji, but must be taken to be Pārimda, whatever that may be. Now, as this Pārimda has been associated with Aṃdhra, it must denote some tribe or people situated in the south-east or eastern part of Aśoka's empire.

[1] EHI., p. 217.

And if a conjecture may be hazarded, the Pārimdas may be identified with the Bārendras, the people of V(B)arendrī, which formed the north and north-east parts of modern Bengal. It is true that the name Bārendra has not so far been traced to any period earlier than that of the Senas. But the same is also the case with Rāḍha which corresponds to West Bengal and which has not been traced prior to the 11th century A.D. Nevertheless that has not prevented scholars from identifying Rāḍha with Lāḍha of the Āyāraṅga-Sutta, or even Lāḷa, the home of Mahendra, who, according to the Sinhalese Chronicles, colonised Ceylon. Similarly, there can be nothing against the Bārendras of the 11th century being identified with the Pārimdas of the Aśoka inscriptions. While some of the outlying peoples and tribes on the north-west, west and south of his dominions have been specified, it seems strange that not a single people on the eastern frontier should have been named. But this omission is forthwith removed if we hold that the Pārimdas are the same as the Vārendras or, at any rate, were situated on the eastern outskirts of the Mauryan dominions.

The peculiarity with Aśoka's Rock Edicts is that they are found on or about the frontiers of his dominions. There is, however, this difference, namely, whereas the Fourteen Rock Edicts seem to be engraved in the capitals of the outlying provinces, the Minor Rock Edicts are mostly found at places which separate his territory from those of his independent or semi-independent neighbours. That Dhauli and Jaugaḍā, where the south-easternmost copies of the Fourteen Rock Edicts have been discovered, represent Tosalī, the capital of an outlying province, and Samāpā, the headquarters of its sub-division, is known to us beyond all doubt. A third version of these edicts has been found at Junāgaḍh, the ancient Girinagara, the capital of Surāshṭra, which, as we know from the inscription of the Kshatrapa ruler, Rudradāman, continued to be so till the middle of the second century A.D. A fourth copy, we have seen, was brought to light at Sopārā near Bombay, which we know was the principal town of Aparānta. When no less than four of these versions are at places which are known to be the capital towns of ancient provinces, it is not unreasonable to suppose that the remaining four copies also must have been engraved at the headquarters of frontier districts. Of these Shāhbāzgarhī, for the reasons stated above, seems to be the chief town of the Yona province. And we need not be surprised if Kālsī, Mansērā, and Yerraguḍi are in the near future found to be the headquarters of similar outlying districts of his dominions. The case is somewhat different in regard to the find-spots of the Minor Rock Edicts, most of which have been found in the midst of dense jungles with no ancient remains close by. There are only two exceptions here, namely, Bairāṭ and Maski. The former is known to be Virāṭapura, the capital of Virāṭa, king of Matsyadeśa. The latter has been called Piriya-Māsaṅgi in the Chālukyan records of the place. In all other places it appears that these inscriptions were put up almost on boundary lines which demarcated the kingdom of Aśoka from those of the independent or quasi-independent states. In Minor Rock Edict I, Aśoka expatiates on the paramount necessity of strenuous endeavour if the spiritual elevation of the people is to be accomplished and tells us that he was able to achieve a great deal even within a short space of time. And he causes this important fact to be notified with a two-fold object in view, in order first that all his officials, whether of the higher or the lower grade, may endeavour for the spiritual weal of the subjects, and secondly, that the Antas or rulers of the bordering states may also know of this, probably because they also may induce their officials to put forth effort with a similar object in view. In order that Aśoka's officials might exert themselves assiduously in this direction, it was not necessary for Aśoka to inscribe these edicts. Like all his behests he must have communicated this order also to them through the proper channel. The Minor Rock Edicts thus appear to have been engraved for the information of his independent neighbours either in the heart of their capital towns or on the frontiers common to their and Aśoka's dominions. This point will clear itself up as we proceed to consider who these Antas or kings of the bordering realms were.

It has been stated above that Rock Edicts II and XIII enumerate the Antas with whom he was on terms of independence and equality.[1] They fall into two groups, according as they had their dominions in or outside India. The rulers constituting the first group, as we have seen above, are the Choḍas, Pāṃḍiyas, Keralaputra, Sātiyaputra, and Taṃbapaṃṇī. In the first place, it is worthy of note that while Choḍas and Pāṃḍiyas are mentioned in the plural, Sātiyaputra and Keralaputra are in the singular. The very fact that each one of the latter is spoken of in the singular also shows that Aśoka is here referring not to the peoples but to their rulers. When, therefore, he is referring to individual rulers and also speaks of the Choḍas and Pāṃḍiyas in the plural,

[1] Over and above the Antas or the people of the independent bordering dominions, Prof. Mookerji acknowledges the existence of a class of peoples called the Aparāntas (*Aśoka*, pp. 166-7, ns. 2 and 4) who were 'lying outside his "conquered country" (*vijita*) or direct dominion [Rock Edict XIII]' and who were thus 'like protected peoples.' These peoples are "the Yavanas (Greeks), the Kaṃbojas, the Nābhapantis of Nābhaka, the Bhojas and Pitinikas, the Andhras and Pulindas" (*ibid.*, p. 21). This is somewhat confusing. Because, in the first place, RE. XIII, on which he relies, includes them in *idha rājavisayamhi*, which he admits to be the antithesis to the Antas. The word *rāja-visaya* clearly shows that they formed part of the royal empire. Secondly, it is not clear why they have been all called Aparāntas by him. He takes the word Aparānta to denote 'the definite geographical region called *Aparānta*' such as has been mentioned in the Purāṇas and the Kāvyamīmāṃsā (*ibid.*, pp. 140-1, n. 6). But this Aparānta cannot be taken as 'a stock word for western India' as supposed by him and cannot thus include the Kaṃbojas and the Gaṃdhāras. And even if we take it to stand for 'Western India,' how it can include the Andhras and Pulindas is inexplicable. It is impossible to take these Andhras as a people of Mahārāshṭra (*ibid.*, p. 33, n. 3) setting at naught the testimony of Megasthenes and the Purāṇas. All these countries formed the outlying provinces of Aśoka's dominions, and he mentions them to show that his Dhaṃma and humanitarian measures, so far as his empire was concerned, were spread to its extreme limits.

the only reasonable inference is that in Aśoka's time there were more than one Choḍa and one Pāṃḍiya king. The territories of three of these four have been identified on the data supplied by Ptolemy and the author of the Periplus. But it has not yet been noticed that the former speaks not of one but two Choḍa kingdoms. The first is represented by "Orthoura, the royal city of the Sornagas," comprised in Soretai.[1] The word Sor in Sornagas and Soretai can easily be recognised to be the Tamil Soṛa or Choṛa. And the name Sornagas clearly shows that the prince whose capital was Orthoura was of the Nāga tribe, but was called Sor (Choṛa), because he was a ruler of Soretai (Choṛatrā). Orthoura has been identified by Cunningham with Uraiyūr near Trichinopoly. This was, therefore, the southern Choḍa kingdom. The clue to the location of the northern kingdom is furnished by Ptolemy's remark that between Mount Bettigo and Adeisathros are the Sorai nomads, "with Sora, the capital of Arkatos."[2] "Sora, the capital of Arkaṭos" is considered to be a mistake for "Arkatos, the capital of Sora." Caldwell identifies Arkatos with modern Ārkāḍ (Arcot). The Sorai were most probably not nomads at all, but have been so called to indicate the Aryan contempt for the aboriginal tribes just as their name, namely, Choṛa (Soṛa), was used to denote "a robber."[3] There were thus two Choḍa

[1] IA., XIII, p. 368.
[2] *Ibid.*, p. 362.
[3] CL., 1918, pp. 8-9.

kingdoms, with capitals at Orthoura (Uraiyūr) and Arkatos (Arcot). As regards the Pāṇḍyas Ptolemy speaks of them as "Pandinoi" and of "Modoura" as "the royal city of Pandion." This Modoura is, of course, the same as Madurā of the Madras Presidency. The Pāṇḍya country according to Ptolemy included Tinnevelly on the south and extended as far north as the highlands in the neighbourhood of the Coimbatore gap. It is true that Ptolemy does not speak of two Pāṇḍya kingdoms as he does of two Choḍa countries. But that does not necessarily mean that there were no two Pāṇḍya kingdoms in Aśoka's time. Even as late as the sixth century A.D., Varāhamihira speaks of Uttara-Pāṇḍyas,[1] which shows that in his time there were two—the northern and the southern—Pāṇḍya countries. The same may have been the case when Aśoka promulgated his edicts. At any rate, if it is assumed even for the moment that in his time there was only one Pāṇḍya kingdom, the tract of land represented by the Mysore State remains unaccounted for. On the other hand, if the existence of a Northern Pāṇḍya kingdom is presumed, this location can fit in splendidly. Two of the remaining southern states are Keralaputta and Sātiyaputta. The ending *putta* reminds us of its Prākṛit equivalent *ot* (=Sk. *putra*) occurring in the names of some Rajput sects such as Bhārmalots, Bhūcharots, Bālots, and so on, and corresponding to the English ending "son" in such family

[1] *Bṛihat-saṃhitā*, XVI. 10.

names as Robertson, Stevenson, and so forth.[1] It, therefore, appears that tribes of the names of Kerala (Chera) and Sātiya were originally living in North India from which they migrated to the south or established colonies which in the early period at any rate were known not as Keralas and Sātiyas but rather as Keralaputtas and Sātiyaputtas. Instances are not wanting even in modern times of provinces being called after a migrating people who are themselves known by a name derived from that of their original tribe.[2] The same thing must have happened in the case of Kerala (Chera) and Sātiya. From the Aitareya-Âraṇyaka [3] we know that the Cheras were settled not far from Magadha. These were probably the Cheros of the Mirzāpur District, U. P., and one of their movements to tho south before they were settled in Malabar is indicated by the mention of Keralas, in the *Pavana-dūta* of Dhoyika,[4] as being situated in Yayāti-nagara, which has been identified with a small town near Sonpur in the eastern part of the Central Provinces.[5] Similarly may not the original Sātiyas be the same as the Setæ placed by Megas-

[1] JAṢB., 1909, p. 168 & n. 4. *Cf.* Bhojaputta, Videhaputta and so forth o' the Pāli Jātakas.

[2] The tracts of land, Śekhāvāṭī and Bidāvāṭi, in Western Rajputāna have been named after the Śekhāvats and Bidāvats who themselves were the descendants of Śekhā and Bīdā.

[3] II. 1. I.

[4] JASB., 1905, p. 44. See also the edition which forms No. 13 of SSPS., Intro., p. 24 and Text, p. 9. The word here is Keralī, which occurs in v. 26. It cannot refer to any 'settlement of Keralī courtezans at Yayātinagara,' becauso the same word is found also in v. 16, where it cannot but signify the women of the Kerala country.

[5] EI., XI, p. 189: *Descriptive Lists of Inscriptions in the C. P. and Berar* by Rai Bahadur Hiralal, p. 95 & note.

thenes in the north [1] and mentioned in the Vishṇu-Purāṇa [2] and the Bhīshma-Parvan [3] but misspelt Satīpa or Sanīya? Where their colony in South India was planted is doubtful. Perhaps a critical examination of the data furnished for South India by Ptolemy and the author of the Periplus may afford us a clue. They speak of four countries in South India, Limyrike, Aioi, Pandioni, and Soretai. The last two, we have seen, are the Pāṇḍya and Choḍa countries respectively. Limyrike is taken to be equivalent to Damir-ike, the greater portion of which, however, was subject to Keralaputra. What about Aioi? If Andrakottos is sometimes written for Sandrakottos and Abiria for Sabiria, can Aioi be really Saioi (=Sātiya)? If this surmise is correct, the kingdom of Sātiyaputta may be represented by modern Travancore. As Damir-ike was held by Keralaputta, the latter's dominions must have included South Canara, Coorg, Malabar, and north-west parts of Mysore with perhaps the northernmost portion of Travancore. In the time of the author of the Periplus, Mouziris (=Muyiri-koḍu) or modern Kranganur [4] was the seat of Keralaputta's government which when Ptolemy wrote was in the interior at Karoura, that is, Karūr on the Amarāvatī in the Coimbatore District.[5] It is really very difficult to fix the exact boundaries of

1 IA., VI. 339.
2 VP. (Wilson), II. 180.
3 Chap. IX., v. 63.
4 IA., VIII. 145.
5 *Ibid.*, XIII. 367-8.

the southern states referred to by Aśoka, but it seems that they met one another and also those of his Empire, in the north of the Chitaldrug District of Mysore. For it is here, as we have seen, that four copies of his Minor Edicts have been found. What could be Aśoka's object in incising these copies in close proximity to one another unless in that tract of land the southern kingdoms touched his dominions? These kingdoms almost certainly were those of the Choḍas (the northern), Pāṇḍya and Keralaputra.

In this connection is worth noting another people or country to which Aśoka refers in Rock Edict XIII. It is the country called Āṭavī or Āṭavya. In regard to it he says: "If any one does (him) wrong, the Beloved of the gods must bear as much as can be borne.[1] And (the people of) the Forests which are in the dominions of the Beloved of the gods he conciliates. The might of the Beloved of the gods, though he is repenting, is told them in order that they may express sense of shame, and not be killed." It appears from this that the Āṭavyas or the people of the Forest Country were not altogether subordinate to Aśoka, but enjoyed some degree of independence. Otherwise there is no meaning in the statement that they have done him wrong, and that although he has the might to punish them, he is resorting to the *sāman*

[1] Compare this with *khamisati ne devanaṁ-piye aphākaṃ ti e chakiye khamitave,* said by Aśoka with reference to the subjects of the Anta or bordering rulers in Dhauli and Jaugaḍā Separate Edicts (*Ins. A.*, pp. 89-90).

or friendly mode of winning them over to his side,—a mode, no doubt, which suggested itself to him on account of his having become an ardent follower of Dhaṃma. Who were these Āṭavyas? In the Purāṇas they are mentioned side by side with Pulindas, Vindhyamūlīyas and Vaidarbhas. And one copper-plate grant describes a Parivrājaka king, Hastin, as master of the Ḍabhālā kingdom together with the Eighteen Forest Kingdoms (Āṭavī-rājya).[1] Ḍabhālā must be the older form of Ḍabhālā the modern Bundelkhaṇḍ. The Āṭavī Country, which comprised no less than eighteen tiny kingdoms in the Gupta period must have extended from Bāghelkhaṇḍ right up almost to the sea-coast of Oṛissā. And this may explain why two copies of his Minor Rock Edict I. are at Rūpnāth and Sahasrām, which were on the eastern and western frontiers of the Āṭavī country. In the Separate Rock Edicts of Dhauli and Jaugaḍā, Aśoka exhorts his officials to announce his policy of sympathy and love to the people of the bordering territory. In Oṛissā there could be no kingdom adjoining to Aśoka's empire except the independent or quasi-independent country of Āṭavī.

We thus obtain a fairly accurate idea of the extent of Aśoka's dominions. They included the whole of India except the southern extremity of the peninsula held by the Choḍa, Pāṇḍya, Sātiyaputra and Keralaputra kings. This southern boundary is marked roughly by a line drawn

[1] GI., p. 114.

from Pulicat near Madras in the east, to Gooty and Chitaldrug in the north where the four copies of Aśoka's Minor Rock Edicts have been discovered right up to the northern point of the South Canara District on the west.

Let us now see what Greek princes have been mentioned by Aśoka as his contemporaries, and try to identify them. They have all been named in Rock Edict XIII. Of course, Aṃtiyoka is the first to be named as he was a neighbour of Aśoka. Beyond his kingdom, we are told, were ruling the four princes Turamāya, Aṃtekina or Aṃtikini, Maga and Alikasu(ṃ)dra. Aṃtiyoka is, of course, Antiochus II. Theos (B.C. 261-246), king of Syria, and Turamāya, Ptolemy II. Philadelphos of Egypt (285-247). Aṃtekina or Aṃtikini, as Bühler has remarked, corresponds to the Greek Antigenes rather than to Antigonus.[1] But as no king named Antigenes is known, Aṃtekini has been identified with Antigonus Gonatas of Macedonia (276-239). Maga is obviously Magas of Cyrene (*c*. 300—*c*. 250), but there is some doubt about Alikasuṃdara, who, according to some, was Alexander of Epirus (272—*c*. 255), and, according to others, Alexander of Corinth (252—*c*. 244).[2] In Rock Edict II. Antiochus alone is mentioned, and the other princes referred to as his *sāmantas* or bordering kings. There can be no doubt that of these Greek princes Antiochus alone had his dominions conterminous with those of Aśoka. And we also know that there had been friendly

[1] ZDMG., XL. 137.

[2] JRAS., 1914, p. 945.

relations and dispatch of embassies between the Seleukidan and Mauryan Houses since the time of Chandragupta. But was Aśoka in any way an ally of the other Hellenic kings? Did he enter into any diplomatic intercourse with those powers? The distance which separated them from the dominions of Aśoka must have been enormous, and, *primâ facie* it does not appear probable that there was any political intercourse between India and the Hellenic kingdoms beyond Syria. But Rock Edict XIII. clearly implies that he was in the habit of sending *dūtas* or envoys to the courts of these Greek rulers. And, as a matter of fact, we know that Ptolemy Philadelphos, Aśoka's contemporary, dispatched an envoy called Dionysios to the Mauryan court.

The reference by Aśoka to his contemporary Greek rulers has been made the basis of calculation for arriving at his date more accurately. But our calculation, in the first place, must rely upon the regnal years to which the edicts referring to or mentioning the Hellenic potentates must be assigned. We have seen that these records are Rock Edicts II. and XIII. But to what regnal years can they be presumed to belong? Senart is of opinion that the whole set of Rock Edicts was engraved in the fourteenth year of Aśoka's reign, and all European scholars have endorsed this view. But one Bengali scholar has questioned its reasonableness, and has adduced reasons, which appear to be cogent, to show that at least Rock Edicts II. and XIII. could not have been promulgated prior to the twenty-seventh regnal year.[1] Supposing that both these Rock Edicts were issued in the twenty-eighth year, the date must correspond to a year when the five Greek rulers were alive. If Alikasuṃdara of Rock Edict XIII is Alexander of Epirus, this year would fall between 272 and 255, but if Alexander of Corinth is intended, then between 252 and 250. The latter supposition is more probable.[2] So that we may take it that the twenty-eighth regnal year of Aśoka corresponds to 251 B.C. If this calculation is correct, Aśoka probably ascended the throne *circa* 279 B.C. Whatever the actual result of such a calculation may be, it is based upon two things namely, the date of Rock Edicts II and XIII and the identification of the Alikasuṃdara of the latter edict. And as these are factors of more or less uncertain character, we cannot possibly arrive at the date of Aśoka's accession to the throne with any accuracy.

[1] *Aśoka's Dhaṃmalipis* by Haritkrishna Deb, M.A. His main contention is as follows : Pillar Edict VII is dated in the 27th year and is admitted by all to be a resumé of the multifarious measures which Aśoka adopted up till that year for the dissemination of his Dhaṃma. It is puerile to suppose that PE. VII is a mere resumé of the domestic measures he adopted for his subjects, and not also of what he did for foreign peoples. The field of Aśoka's activity is *all* mankind, and he never draws any factitious distinction between his subjects and foreign peoples so far as Dhaṃma is concerned, his ideal being that of Chakravartī Dhārmika Dharmarāja. The carrying out of philanthropic works (RE. II) and the propagation of Dhaṃma (RE. XIII) in the realms of the Greek rulers are such important things that Aśoka would most certainly have made mention of them in Pillar Edict VII if he had heard, when it was engraved, that they had met with any appreciable measure of success in those foreign countries. The omission is significant, and shows that Rock Edicts II and XIII could not have been promulgated prior to Pillar Edict VII, that is, the 27th regnal year.

[2] JRAS., 1914, p. 945.

We have thus obtained a fairly good idea of the extent of Aśoka's dominions. We will now try and see how they were administered. What the system of the Mauryan administration was in general we know from Kauṭilya's Arthaśāstra and also from the account left to us by Megasthenes. But our object here is to see what the Aśoka inscriptions themselves teach us about this matter. This will not be a superfluous inquiry, and is sure to throw light upon new points, not known previously.

That Aśoka had a vast empire cannot be doubted. That such an extensive empire cannot be successfully administered by one single individual will also be admitted. The empire must therefore have been split up into a number of viceroyalties, corresponding to the *subahs* of the Mughal period. And the Aśoka inscriptions clearly prove that the system of provincial government existed under his rule. But the provincial governors appear to have been of two classes in his time as also in the later imperial Gupta period. The provinces which were of political importance and which therefore required loyal and tactful administration were assigned to the princes of the royal blood designated Kumāras. Three such Kumāra viceroyalties are referred to in the edicts. One Kumāra was stationed at Takshaśilā the headquarters of Gandhāra, which being a frontier province required a careful and trustworthy administrator. A second Kumāra was in charge of Kaliṅga, with his headquarters at Tosalī, no doubt, Dhauli, where one set of Rock Edicts was found. Just because it was a newly conquered province, it stood in necessity of being entrusted to a faithful and vigilant ruler and must therefore have been converted into a Kumāra viceroyalty. There was a third province which was also held by a Kumāra. This was the province with its capital at Ujjain. It was neither a frontier nor a newly conquered province, but still it must have possessed sufficient political importance to be administered by a prince of the royal blood. But these could not have exhausted the list of the provincial governors in Aśoka's time. Just as some provinces were ruled over by Kumāras, there must have been others which were governed by persons not related to the royal family. It is true that no instance of such a provincial governor is known from Aśoka inscriptions, but one such instance has been supplied by the celebrated Junāgaḍh inscription of Rudradāman. This epigraphic record tells us that the province of Surāshṭra or Kāṭhiāwāṛ was governed by Vaiśya Pushyagupta in Chandragupta's time and by the Yavana king Tushāspa when Aśoka was king.[1] How a chief and, above all, a Yavana ruler can be a provincial governor need not surprise us. The case is not at all unlike that of Rājā Mān Singh, Chief of Amer, appointed by Akbar to govern the province of Bengal. In the Gupta period also we know that some of the provincial governors were designated Mahārājas.[2]

In regard to the provincial government by princes just referred to, it is worthy of note that

[1] EI., VIII. 43 & 46-7. [2] *Ibid.*, XV. 136 & 138.

the Kumāra did not always exercise full autonomy in the province. In the case of Ujjayinī and Takshaśilā, the Kumāras seem to have been regular viceroys with their power unfettered, but it was not so in the case of Tosalī. Thus from Separate Kaliṅga Edicts it appears that although the Kumāras of Ujjayinī and Takshaśilā were to send on tour a Mahāmātra of their own every three years to make sure that there was no maladministration of justice, in the case of the Tosalī province, this Mahāmātra was to be deputed, not by the Tosalī Kumāra, but by Aśoka himself. Secondly, in connection with the dispatch of such an Officer, the Kumāras of Ujjayinī and Takshaśilā are mentioned by themselves and not associated with any state dignitaries, whereas, in Separate Kaliṅga Edict II (Dh. version) where alone the Kumāra of Tosalī is referred to, he is mentioned not by himself but associated with the Mahāmātras. Again, in regard to the latter province we find that Aśoka issues admonitions or instructions to the Nagara-vyavahārikas and others directly and not through the Kumāra-Mahāmātras. It is thus evident that while the provinces of Ujjayinī and Takshaśilā were in charge of Kumāra viceroys who wielded practically independent authority, the province of Tosalī was placed under the joint rule of the Kumāra-Mahāmātras, which was again not left unfettered, but made subject to the control of the king himself.

There is yet a fourth prince who has been referred to in Aśoka's inscriptions. He has been mentioned in the Mysore copies of Minor Rock

Edict I. The preamble of these recensions introduces us to an Āryaputra and Mahāmātras stationed at Suvarṇagiri who communicate certain orders of Aśoka to a Mahāmātra in Isila. It is generally assumed that Suvarṇagiri was the capital of a fourth province, under the jurisdiction of a Prince of the Blood Royal, which was the southernmost part of the empire, and included the Isila district, apparently, touching the frontiers of the independent Choḍa and Pāṇḍya kingdoms. In support of this conclusion, some texts are quoted from the Khaṇḍahāla-Jātaka[1] where the word *ayyaputta* is used to signify 'a prince' But it is worthy of note that in Separate Kaliṅga Edicts I and II, *kumāra*, and not *ayaputa*, has been employed to denote 'a prince' appointed as a provincial governor. And it is, indeed, curious if we suppose that there were two different designations for one and the same office. Besides, we have to remember that *ayyaputta* does not occur, in the Pāli literature, only in the sense of a 'prince'. The same word occurs also in the Mahāvagga in connection with the incident where the Lichchhavis and the courtezan Ambāpālī vie with one another in inviting Buddha to dinner. In the dialogue that is reported to have ensued, the Lichchhavis have twice been addressed by her as *Ayyaputta*[2] which has been translated as 'My Lords'[3] by Oldenburg and Rhys Davids. Surely the Lichchhavis were not *rājakumāras* or princes but rather *rājans* or

[1] See below n. 1 on MRE., I.
[2] *Vinaya-P.*, I. 232, 4 & 7.
[3] SBE., XVII. 107.

rulers, the joint but independent rulers of a tribal oligarchy. Similarly, the Vatsa king, Udayana, has been addressed *Āryaputra* thrice in Bhāsa's *Svapna-Vāsavadattā*.[1] Udayana figures in this drama not as a 'prince' but as 'a king'. It is therefore more reasonable to suppose that the term *ayaputa* of the Mysore edicts denoted a 'Prince of the Royal Blood' who was higher in rank than a prince-viceroy. And we shall perhaps not be far from right if we hold with J. F. Fleet that this Āryaputra was a vice-regent who represented king Aśoka for some time. Fleet, however, wrote long before Hultzsch published his authoritative transcripts of the various versions of Minor Rock Edict I, and was therefore led astray in regard to the time of this Edict. But we now know that this edict was issued when Aśoka was with the Buddhist Saṃgha and visiting the different places of pilgrimage. To enable him to do this, it was necessary that there should be some deputy to act for the king. It thus seems that Āryaputra here denotes the *Yuvarāja* or crown-prince who carried on the administration during the temporary absence of Aśoka from his capital. It further seems that this Yuvarāja was stationed at Suvarṇagiri in Rājagṛha, the old capital of Magadha, just as the Yuvarāja of the imperial Gupta dynasty was posted at Vaiśāli, the old capital of the Lichchhavis, from whom practically the Guptas received sovereignty. The language, again, of the preamble of the Mysore copies is almost exactly the

[1] (Trivandrum Sk. Series), pp. 60 & 69.

same as that of a Nāsik Cave Inscription in which Gautamīputra Śātakarṇi issues an order to his *amātya* at Govardhana.[1] The former was the ruler, and similarly the Āryaputra-Mahāmātras of the Mysore edicts, being the vice-gerent, formed naturally the ruling authority for the time being at least.

In Rock Edict III, Aśoka specifies three classes of officials, namely, Prādeśikas, Rājūkas, and Yuktas. Dr. F. W. Thomas was the first to draw our attention to the word *yukta* occurring in this sense in Kauṭilya's Arthaśāstra.[2] But he takes it to mean a subordinate official in general though Kauṭilya enables us to understand more precisely which class of officials the Yuktas denoted. Kauṭilya speaks of both the Yuktas and their Assistants the Upayuktas. Their duties, however, were of the same kind and are described in two consecutive chapters, a careful reading of which leaves no doubt as to their being principally district treasury officers who managed the king's property, received and kept account of revenue, and had power to spend where expense was likely to lead to an increase of revenue. The verse quoted about the Yuktas by Dr. Thomas from the Mānava-dharmaśāstra confirms this idea. For Manu says that lost property, when recovered, should remain in the charge of the Yuktas. These officers were therefore in charge of the receipts of all revenue and property of the king. Curiously

1 EI., VIII, 73.

2 JRAS., 1909, 466-7; 1914, 387-91.

enough, the designations Yukta and Upayukta survived to a late period. Thus in a grant of the Rāshṭrakūṭa king, Govinda IV, dated Śaka 853 (=A.D. 930), mention is made of Yuktaka and Upayuktaka along with the officers, Rāshṭrapati, Grāmakūṭa, and Mahattara.[1] Instead of Yukta and Upayukta we sometimes have Āyukta and Viniyukta. Thus Āyuktas are mentioned in the Allāhābād Pillar Inscription of Samudragupta as "restoring the wealth of the various kings, conquered by the strength of his arms."[2] An Āukta is mentioned also as a Vishaya-pati or Head of a district in a copper-plate grant of Budhagupta.[3]

As regards the Prādeśika Dr. Thomas identifies him with the officer Pradeshṭri mentioned in the Arthaśāstra. He has culled several passages from this work which go clearly to show that Pradeshṭri was an officer "charged with executive duties of revenue collection and police."[4] It is, however, safer to take Prādeśika in the sense of "an Officer in charge of a Division (*pradeśa*)." Most probably he corresponds to a Provincial Governor, as suggested by Kern.

Who the Rājūkas were has been partly explained by Bühler.[5] From quotations in the Kurudhamma-Jātaka he has shown that Rājūka corresponds to Rajjuka or Rajjugrāhaka as he is therein more fully called. His duty, as described

[1] EI., VII. 39-40.

[2] CII., III. 14.

[3] EI., XV. 138.

[4] JRAS., 1914, 383 & ff.; 1915, 112.

[5] ZDMG., XLVII, 466 & ff., Fick's *Social Organisations*, etc. (trans.), 148-9.

in the Jātaka, seems to have been that of measuring land by means of a cord (*rajju*) and fixing its boundaries. As he is styled *amachcha* it seems he was a big officer, corresponding perhaps to the modern Revenue Settlement Officer. That he was an officer of a very high grade is also shown by the fact that Aśoka speaks of having appointed Rājūkas over hundred thousands of men. In his time the Rājūka was entrusted with the power of giving awards and punishments and was to see that uniformity of *vyavahāra* and uniformity of *daṇḍa* were preserved. They were also to ascertain what gave happiness (*sukhīyana*) to the provincials and confer favours upon them. Pillar Edict VII clearly shows that by *sukhīyana* Aśoka means the works of public utility, the digging of wells on roads, and such other charities as he has specified in that Edict. Now Megasthenes[1] refers to a class of high officers of state whose duties, curiously enough resemble very closely those of the Rājūkas. Thus we are told that they measure the land, collect the taxes and superintend the occupations connected with the land. This seems exactly to be the function of the Rājūka described in the Kurudhamma-Jātaka. Again, these officers of state, Megasthenes informs us, "*have the power of rewarding or punishing* those who merit either,"[2] superintend the rivers, inspect sluices, construct roads, and carry out such other works of public utility. It will be seen that these are exactly the duties which Aśoka has assigned to the Rājūkas. Further we

[1] IA., VI. 238.

[2] *Ancient India* by J. W. M'Crindle, pp. 53-4.

have to note not only that they were appointed over hundred thousands of men but also that they were placed in direct charge of the provincials (*jānapadajana*). It therefore seems that they were the highest district, not divisional, officers.

There is yet another officer whom we have to know in this connection. He is mentioned as *Nagala-viyohalāka* (Nagara-vyāvahāraka) in Separate Kaliṅga Edict I. He is doubtless the same as the Paura-vyāvahārika referred to in the Arthaśāstra,[1] and appears to have been a judge for district towns only. The same edict informs us that these officers were appointed over many thousands of men. They thus seem to be inferior in rank to the Rājūkas who ruled over many thousands. While the latter were district magistrates and heads, the former seem to be town magistrates.

There are two or three other classes of officials mentioned in the Aśoka inscriptions. They are all referred to at the end of Rock Edict XII. They are Dhaṃma-Mahāmāta, Ithijhakha-Mahāmāta and Vachabhūmika. Who the Dhaṃma-Mahāmātas were we shall see shortly. Ithijhakha-Mahāmātas are Stryadhyaksha-Mahāmātras, that is, the Mahāmātras who were Superintendents (*adhyakshas*) of women. Hultzsch compares this officer to the Gaṇik-ādhyaksha or Overseer of Courtezans mentioned in the Kauṭalīya (II. 27). This is not impossible, but anybody who has studied the Arthaśāstra knows full well what different and compli-

[1] Pp. 20 & 245.

cated questions connected with woman such as her maintenance, transgressions, elopement and so forth have been discussed under the section 'Dharmasthīya'. The state also recognised its duty of providing subsistence to helpless women when they were carrying and also to children they might give birth to. It is quite conceivable that there was appointed an officer specially for this purpose who was called Stryadhyaksha. It is, however, somewhat difficult to understand who the Vacha-bhūmikas were. The first part of this designation has been taken as equivalent to *vraja* mentioned twice in the Arthaśāstra in the sense of "herds of cows and buffaloes, goats and sheep, asses and camels or horses and mules."[1] It seems that there were different castes which reared different flocks of cattle, that they were settled on grounds (*vraja-bhūmi*) round about towns and villages, and that the state realised some revenue by levying light taxes[2] on them. There certainly were more than one officer connected with *vrajas*, such as Samā-hartṛi, Godhyaksha and so on. The latter maintained the king's *vraja*, carried on cattle-rearing, and ran the dairy work of the Royal Household.[3] This seems to be the *vraja* or stud where Aśoka beguiled his time as he tells us in Rock Edict VI. But as there was a plurality of officers concerned with *vrajas* spread all over the country, that is, concerned with their supervision, assessment and so forth, they all seem to have been referred to by

1 *Ibid.*, pp. 47, 311 &c.
2 *Ibid.*, pp. 128 & ff.
3 JRAS., 1914, pp. 386-7.

Aśoka in Rock Edict XII under the generic designation Vrajabhūmikas.

There now remains only one officer for us to note here. He is designated Aṃta-Mahāmāta, that is, Anta-Mahāmātra. This phrase has been taken to mean 'High Officers of the Frontiers,' 'Wardens of the Marches.' They have been mentioned in Pillar Edict I. There Aśoka seems to imply that just as his officials of whatever rank are inducing the fickle-minded people in his territory to follow Dhaṃma, the Anta-Mahāmātras are attaining the same object apparently outside. This indicates that these latter officials were not in charge of the frontier provinces of Aśoka's empire but rather those sent to the neighbouring states and charged with the carrying out of Aśoka's programme of Dhaṃma. This agrees with the fact that in the same edict he distinguishes Anta-Mahāmātras from Purushas or officers of his dominions. It further agrees with the fact that in Aśoka inscriptions wherever the word *amta* occurs, it has the sense of either 'a bordering king' or 'people of a bordering kingdom.'

It will be seen that the last four classes of officials, though their functions are so diverse, have all been designated Mahāmātras. The term *mahāmātra* must therefore be understood to mean 'a high official' or 'dignitary' only. This is also clear from the fact that in the Dhauli and Jaugaḍā Separate Edict I, Nagaravyāvahārikas also have been called Mahāmātras. There is also another general term which we find used in Aśoka inscriptions. It is the word *purusha*, which denoted district officials of whatever description, but below the rank of the Rājūkas who are contrasted from them in Pillar Edict VII and who seem to be the highest district officials.[1] This is evident from the fact that in Pillar Edict I, Aśoka divides his *purushas*[1] into three classes, according as they are of the high, middle, and low rank. According to both the edicts they took part in the dissemination of Dhamma.

Aśoka refers to his dominions four times as *vijita* (RE. II, III, XIII, & XIV) and only once as *rāja-vishaya* (RE. XIII). If we leave aside the capital of the empire and the provinces which were ruled over more or less independently by the viceroys and governors, the territory which was under the direct sway of the king is called *janapada*. This *janapada* seems to have been split up into *pradeśas* or Divisions, each *pradeśa* into *āhāras* or Districts, and each *āhāra* into *vishayas* or *Tāluks* (Sārnāth PE.). The principal town of each *Tāluk* or Sub-division seems to have been a fortified place and called *koṭṭa*. The heads of the Divisions or Provinces are the Prādeśikas ; and those of the Districts, the Rājūkas. Below the Rājūkas came the Purushas, who appear to have been entrusted with the administration of the Sub-divisions.

Now the question arises : "How was the king connected with these Mahāmātras?" Aśoka had a very wide empire, and the number of the

1 Hultzsch takes these *purushas* in the sense of 'agents,' *i.e.*, 'spies'. But as they were also open preachers, it is not clear how they could remain undetected as they should if they were to play the rôle of 'spies' effectively.

Mahāmātras appointed must have been a big one. How could one single ruler be in direct touch with these officials? Do the inscriptions speak of any intermediate body which was in close touch with the king on the one hand, and with the officials on the other? Yes, this body is the Parishad, which is mentioned in two edicts. This is evidently the Mantri-parishad of the Arthaśāstra. It was the council of ministers, whose duty, as Kauṭilya tells us,[1] was to start the work that was not begun, to complete what was begun, to improve what was accomplished, and enforce strict obedience to orders. Another important duty of the Parishad was to dispose of work in conjunction with the officers that were near and advise those that were far off, through official communication. And *when any emergent work arose*, the king was to call not only his counsellors but also the assembly of ministers, to do what the majority of the members suggested, or whatever course of action, leading to success, they pointed out. This is what Kauṭilya says, and it agrees with what has been stated about the Parishad in the edicts. Thus in Rock Edict III, Aśoka specifies 'small expense' (*apavyayatā*), and 'small accumulation' (*apabhāṇḍatā*), as two of the practices constituting Dhaṃma, and apparently entrusts to the Yukta officers the work of fostering these virtues among his people. But as no two households can agree in regard to the necessaries of life, no hard and fast rule can be laid down for all households in regard to the amount

[1] *Arthaśāstra*, p. 29.

they ought to accumulate or expend. And Aśoka therefore orders the Parishad to advise and help the Yuktas to execute his order in this respect so that the spirit of it was carried out. This shows in the first place that the Parishad is to see that every order of the king is put into execution and secondly that it was a body which dominated and guided the action of the officials, as the Arthaśāstra tells us. Another function of the Parishad detailed in this work, that is, in respect of the emergent work cropping up, is also emphasised by Rock Edict VI which is an administrative edict. There Aśoka says: "And when in respect of anything that I order by word of mouth, for being personally issued or proclaimed, or again in respect of any emergent work superimposing itself upon the Mahāmātras, there is any division or consensus of opinion in the Parishad, I have commanded that it should forthwith be reported to me at all places and at all hours." What he means is that when he issues an oral order or when any pressing matter devolves upon a Mahāmātra, the Parishad has to meet and discuss it. If they come to a unanimous decision, no question can arise as to its being carried out. But if there is a divergence of opinion or even unanimous opposition, it is for the king to see what this difference or opposition is and find out which of their counsels is most likely to be efficacious. But he must have the benefit of the views of the Parishad before he can take action, and in order that no delay may occur in the matter of his taking action, he commands the Prativedakas to report to him as soon as the views of the council are formed, whatever the hour when and whatever the place where he may be. The Parishad was thus like a modern Executive Council which was an intermediate administrative body between the king and the Mahāmātras, and it appears that whereas, on the one hand, it saw that the written orders of the king were carried out by the different officials, it had, on the other, the power to scrutinise his oral orders before they were executed and to suggest what course of action could meet what pressing contingencies of the Mahāmātras—for the information and approval of the king, who was, of course, the final arbiter.

One interesting point to be noticed in connection with the administrative system of Aśoka is that some of his officers had to undertake tours for the dispatch of their business. This is clear from the Sārnāth Edict where the local Mahāmātras have been instructed to go out on tour as far as their jurisdiction went. The same instruction has been issued in the Rūpnāth Edict. And, as a matter of fact, the Prādeśikas, Rājūkas and Yuktas have been mentioned in Rock Edict III as going out on tour for their routine work, and, we know that they were dignitaries of a high class. The touring Mahāmātras or higher officials were expected to return to the district headquarters by turns on the Uposatha or fast days, as may be inferred from the Sārnāth Edict. But they had all to be present at the headquarters on the day of the *Tishya nakshatra*—that is the king's birthday,[1]

[1] Above, p. 11.

as we may see from the Dhauli and Jaugaḍā Separate Edicts.

Let us now see what Aśoka was as a ruler. To begin with, it is interesting to note with what feelings he looked upon his subjects. He gives us an insight into his mind by what he says in the Separate Kaliṅga Edicts. "All men", says he therein, "are my children ; and, just as I desire for my children that they may obtain every kind of welfare and happiness both in this and the next world, so do I desire for all men." He expresses the same sentiment also in Pillar Edict IV. Aśoka evidently had a paternal conception of the king's duty, pointing clearly to the royal absolutism of the Mauryan period.[1] Just as children are solely dependent upon their parents who can do to them just what they like, the subjects were at the mercy of the king who was thus no better than a despot. This presents a strong contrast to the notion, that was prevalent before the rise of the Mauryan power, and according to which the king was considered to be a mere servant of the state and was allowed to levy the prescribed taxes in order that he might receive the wage due to him for his services.

As regards the reforms he introduced in his government, one thing to which Aśoka paid special attention and to which he was particularly sensitive was the administration of justice. No wonder if

1 This agrees also with the spirit of Kauṭilya's Arthaśāstra, wherein at least two places (pp. 47 and 208) the relation of the king to his subjects is described as that of the father to his children, as has been pointed out in MCNL., p. 164 ff.

he kept a watchful eye when the newly conquered territory of Kaliṅga was formed into a province of his empire. In Separate Edict I, found at both Dhauli and Jaugaḍā, he takes Nagara-vyāvahārikas severely to task, because some people of the district towns of Tosalī and Samāpā were subjected to arbitrary imprisonment or harassed without any cause. He plainly gives them to understand that they have not fully grasped the meaning of his words when he said that all men were his children and that he desired for them as for the latter both material and spiritual happiness. When his expostulations are over, he gives them a healthy piece of advice. Earnestly and fervently he directs them to studiously guard themselves against "envy, lack of perseverance, harshness, impatience, neglect of repeated effort, idleness, and sense of weariness," and develop in themselves "perseverance and patience." He presses on their attention the fact that unless they performed their duties sedulously, they would neither gain heaven nor discharge their debt to the king. Still fearing that notwithstanding all these remonstrances the condition of things might not improve and that arbitrary imprisonment and causeless harassment might continue, he threatens them with sending forth a Mahāmātra every five years to see that all his injunctions for the proper administration of justice are carried out. Thinking that in other provinces also it was not prudent to wait for similar maladministration to take place in order to remedy it, he proposes to issue orders to the princes stationed at Takshaśilā and Ujjain to dispatch similar Mahāmātras on tour with the same object in view in the provinces of their jurisdiction.

The question arises: who were these Mahāmātras that were commissioned to detect cases of arbitrary imprisonment or harassment in the districts? One point to note about them is that they have been instructed to attend to this new duty without neglecting their routine work. And it seems almost certain that they were the Dharma-Mahāmātras for the first time mentioned in Rock Edict V. In this edict Aśoka tells us that he was the first to create this class of officials, and specifies their duties. As the Dhaṃma of Aśoka was directed towards the generation and development of not only the material but also the spiritual good of the people, the duties of the Dharma-Mahāmātras also fell under these two heads. In what manner Aśoka instructed them to cause and promote the spiritual good of his people we will see when we come to discuss Aśoka's achievements as a missionary. Here, of course, we are concerned with their duties in so far as they relate to the material good. And one of the duties they had to discharge in this connection was to inspect those who were put into prison and to make money grants if any one of them was encumbered with a big family, to free him from shackles if he was oppressed, and even to release him if he was very aged. This clearly shows in the first place that supervision, by a touring Mahāmātra, of the administration of justice in the provincial towns, which Aśoka says in the Separate Kaliṅga Edicts that he is going to enforce, has actually been assigned to the Dharma-Mahāmātras. What is worthy of note is that they have been authorised not only to set right the violation of justice by freeing a person from fetters who may have been subjected to oppression but also to temper justice with mercy by making money grants for the maintenance of a culprit's family if it was in a helpless condition or even by releasing him if he was stricken with years and not fit to be confined in a dungeon. They had also a humanitarian function to discharge in the outlying parts of Aśoka's empire, such as the districts of the Yavanas, Kaṃbojas, Gandhāras, Rāshṭrikas and other Aparāntas. They were to look to the welfare and happiness of such among the Brāhmaṇ and Gṛihapati classes as had been reduced to a servile condition and to occupy themselves with the helpless and the aged in general. The idea of the state providing the helpless and the aged with maintenance is not a new one, and was known even before the time of Aśoka. Thus Kauṭilya's Arthaśāstra says:[1] "The king shall maintain the orphan, the aged, the infirm, the afflicted and the helpless." It is possible that this duty of the state up to Aśoka's time was observed more in the breach, and in order to renew the practice and ensure its continuance, Aśoka entrusted it to the Dharma-Mahāmātras, who were created by him. And even if we suppose for the moment that this humanitarian measure was not for the first time devised by Aśoka, it was no insignificant thing that he attempted to revive

[1] P. 47.

it and ensure justice where it was set at naught and soften it with clemency where it was likely to hit severely. This is one sidelight we obtain into Aśoka as a ruler.

The Dharma-Mahāmātras were Aśoka's own creation, and he appointed them for the first time in the thirteenth year of his reign as he tells us in Rock Edict V. About this time he seems to have introduced another administrative reform. This has been described in the edict following it, and relates to the prompt dispatch of business. Accessibility to the subjects is looked upon as a paramount virtue with a ruler in the oriental countries, and especially so it was in ancient India. But it is perhaps impossible to surpass Aśoka in the degree to which he seems to have exhibited it. In Rock Edict VI, he notifies his willingness to receive reports at all hours and at all places, whether he is taking his meals or is in the ladies' apartments, his inner chamber, in the stud, on horseback, or in pleasaunces. It is in this connection that he speaks of the Prativedakas or Reporters and the deliberations of the Parishad to which we have adverted above. The earnestness and fervour with which he made himself accessible are clearly and indelibly depicted in the words he has used. "I am never satisfied," says he, "with (my) exertion or with (my) dispatch of business. The welfare of the whole world is an esteemed duty with me. And the root of that, again, is this, namely, exertion and dispatch of business. There is no higher work than the welfare of the whole world. And what little effort I make is for the purpose that I may be free from debt to the living creatures, that I may render them happy here and that they may gain heaven in the next world. For this purpose have I caused this document of Dhaṃma to be engraved, in order that it may endure for a long time and that my sons and grandsons may similarly exert themselves for the welfare of the whole world. This, however, is difficult to carry out without the utmost exertion."

For about thirteen years after this Aśoka does not seem to have adopted any important measure connected with his administrative system. In the twenty-sixth year of his reign, however, he took an important step for further ameliorating the administration of justice, especially so far as the provinces were concerned. Pillar Edict IV informs us that in that year he placed "Rājūkas in sole charge of reward and punishment in order that they may perform their duties with confidence and without fear, cause welfare and happiness to the people of the provinces, and confer favours (on them)." The same edict continues by saying that the Rājūkas "shall make themselves acquainted with what gives happiness or pain, and exhort the people of the provinces along with the faithful, so that they may gain happiness in this world and in the next." Evidently, the Rājūkas in the twenty-sixth year of his reign had a twofold duty to perform,—to cause and promote not only the temporal but also the spiritual good of the provincials. How exactly they were expected to fulfil this second object we will see when we treat of

"Aśoka as a Missionary" Here we will try to find out by what administrative reform the Rājūkas were expected to achieve the first object. They were put in sole charge, we are told, of the reward and punishment of the muffasil people. Two questions may arise here. The first is: Why were they placed in sole charge of this? Aśoka gives a reply to it, namely, in order that there may be uniformity in administration (*vyavahāra*) and uniformity in punishment (*daṇḍa*). The second question that now arises is: What did Aśoka mean by 'uniformity' here? This is rather a difficult question to answer. But what he probably meant was this. The Rājūkas were not the only officers who were connected with the administration of justice. We have seen above that there were at least two more officers,—the Nagara-vyāvahārika and the Prādeśika (Pradeshṭri), who also performed the function of a judge. As there were thus three classes of officials in one and the same province who performed judicial as well as other duties, uniformity in respect of *vyavahāra* and *daṇḍa* was not possible. The administration of justice could not consequently be expected to be uniform even so far as the people of one province were concerned. This was a veritable evil, and Aśoka tried to remedy it by handing over to the Rājūkas the sole charge of the judicial department and by relieving the other two classes of officials of this work. Well could Aśoka therefore say: "Just as a (person) feels confident after making over his offspring to a clever nurse, saying unto himself: 'the clever nurse desires to bring up my offspring', even so have I appointed the Rājūkas for the welfare and happiness of the provincials, in order that they may perform their duties without fear, with confidence, and without perplexity.'"[1]

Just in the year when Aśoka effected the above reform in the administration of justice, he made an attempt to mitigate the rigours of the penal code. The same edict, that is, Pillar Edict IV, informs us that he granted a respite of three days to men condemned to the sentence of death. The object of it was to afford them an opportunity to think about, and make themselves fit for, the next world before they were executed.

---

[1] It appears from this passage that the Pājūkas were made supreme in the execution of the judicial function and that Aśoka abolished all appeals to higher authorities. It looks that the revision of justice by the Dharma-Mahāmātras was abrogated by the king in the twenty-sixth year when its administration was consigned solely to the Rājūkas. He must have taken particular care in the selection of these officials, who were the highest district officers.

CHAPTER III

Aśoka as a Buddhist

It is scarcely necessary to state that Aśoka was a follower of Buddhism. All Buddhist records tell us that he had espoused that religion. On the other hand, there is no work, literary or scriptural, which says that he had embraced any other faith. But what do his inscriptions teach us? This is the only and real question we have to answer. When the inscriptions of Aśoka began to be studied and only a few were known, H. H. Wilson ventured to dispute his Buddhist faith, and Edward Thomas held that Aśoka was a Jaina at first but became a Buddhist afterwards.[1] But it is no longer permissible to call in question the Buddhist faith of Aśoka. That is now established beyond all doubt by the Bhābrū Edict, otherwise called the Second Bairāṭ Edict. It opens with Aśoka expressing his reverence for Buddha, Dhaṃma, and Saṃgha, exactly in the well-known trinitary formula of Buddhism. There are other records too, which point to the same conclusion. The views of Wilson and Thomas were based upon unreliable readings and

[1] JRAS. (NS.), Vol. IX, pp. 155 and 187. H. Heras is recently reviving Wilson's theory that Aśoka was Brāhmaṇical till the end of his days, but see B. M. Barua's *Religion of Aśoka* (Mahābodhi Pamphlet Series, No. 7.).

inaccurate interpretations, and are no longer countenanced by scholars. The question regarding which difference of opinion is now possible is: when did Aśoka become a follower of Buddhism? The scholar who considered this question last was the late Dr. J. F. Fleet. He held that the Dhaṃma inculcated in the rock and pillar edicts was in no way the Buddhist Dhaṃma, because in them Buddha is not mentioned at all and the Samgha only once and in such a way as to place it on a par with other creeds. The object of these edicts, says Dr. Fleet, was thus " not to propagate Buddhism or any other particular religion, but to proclaim the determination of Aśoka to govern his kingdom righteously and kindly in accordance with the duty of pious kings ".[1] In other words, the term dhaṃma, used in the rock and pillar edicts, Fleet takes as the 'ordinary *dharma* of kings, which is laid down in the Mānava-dharmaśāstra, I, 114, as one of the topics of that work.' According to him, Aśoka was converted to Buddhism in the thirtieth year from his coronation, that is, two years after the pillar edicts were engraved. Evidently, Fleet ignores the fact that the Dhaṃma Aśoka refers to in his rock and pillar edicts is intended for being put into practice, not by himself or his officers, but by all men. Obedience to parents, respect for teachers, seemly behaviour towards relatives and so forth, as we shall see later on, are some of the practices of Dhaṃma taught by Aśoka. This Dhaṃma cannot

[1] JRAS., 1908, pp. 491-2.

possibly be *rāja-dhaṃma*, which represents a code of duties for a king and his officers to perform and not for his people. The Rummindēī inscription, again, informs us that in the twentieth year of his reign Aśoka visited in person the place where Buddha was born and did worship there. It is evident from this that already in his twentieth regnal year he was a Buddhist. The words of the inscription clearly mean that Aśoka went to Buddha's birthplace in person and performed worship, and not that he did the place the honour of going there in person, as Fleet has understood it. Again, in Rock Edict VIII, Aśoka says that in the tenth year of his reign he repaired to Saṃbodhi. Whether Saṃbodhi here means 'supreme knowledge' or something like it as scholars take it, or 'the place where Buddha obtained enlightenment' as I and, following me, Hultzsch, understand it, this much is admitted on all hands that it is a word technical to Buddhist scriptures, and cannot possibly be taken as equivalent to the ordinary Sanskrit word *saṃbodha* as proposed by Dr. Fleet. This rock edict thus proves that in the tenth year of his reign Aśoka was already a Buddhist.

There is, however, evidence that Aśoka was converted to Buddhism about one year earlier. This evidence is supplied by Minor Rock Edict I, copies of which have been found at no less than nine different places. He begins this edict by saying: "It is more than two years and a half that I am a lay worshipper, but did not exert myself for one year. But, indeed, for more than one year that I have been living with the Saṃgha I have exerted myself strenuously."[1] When, therefore, this edict was engraved, he had already been a Buddhist for just less than three years. This edict, again, describes his work as that of a zealot in such terms that it reminds us of his Rock Edict IV, as pointed out by Senart, and a little comparison is enough to convince any one that in both Aśoka gives an account of one and the same thing, namely, his achievements as a missionary. Now, it is worthy of note that Rock Edict IV, refers itself to the twelfth year of his reign. He therefore must have embraced Buddhism not more than three years before this date, that is, in the ninth year. The principal events of this period of Aśoka's life may be thus briefly narrated. He became a Buddhist, as we have just seen, in the ninth regnal year. But for one year he was lukewarm and did little for the propagation of Buddhism. Then he lived with the Saṃgha for over a year and put forth such missionary activity that at the end of this period, that is, in the twelfth year of his reign, he could say in all good conscience that he achieved the progress of the people in Dhamma, such as never happened before.

[1] I have accepted the interpretation of Hultzsch which seems to be the only possible one, as the word *sumi* in this passage shows. It will thus be seen that the Kaliṅga war which took place in the eighth year was in no way connected with his conversion to Buddhism in the ninth, as shown above in the sequel. It is therefore strange how Prof. Mookerji puts this conversion two years and a half even before the Kaliṅga-conquest (*Aśoka*, p. 18). He gives no word of explanation to show why he rejects Hultzsch's interpretation, though it is the only logical one in the circumstances (ABORI., Vol. X, pp. 247-8).

Now, what does Aśoka mean by saying that he had been living with the Saṃgha for over a year? Senart thinks that this refers to the state visit of the king to the Saṃgha, in the midst of which he took his seat and made a public profession of his Buddhist faith, as the Sinhalese Chronicle Mahāvaṃsa informs us.[1] It was on this occasion that he showed the genuineness of his devotion by making his son and daughter enter the religious order. Recently Prof. B. M. Barua, and following him, Prof. Radhakumud Mookerji have attempted to revive Senart's theory, by expressing the opinion that Aśoka is here distinguishing between two stages of his life, of course, as *upāsaka* that he was for his whole lifetime,—one, the stage of inaction for over two years and a half in which he was merely the personal admirer of an individual monk Nigrodha (then just seven years old!!!), and the other for over a year, the stage of exertion, when he visited the Saṃgha and became identified with its cause. In the first place, it is unfortunate that the interpretation of Hultzsch, though it is of such paramount importance for the religious history of Aśoka, has not been even so much as referred to by these scholars. Secondly, nowhere do the Pāli Chronicles describe any part of Aśoka's life which was a stage of inaction. For even long before Aśoka paid a state visit to the Saṃgha, we find him bestowing alms on 60,000 Buddhist monks in his own palace and building 84,000 *vihāras*. Thirdly, it was not during the second stage that he

[1] I.A., 1891, pp. 233-4.

first visited the Saṃgha, as implied by them. As a matter of fact, his first visit came off immediately after his conversion by Nigrodha,[1] as has been pointed out by Hultzsch himself.[2] In fact, any scholar, who reads the Pāli chronicles carefully and impartially, will find that no two stages in Aśoka's life after his conversion have been contrasted and that his career as a Buddhist is one of uniform unflagging zeal. Finally, what is here most important to remember is that the *saṃgham-upagatatva* of Aśoka had lasted the whole period of his second stage,[3] namely for more than one year. We cannot therefore say that the king *visited* the Saṃgha for over a year (which is nonsensical), but rather *lived* with it for that period.

The second period of Aśoka's religious life began with a course of action which he thus describes in Rock Edict VIII :

"For a long time past, kings used to go out on tours of pleasure (*vihāra-yātrā*). Here there were chase and similar diversions. Now, king Priyadarśin, Beloved of the gods, repaired to Sambodhi (Bodhi Tree) when he had been consecrated ten years. Hence, this touring for Dhamma (Dhamma-yātrā)."

Here Aśoka tells us that up till the tenth year of his reign, he, like the previous kings, used to find his relaxation in tours of pleasure where he

1 Dīp., VI. 78; Mahā., V. 76.

2 *Inscr. of Aśoka* (CII., I.), Intro., p. XLV.

3 This is quite clear from the occurrence of the word *sumi*, in no less than two recensions, along with *Sagh[a] up[e]te* or *[S]aṃgha[ṃ] u[pa]gate*.

indulged in hunting and other sports. In that year, however, he gave up the idea of ever going on these pleasure tours, and started religious tours instead. What he actually did in these religious tours and how he was able to foster Dhaṃma not only in himself but also in his subjects we shall see in a future chapter. What we have to note in this place is that in the tenth year of his reign he paid a visit to the Bodhi Tree and that this was his first *Dhaṃma-yātrā* or religious tour. And as this time coincides with that of his second period, it is difficult to avoid the inference that he began his career of strenuous exertion with a visit to the Bodhi Tree along with a Saṃgha of Bhikshus, and that the various spiritual benefits conferred upon him and also his people induced him to repeat this *Dhaṃma-yātrā* so that it became a regular fixture with him. The reminiscence of a later *Dhaṃma-yātrā* or pious tour certainly appears to be preserved in two pillar inscriptions found in the Tarāi region of Nepāl. One of these is engraved on a column found at Rummindēī, and the other at Niglīvā, thirteen miles north-west of the former. The first of these records tells us that in the twentieth year of his reign Aśoka came in person to the locality where the inscribed pillar stands, did worship, and, as that was the place where Buddha, the sage of the Śākya family, was born, he constructed huge stone walls and set up the pillar there. The inscription further informs us that because the Blessed One was born there, the village of Luṃminī was freed from all religious cess (bali) and was required to pay only one-eighth of the produce as land revenue (*bhāga*). What the epigraph means is that in his twentieth regnal year Aśoka visited the garden of Lumbinī, where according to Buddhist tradition, Prince Siddhārtha, the founder of Buddhism, was born, and that he did not rest contented with merely performing worship there, but put up a stone enclosure round the birth-spot of Buddha and erected a column there. But this was not all. Even to this day we know pilgrims have to pay religious cesses at certain holy places, such, for instance, as Dwārkā in Kaṭhiāwār. The village of Lumbinī, just because it was the birthplace of the founder of Buddhism, must have become a sacred place and been visited by all sorts and conditions of Buddhists even before the time of Aśoka, and, must therefore have been saddled with a similar cess. Aśoka, being a Buddhist, naturally did not like the idea of his co-religionists being compelled to pay any kind of impost just at the place where the founder of their religion was born, and so abolished it. But that was not the only boon he conferred upon Lumbinī. Every village of ancient India had to pay one-fourth or one-sixth of its produce as revenue to the king in whose dominions it was comprised. The village of Lumbinī, being subject to Aśoka's rule, had to pay some part of its produce as revenue to him. What portion of the produce he was actually receiving we do not know, but certainly it could never have been less than one-sixth. And what he did was that he reduced it to one-eighth. The other pillar of Aśoka in the Nepālese Tarāi is at Niglīvā. The inscription on it says that in the fourteenth year of his reign he enlarged the second Stūpa of the Buddha Konāgamana, but that he visited the place itself and did worship in the twentieth year. It is therefore quite plain that Aśoka undertook his pious tour in Nepāl in his twentieth regnal year. Perhaps one may wonder why Aśoka visited the birthplace of Buddha so late, that is, eleven years after he became a Buddhist. If Buddha was born in the garden of Lumbinī, as the Buddhist tradition tells us, one is apt to expect Aśoka to go to the Nepālese Tarāi first and perform worship at the spot where the founder of the religion was born. But it is worthy of note that with the Buddhists the most holy is the place where Prince Siddhārtha saw the light, visible, not to the sensuous, but to the spiritual, eye. And this is just the reason why we see that Aśoka's shaking off his indifference and adopting the hard and strenuous life of a missionary synchronized with his pilgrimage to Sambodhi, where the originator of Buddhism became illumined, that is, became Buddha.

We thus see that Aśoka became a convert to Buddhism in the ninth year of his reign, that for one year he did not much exert himself for his faith, and that in the tenth year he adopted a strenuous career, which he signalised with a pilgrimage to the Bodhi Tree. He was now so full of solicitude and unflagging zeal for the propagation of his faith that hardly a year or so had elapsed when he could not help wondering at the amount of work he was able to accomplish. His work, of course, was the dissemination of Dhaṃma. What the exact nature of this Dhaṃma was we will see in the next chapter, where also we shall show that it was a code of morals, not such as could be deduced from all religions and made the basis of a universal religion, but rather such as has been recommended by Buddhism to its lay followers in general, as no doubt may be inferred from the fact that Aśoka preached it as a layman. But in this chapter where we are concerned with Aśoka as a Buddhist we are to take cognisance of those of his edicts only where he shows himself to be a sectarian.

The first inscription that has to detain us here is the Bhābrū Edict. This is really an epigraph discovered in the ruins of a hill monastery at Bairāṭ in the northern part of the Jaipur State, Rājputānā. It is a missive from Aśoka to the Buddhist Saṃgha, a copy of which must have been inscribed and deposited by him at every monastic establishment of importance, and the Bhābrū Edict appears to be only one such copy at present discovered. The epigraph opens with a declaration of Aśoka's faith in Buddha, Dhaṃma and Saṃgha according to the well-known Buddhist formula and of his conviction that the utterances of Buddha are gospel truth. No doubt can possibly be entertained in regard to the sectarian character of this record. The object of this missive is to enumerate certain *Dhaṃma-pariyāyas* or canonical texts, which he earnestly wished to be listened to and retained in memory not only by monks and nuns but also by the lay people of both the sexes, in order that the Good

Dhaṃma might long endure. The texts referred to by Aśoka are as follows :—

1. Vinaya-samukase.
2. Aliya-vasāni = Ariya-vaṃsā (Aṅguttara N., II. 27).
3. Anāgata-bhayāni (*ibid.*, III. 103).
4. Muni-gāthā = Muni-sutta (Sutta-nipāta, p. 36).
5. Moneya-sute = Nālaka-sutta (*ibid.*, pp. 131-34).
6. Upatisa-pasina = Rathavinīta-sutta (Majjhima N., I. 146-51).
7. Lāghulovāda = Rāhulovāda-sutta (*ibid.*, p. 414).

All these texts have been satisfactorily identified except the first. Buddhaghosha, in his *Visuddhimagga*, narrates a beautiful story of a young monk, who, although he ate for three months in the house of his mother, never said, 'I am thy son and thou art my mother,' showing clearly that to a conscientious monk mother and father are no hindrances.[1] The young monk lived this exemplary life, because he lived up to the courses of conduct preached by Buddha in the Rathavinīta-sutta, the Nālaka, the Tuvaṭaka, and the Mahā-Ariyavaṃsa. The Suttas in which Buddha is represented to have preached to the Bhikshus are many, but as this story lays emphasis on only four, it appears that up till the time of Buddhaghosha the four Suttas just referred to were looked upon as of paramount importance to a

[1] Warren's *Buddhism in Translations*, pp. 434-36.

Buddhist Bhikshu. That the Aliya-vasāni, Moneya-sutta and Upatisapasina of Aśoka correspond to the Mahā-Ariyavaṃsa, Nālaka-sutta, and Rathavinītá respectively of Buddhaghosha's story has now been accepted by most scholars.[1] If three of the four Suttas referred to by Buddhaghosha have been identified with three of the *Dhaṃma-pariyāyas* mentioned by Aśoka, it is very strange that the fourth, namely, the Tuvaṭaka cannot be recognised in any one of the texts named by Aśoka. From verse 7 of this Sutta, however, it appears that Buddha is here expounding religious practices (*paṭipadā*), precepts (*pātimokkha*), and contemplation (*samādhi*).[2] And the words *paṭipadā* and *pātimokkha* used here lead to the surmise that in the Tuvaṭaka Sutta we have Aśoka's *Vinaya-samukase*, Vinaya *par excellence*.[3]

It will be seen from the above identifications of the *Dhaṃma-pariyāyas* referred to by Aśoka that sometimes one text was known by more than one title. Thus *Moneya-sute* is but another name for the Sutta which is now known as the *Nālaka-sutta*. This was not, however, the peculiar feature of the canonical texts cited by the king. Several others are known, and have already been pointed out.[4] The mention of these texts by Aśoka, again, does not prove anything against the existence of the whole body or any part of the Tipitaka in his time,

1 I.A., 1912, pp. 37 and ff.; Neumann, *Buddhist Renden*, Vol. I, p. 152.

2 *Sutta-nipāta*, p. 171; SBE., Vol. X, Pt. II, p. 168.

3 For a different identification see Mr. Sailendranath Mitra's paper on this subject in JDL., Vol. XX.

4 I.A., 1912, p. 40.

for Aśoka is here recommending a few sacred texts only, and what he is here not citing or selecting from cannot be regarded as non-existent in his time.

The scriptural texts selected by Aśoka show what sort of Buddhist he was. His mind was ravished not by the ritualistic or metaphysical elements of Buddhism, but rather by the fundamentals of that religion, or for the matter of that, any religion. He was fascinated not by any specification of rules and regulations to be observed externally and mechanically, but rather by what constitutes and conduces to real inner growth. Take for instance the *Ariyavaṃsā*, one of the texts cited by Aśoka. It lays down four courses of conduct for a monk. A monk, says the Sutta, should be (1) content with simple raiment, and (2) with plain food, obtained in the proper way, (3) should be satisfied with the humblest habitation, and (4) should delight in meditation. The text thus tells us in a nutshell how a Bhikshu should be or ought to live. There are two or three other texts, such as Munigāthā and Moneya-sutta which tell us practically the same thing. And there is no sacred text referred to by Aśoka which is connected merely with the externals of a religion, with the mere disciplinary rules of a religious order, the observance of which may make a Bhikshu an outwardly perfect monk but not necessarily an inwardly good man. All the Suttas adduced by the king relate to the elevation of the soul and are applicable not only to the clergy but also to the laity. This is just the reason why he expressly says that his Suttas should be listened to and pondered over not by monks and nuns alone but also by male and female lay-worshippers. Again, in the Suttas selected by Aśoka he is not content with including those which merely depict a higher mode of life or describe the constituents of lofty and sublime character, but he is careful enough to specify also those which are helps and guides in the path of spiritual elevation. One such Sutta is *anāgata-bhayāni*, which depicts the 'fears and dangers of the future' that may at any moment arise and frustrate the realisation of the goal of a man's religious strivings. It contains a series of admonitions to exercise all energies and lead a heedful and strenuous life in view of the adverse contingencies forthcoming, such as age, disease, famine, war and schism. Aśoka is thus not satisfied with merely adducing a text which describes the highest mode of living but also lays stress on a Sutta which warns a man against the dangers that threaten and tend to prevent the actualisation of this end if he is not always on the alert and watchful. But these dangers after all are of an external nature. It is true that we ought to be constantly on our guard and strive most assiduously to avoid them. Nevertheless, they are dependent on extraneous circumstances over which we have no control. But there are other dangers which are of an inner character and which with equal if not greater violence threaten the attainment of spiritual elevation. And the king has therefore done a most wise thing in drawing attention to a sacred text, Rāhulovāda-Sutta, a discourse where Buddha is represented to have exhorted one Ambalaṭṭhika Rāhula and expatiated on the supreme necessity of rigorously scrutinizing (*pachchavekkhana*) every act of the body, speech and mind both when and after it is initiated. A reading and contemplation of the religious texts recommended by Aśoka is sure to be edifying to any earnest soul that strives for a higher and nobler life, to whatever religion or creed he may belong.

The second document of a sectarian character which we have to note here is the *śāsana* or order of Aśoka which we find engraved on pillars at three different places, namely, Sārnāth, Sāñchī and Allahābād. The pillars at the former two places are believed to be *in situ*, but that at present existing at Allahābād is rightly regarded as having originally been at Kauśāmbī. Through this *śāsana* Aśoka aims at preserving the unity of the Buddhist Church by putting down all attempt at schism. "Whosoever," says he, "breaks up the church, be it monk or nun, shall be clad in white raiment, and compelled to live in what is not a residence (of the clergy). Thus should this order be respectfully communicated to the congregation of the monks and the congregation of the nuns." This order has been addressed to the Mahāmātras, as is clear from two of these inscriptions. One of these, again, shows, that in one case at least, these Mahāmātras were those stationed at Kauśāmbī. And it is not at all improbable that in other cases too the Mahāmātras addressed were those belonging to the Muffasil Districts, where the old Buddhistic clerical establishments now represented by the remains at Sārnāth and Sāñchi were originally situated. The prevention of schisms in the Buddhist Church was of extreme importance. It was not therefore enough that orders in that connection should merely be issued to the Mahāmātras of the districts. He therefore further says as follows in the same edict: "One such document has been deposited in (your) office (*saṃsaraṇa*) in order that it may be accessible to you. And deposit just another such document so as to be accessible to the laity. And the laity should come every Fast day in order to assure themselves of that same order. And certainly on all Fast days as each Mahāmātra comes in his turn (to the head-quarters) for Fast, he should assure himself of that same order and understand it. And so far as your jurisdiction goes, you must set out on tour with this specification (of my order). So too in all fortified towns and the district sub-divisions you must cause (subordinates) to go out on tour with this specification (of my order)."

The contents of this edict are enough to convince anybody that Aśoka was bent upon eradicating all apostasy and division in the Buddhist Church. To gain this end he resorts to a threefold method. He of course issues the order that he who tries to create a schism shall be clad in white garments, that is, shall be dispossessed of his yellow robes—the monkish garb, and shall be transported to a place where monks do not reside. In other words, he is at once cut off from all intercourse with his fraternity. And as Aśoka's order is to be communicated to every Buddhist Saṃgha, that must naturally deter a bellicose monk from obtruding his heretic doctrines on the attention of his brethren. This dispels three-fourths of the danger of schism. But the heretic, though ostracised, may gain the ear of the lay people, and with their following create a split in the community. Aśoka is alive to this danger, and has therefore instructed the Mahāmātras to post a copy of his order on this subject so as to be accessible to the laity. Where exactly this order was to be put up for their knowledge we are not told. But it is not unlikely that it was intended to be posted in the town hall (*nigama-sabhā*) of which we hear so much both in inscriptions and literature.[1]

The Sārnāth-Kosāmbī-Sāñchī edict leaves no doubt as to the firm determination of Aśoka to put down all attempt at creating a schism in the Buddhist Church. The earnest, almost severe tone of the edict and the fact that copies of it are found at places of important Buddhist monastic establishments presupposes that in his time the Buddhist Church was at least threatened with disruption, to prevent which he was straining every nerve. But were there, as a matter of fact, any divisions of the Buddhist Saṃgha obtaining in Aśoka's time? The edict was no doubt intended to arrest disruption, but that does not preclude us, it may be contended, from supposing that the Saṃgha had already broken up into a number of sections, and Aśoka's endeavour was directed against further division.

[1] CL., 1919, p. 82.

The Buddhist tradition, preserved in the Singhalese chronicles, which says that a Buddhist council was held at Pāṭaliputra eighteen years after Aśoka's coronation, also says that at that time the Saṃgha was split up into the two main divisions : (1) Theravāda and (2) Mahāsaṃghika and that the first division had branched off into two and the second into four sections.[1] If we accept this tradition, we have to suppose that already in Aśoka's time there were not only divisions but also subdivisions in the Buddhist Church. What could then be the meaning of the edict which aimed at preventing schism? Are we to suppose that Aśoka intended to nip schism, not in the Buddhist Church as a whole but rather in that division or subdivision of it, to which he individually belonged? Of course, it is quite possible to contend that in this edict by Saṃgha Aśoka means only that sect of Buddhism of which he was a member. But if we once countenance this view, we are compelled to hold that wherever Aśoka uses the word *saṃgha* he means by it that section of the Buddhist Church to which he pertained. This conclusion cannot, however, commend itself to us. For in Pillar Edict VII. where Aśoka speaks of the Dharma-Mahāmātras, he speaks of the Saṃgha side by side with the Ājīvikas and the Nirgranthas. And are we to suppose here that whereas these Dharma-Mahāmātras were to look to the welfare and progress of the Ājīvikas and Nirgranthas without distinction of creed and division, in the case of the Buddhists

[1] Kern, *Manual of Indian Buddhism*, pp. 110-1.

only they were to confine their activities not to the Buddhist Church as a whole, but to that division of it of which the king was a follower, all the other divisions or subdivisions of the Saṃgha being consigned to neglect and indifference? Similarly, in the Bhābrū Edict, he refers, as we have seen, to certain scriptural texts which he recommends for perusal to the Saṃgha. These texts are so free from sectarian elements that they will bear recital even to those monks who are not Buddhists. And are we to suppose that in the case of the Buddhists alone they are to be recited not to the Buddhist monks and nuns in general but to those only who belonged to Aśoka's denomination? If we are not to land ourselves on such absurdities, it seems disirable to hold that in Aśoka's time the Buddhist Church was not divided and that wherever he uses the word *saṃgha*, he means the whole undivided Church. What then becomes of the Buddhist tradition? Scholars who have investigated these traditions about the Buddhist councils have lighted upon such downright absurdities and inconsistencies and detected so much of dogmatical and sectarian tendency that very little that is contained in these traditions may be accepted as historical truth.[1] Thus the Council of Pāṭaliputra is not looked upon as any general council at all but a party meeting, and the Second General Council which was held at Vaiśālī came off, in all probability, not one century after Buddha but in the time of Aśoka, who is the real Kālāśoka of the

[1] *Ibid.*, p. 110, which contains the late Prof. Kern's opinion on the subject.

tradition, that is, Black Aśoka, as he is painted to be before his conversion to Buddhism.[1] This inference is more in consonance with his edicts. For, at the time of the Second General Council, the Buddhist Church was still undivided, though it was threatened with a schism on account of the Ten Points about discipline raised by the Vṛijian monks.[2] The latter were defeated, and the split of the Saṃgha for the time averted. This is borne out also by the epigraphic records of Aśoka. Special attention may be drawn in this connection to the words *saṁghe samage kaṭe*, 'the Saṃgha has been made whole and entire,' which occur about the beginning of the Sāñchī and Allāhābād Edicts. This no doubt shows that the Buddhist Church was then divided, but certainly not to such a serious extent as is implied by the Sinhalese tradition connected with the Council of Pāṭaliputra. The differences were unquestionably of small importance, such as they were when the Council of Vesāli was convened. It seems that these differences were made up, that the whole Church was again united by Aśoka, and that it continued to be so till at least the 27th year of Aśoka's reign.

It is worthy of note that the Sārnāth, Kosāṁbī and Sāñchī Edicts contain a *śāsana* or order to the Mahāmātras of the districts concerned to expel a Bhikshu or Bhikshuṇī as soon as he or she is detected in the act of creating a schism. Many other Mahāmātras must have been similarly in-

1 *Ibid.*, p. 109; JRAS., 1901, pp. 855-8.

2 Kern, *op. cit.*, p. 103.

structed by the king. But the question arises how were the Mahāmātras to decide whether any particular Bhikshu or Bhikshuṇī was an apostate or not. Was the Saṃgha to decide this matter by a majority, and were the Mahāmātras merely to carry out their decision? If this was so, it could be done by a general conference of Bhikshus for every such matter as would arise. The holding of such an unwieldy conference of Bhikshus from the different parts of India for every such occasion, especially at that time when there was no quick conveyance or communication, would be exceedingly cumbrous, nay impracticable. Are we then to presume that Aśoka had some Theras or seniormost Bhikshus at his capital to instruct him as to what constituted heresy in any particular case? But this sort of religious autocracy or oligarchy was utterly unknown to early Buddhism. What we might reasonably suppose is that, as a matter of fact, there was a council of Buddhist Bhikshus held at Pāṭaliputra as is reported by the Singhalese tradition, and that the canonical literature was definitively and finally settled by them, so as to eliminate all disruptive tendencies. It is only on the supposition that such an authorised text of the canon was before the Mahāmātras that we can understand how it was possible for them to detect, prove and punish apostasy.

That a Council of Buddhist Bhikshus was held in the time of Aśoka seems to be hinted at even in the Bhābrū edict. This edict is a missive addressed by the king to the Saṃgha The question arises: which Saṃgha is here intended? In one sense, the Saṃgha was spread over the whole of India. But it is impossible to despatch the missive to a Saṃgha which was not confined to any particular place at any particular time, but was spread over the whole of a country. Nor was any all-India Committee of this body known to which the missive could be addressed. There was a time when the third and fourth words of the edict were read as *Māgadhaṃ Saṃghaṃ*, and it was then possible to say that Aśoka had sent this epistle to the Saṃgha pertaining to the small province of Magadha. But the facsimile which Hultzsch has published leaves no doubt as to *Māgadhe Saṃghaṃ* being the correct reading. *Māgadhe* has thus to be connected with *Piyadasi lājā* and not *Saṃghaṃ*. Which was then the Saṃgha addressed by Aśoka? This question still remains unanswered. The only plausible reply is that the monarch had dispatched this missive to the Saṃgha of the Bhikshus who had gathered as representatives from the various parts of India to attend the Council that had been convened. This also receives confirmation from the fact that here Aśoka calls himself *Māgadhe* = '(king) of Magadha.' In no inscription of his has this king been styled *Māgadho*. Where was the necessity for this in the present instance? The reply is that to the Council must have come many Bhikshus who did not belong to his empire, and to whom it was therefore necessary for Aśoka to introduce himself as King of Magadha.

CHAPTER IV

Aśoka's Dhamma

We have seen in the second chapter what Aśoka did for the temporal good of his people and are in a position to form our own estimate of him as a ruler. He, no doubt, strove very hard for the temporal welfare of his subjects. But what has made Aśoka entitled to world-wide renown, and, in fact, the principal object, which he had invariably before his mind and on the realisation of which he prided himself, was the spiritual good of man, the dissemination of what he loved to call Dhaṃma, not only in his country but far beyond in the dominions of his independent neighbours. It, therefore, behoves us, in the first place, to ascertain what exactly Aśoka understood by Dhaṃma. He is quite explicit on this point, and gives us not only the attributes that fall under the term but also specific practices thereof, which he is never wearied of asking his people again and again to bring into action. In Pillar Edicts II and VII, Aśoka specifies the qualities, which, in his opinion, constitute Dhaṃma. With him Dhaṃma consists of (1) *sādhave* or *bahu-kayāne*, much good, (2) *ap-āsinave*, freedom from depravity, (3) *dayā*, mercy, (4) *dāne*, liberality, (5) *sache*, truthfulness, (6) *sachaye*, purity, and (7) *mādave*, gentleness. But how are these virtues to be put into practice? Aśoka makes several enumerations of duties in this connection, which vary but slightly in different inscriptions. These may be summed up as follows : *anārambho prāṇānaṁ*, non-slaughter of animate beings ; *avihisā bhūtānaṁ*, non-injury to 'existing' creatures ; *mātari pitari susrūsā*, hearkening to father and mother ; *thaira susrūsā*, hearkening to the elders ; *gurūnaṁ apachiti*, reverence to teachers ; *mita-saṁstuta-nātikānaṁ bahmaṇa-samaṇānaṁ dānaṁ saṁpaṭipati*, liberality and seemly behaviour towards friends, acquaintances and relatives and towards Brāhmaṇa and Śramaṇa ascetics ; *dāsa-bhatakamhi samyapratipati*, seemly behaviour to slaves and servants ; and, in one inscription only (R. E. III), *apa-vyayatā* and *apa-bhāṇḍatā*, small expense and small accumulation. This is part of Aśoka's message to the world for all climes and for all ages. It sounds almost a truism, and yet how lucid, simple and true ! He does not rest satisfied by merely telling us to practise *dayā*, *dāna mādava*, mercy, liberality, gentleness, and so forth, but also shows how these virtues are to be translated into action. Thus *dayā*, mercy, means *anārambho prāṇānaṁ*, *avihisā bhūtānaṁ*, non-destruction and even non-injury to creatures ; *dāna*, liberality, means liberality towards friends, acquaintances and relatives and towards ascetics whether they belong to the Brāhmaṇa or Śramaṇa sects ; and *mādava*, gentleness, is to be manifested by hearkening to the parents and the elders, and seemly behaviour not only towards relatives or Brāhmaṇa and Śramaṇa recluses but also towards slaves and servants.

Aśoka is so fond of this part of his message that he takes delight in iterating it again and again in his edicts. In Rock Edict XIV, he frankly confesses that certain words have been repeated over and over again because of the sweetness of their import. The word Dhaṃma and its import are so sweet to him that he not only repeats the code of duties which constitute it, but also extols it by instituting a comparison between Dhaṃma and the ordinary practices of life and establishing the superiority of the former over the latter. Thus in Rock Edict IX he speaks of Dhaṃma, or *Dhamma-maṃgala* as he calls it, in contradistinction with the *maṁgalas* or rites for inducing luck and averting calamities, which, in Aśoka's time as now, obtained in legion in Hindu society. "People perform," says he in that edict, "various (lucky) rites in sicknesses, at marriages, on the birth of sons, and on journey.........In this matter, however, womankind performs much, manifold (but) trivial, useless rites. Rites should undoubtedly be performed. But a rite of this kind bears little fruit. That rite, however, bears great fruit which is *Dhaṃma-maṃgala*," that is, the rite which consists in the fulfilment of Dhaṃma. And after this he goes on inculcating the duties which form the practical character of his teaching and which have just been enumerated. Similarly, in Rock Edict XI he draws a contrast between *dāna* or ordinary gift and *Dhaṃma-dāna* or gift of Dhaṃma. The latter, he tells us, is the highest form of *dāna* and means making one acquainted with Dhaṃma, participate in Dhaṃma, and thus become a kinsman of Dhaṃma. And in order to explain this Dhaṃma he again enumerates his ethical practices, and winds up by saying that this *Dhaṃma-dāna* or alms-giving of Dhaṃma can be conferred by anybody on anybody, by father on his son or *vice versâ*, by brothers and relatives upon one another, and, in fact, by everybody upon his neighbour. Likewise, in Rock Edict XIII Aśoka compares *vijaya* or ordinary conquest with *Dhaṃma-vijaya* or conquest through Dhaṃma and in such a way as to conduce to the exaltation of the latter. In this connection he refers to his territorial conquest of Kaliṅga, and, with great heaviness of heart and even a little sense of shame, he speaks of the terrible massacre he inflicted on soldiers and the acute misery and grief of bereavement he caused to their relatives. These are the diabolical concomitants of a territorial conquest. But the conquest through Dhaṃma, says he, is *prītirasa* or flavoured with love, and can be accomplished anywhere, not only up to the outlying provinces of his empire but also in the dominions of his independent neighbours, whether they are in India or far beyond its north-western frontiers, where rule the Yavana or Greek princes, Antiochus Theos, Ptolemy Philadelphos, and so forth.

We have thus seen what qualities and what practices go to make up Aśoka's Dhaṃma. But this is not all that we have to understand by his Dhaṃma. These qualities and practices form only its positive character. But Aśoka's Dhaṃma has also a negative side, which may be summed up in the one word, *ap-āsinava*, that is, the negation of *āsinava*. But what is *āsinava*? Aśoka gives a reply to this question in Pillar Edict III where he places it side by side with *pāpa*, and specifies the malevolent affections that lead to *āsinava*. They are: *chaṁḍiye*, violence; *niṭhuliye*, cruelty; *kodhe*, anger; *māne*, conceit; and *isyā*, envy. Thus not only the performance of moral duties enumerated by Aśoka, but also freedom from these passions, is necessary for the full and adequate fulfilment of Dhaṃma.

It will be seen that Aśoka had thus a definite message to give to this world. And it is a pity that this has not yet been clearly perceived. In regard to the positive side of Dhaṃma, he specifies not only the attributes that constitute it but also the ethical practices in which they are to manifest themselves. As regards its negative character he has taken care to enumerate the malevolent affections which impel a man to sin and depravity (*āsinava*) and to exhort us to keep ourselves as free from them as possible. But this is not all. Like a true prophet he has clearly apprehended what debars spiritual progress, and has suggested a remedy which enables us to pursue the evolution of piety unhampered. This remedy is the self-examination which he inculcates on our minds as absolutely necessary for the real development of Dhaṃma. It is, however, worthy of note that Buddhaghosha in his *Visuddhi-magga*, distinguishes between various forms of *pachcha-vekkhana*, which has been consecrated to the sense of 'examination of conscience,' 'self-examination.' And this idea of *pachcha-vekkhana* he has adopted from Buddha himself, who taught it to Ambalaṭṭhika-Rāhula. Buddha's discourse to Rāhula occurs in the Majjhima Nikāya, and is no doubt one of the texts referred to approvingly by Aśoka himself in the Bhābrū Edict, as we have seen in the last chapter. Therein Buddha exhorts Rāhula to examine every act of the body, speech or mind before and also after it is initiated. Aśoka, however, is more human and teaches us to examine our character as a whole and thus take a broader outlook of our activities. "Man," says he, in Pillar Edict III, "seeth the good only, saying unto himself: 'this good have I performed.' In no wise doth he see (his) sin (*pāpa*), and say unto himself: 'this sin have I committed,' or 'this indeed is *āsinava*.' This, however, is difficult to scrutinise. Nevertheless, man should see to this, and say unto himself:—'such and such (passions), indeed, lead to *āsinava*, ... and by reason (of them) may I not cause my fall!'" It is in this place that Aśoka enumerates the malevolent affections which conduce to *āsinava*,—and we have already seen what they are. Here Aśoka is evidently referring to the natural tendency of the human being to perceive and chuckle over the good he performs but not to see and regret the ill, the sinfulness, he is committing. Aśoka, therefore, very aptly remarks that it is very difficult for a person to conduct self-examination and see through the evil he has committed. He, however, insists upon self-scrutiny being carried on in order that man may not bring about his own fall. The idea of self-examination is looked upon at present as essentially Christian both in origin and practice. But if Aśoka is not here preaching what the Christians understand by 'self-examination,' it is difficult to see what self-examination really is. What, again, is worthy of note here is the word which Aśoka uses for 'self-examination.' This word is *paṭivekhā*, which, except for a little irregularity of form, is exactly the same as *pachchavekkhana* which, as we have seen, Buddha himself employs in the sense of 'examination of the conscience.' It is not, therefore, permissible to doubt that Aśoka taught 'self-examination' to his people, and regarded it as essential to spiritual progress.

Any one who considers Aśoka's code of Dhamma cannot fail to be struck by the remarkably simple nature of his teaching. His Dhamma may be described as the common property of all religions. The virtues and practices which he tells us to follow are precisely those which all religions specify as worthy of our imitation. One is, therefore, almost tempted to say that there is nothing new or original in what he teaches. He himself admits as much in one of his edicts, Rock-Edict XIII., where he says that "there is no country except that of the Yavanas where there are not the Brāhmaṇa and Śramaṇa congregations and there is no place in any country where men have no faith in one sect or another," and that, in fact, "everywhere dwell these Brāhmanic, Śramanic and other sects and householders among whom are established such practices as hearkening to the elders, hearkening to parents, hearkening to the preceptors, seemly behaviour and steadfast devotion to friends, acquaintances, companions and relatives, and to slaves and servants." Is it not tantamount to

Aśoka's admission that his Dhaṃma, which involves the preformance of these duties, is something which all sects possess in common? This is just the reason why in another place (Rock Edict VII.) he gives expression to his intense desire that "all sects may dwell at all places (in his kingdom), because they all desire self-restraint and purification of heart." "The people, however," he continues, "are of various likings and various attachments. They will perform either the whole or a part (of their duty). But even the lavish liberality, (gratitude and firm attachment) of (a man) who has no self-restraint and purity of heart are quite worthless." What Aśoka means is that *saṃyama*, self-restraint, and *bhāva-śuddhi*, purification of heart, are virtues of such paramount excellence that every individual ought to develop them in himself. These virtues, again, are inculcated by every sect, and form the chief portion of its commandment. Whether the whole commandment will be put into practice by a member of a sect is doubtful. But it is supremely imperative on him to cultivate at least these two virtues, the negation of which can never be compensated by any degree of liberality, gratitude or devotion that he may show to his sect. The same exhortation has been set forth by Aśoka in clearer language and at greater length in Rock Edict XII. This edict is so important, as it faithfully portrays his attitude towards the different religions, that no excuse is needed for giving a full substance of it here. Aśoka says that he does not think of liberality and outward reverence (*pūjā*) to one's own religion so much as of the growth of its essential (*sāravaḍhi*). This growth of the essential is of various kinds, but at the root of it is restraint of speech. In other words, a person must not make an exhibition of reverence to his own sect and condemn another's without any good reason. On the contrary, the other sects should be shown reverence for this and that reason. By so doing a person exalts his own sect, and does service to another's sect. By doing otherwise, he does harm to both. He who shows reverence to his own sect and condemns that of another because he is attached to his own sect and wants to illuminate it, inflicts, in reality, a severe injury on it. What course of action then is commendable in these circumstances? Aśoka replies: "people shall hear and desire to hear further one another's Dhaṃma." What will be the consequence of this? Aśoka describes it as follows. All sects, says he first, will thereby be possessed of much information and knowledge (*bahu-śruta*) and will conduce to the performance of good deeds (*kalyāṇ-āgama*). There will thus arise, he also says, the exaltation of one's own sect (*ātma-pāsaṃḍa vaḍhi*) and the illumination of Dhaṃma (*Dhaṃmasa dīpanā*). This, in fact, is what Aśoka says in Rock Edict XII., and offers pabulum for reflection even to the present age. What he implies is that every religion, or Dhaṃma in its more extensive sense, has two sides: (1) doctrinal and (2) ethical. The first concerns itself with questions of ritual and theology, and appeals to the intellect. The second is represented by Dhaṃma in its less extensive but proper sense, by what a man of sense, a man of right feeling, will naturally do; in other words, it appeals to the conscience as the modern people will say. So far as the doctrinal portion of a religion goes, there will always be diverse and mutually conflicting views not only in regard to the articles of belief but also in regard to the ritual we have to observe. This must be so, because the human intellect varies so widely. So far, however, as the ethical side of a religion is concerned, there is no divergence, no conflict, but perfect unanimity as regards the moral virtues and the moral practices we have to manifest in our conduct. This must be so, because the conscience, the sense of right and wrong, can never vary. What, therefore, the ethical side of a religion teaches cannot be something which is peculiar to that religion, but rather must be the common property of all religions. It is really the essence of all religions and the Dhaṃma, which Aśoka teaches and which we have so far considered is really this essence. On the other hand, the moment we give a loose rein to our intellect, there is no end to the discussion we can carry on in matters connected with ritual and theology; and very often this discussion is nothing but acrimonious wrangling. It is this which tends the people to eulogise their sect even when no occasion calls for it, or run down other sects without any good reason,—a fanatic spirit, in fact, against which Aśoka, as we have seen, has so strongly protested. That there was this propensity to exalt one's own sect and revile that of another, that there were often hot and bitter debates between one sect and another probably over doctrinal points in Aśoka's time which put the essentials of a religion into the background seems to follow from the strong expostulations in which he has thought fit to indulge. It is even possible to be more definite on this point and find out in what quarters exactly this animosity, this carping spirit, prevailed. For Aśoka distinctly tells us that the work of generating sympathy and concord between one sect and another was entrusted to the Dharma-Mahāmātras, Stryadhyaksha-Mahāmātras and Vachabhūmikas. We know that the Dharma-Mahāmātras were occupied with all sects, the most prominent of which were the Brahmanical Ājīvikas, Nirgranthas and Buddhists. And as these officials have been instructed to attain this object, it is plain that there were friction and bitter spirit between those sects. This is clear also from a critical study of the early Buddhist literature which speaks of a number of schools, orders and sects, wrangling often bitterly with one another. Stryadhyaksha-Mahāmātras were, of course, officers who were concerned with the welfare and happiness of women. And as they too have been ordered to attain the same object, it is evident that sectarian fervour and intolerant spirit were being displayed by women also. It is a pity we do not know yet definitely who the Vachabhūmikas were and what their function was. But it is sufficiently clear that the tendency to eulogise one's sect and disparage that of another through religious frenzy was displayed by all the principal sects of the period and that women who are naturally more religious-minded, were by no means free from it. When, therefore, Aśoka lived and preached, theological disputation and sectarian spirit were rampant. And at a time when the people's attention is rivetted not on the essential but on the non-essential element of a religion, it requires the penetrating insight and religious strength of a prophet to distinguish the essential from the non-essential and proclaim it to the world. As a matter of fact, this is what Aśoka has done. What constitutes his originality of mind as of all saints is his concentration on the essence of religion which all sects possess in common, specially at a time when they have lost sight of it.

It is interesting to note by what means he attempted to divert the mind of his people from the non-essential to the essential element of religion. He exhorts the people to hearken and desire to hearken still more to one another's Dhaṃma, by which he here means not only the ethics but also the ritual and theology of a sect. The effect of such a step must be at once to show to them that although one sect differed from another, they agreed in many important points. The attention of the people would thus be drawn to the points of agreement which, they must naturally conclude, constituted the essence of a religion. When the essential is thus selected and emphasised, the people would consider it to be their primary duty to put it into practice, and the result is that there is *dhaṃmasa dīpanā*, illumination of Dhaṃma, and that the sects must thus contribute to benevolent activity (*kalyāṇ-āgama*). But like a true thinker Aśoka did not neglect the non-essential, that is, the sacerdotal, side of a religion which comprised ritual and theology and which appealed more to the intellect than to the moral or religious sense By hearkening to one another's Dhaṃma, as proposed by Aśoka, people have to listen to and consider the doctrinal points also of the various sects. They will thus have for their reflection and judicious selection various forms of philosophy, nature lore and ceremonial developed by the various sects. They must consequently become *bahu-śruta*, that is, possessed of much knowledge and information, and be able to evolve their own system of ritual and theology in a satisfactory fashion. When the people in this manner hearken to one another's Dhaṃma, note the essence of religion, and emphasize it for conduct, and by a careful sifting of the different rituals and theologies of the different sects construct their own creed, they can thereby achieve the *ātma-pāsaṃḍa-vaḍhi*, or the exaltation of their own sect, which was one of the uppermost thoughts in Aśoka's mind. The Dhaṃma of Aśoka is thus the essence of religion, and to perceive it in all religions and single it out for practice, and to study and weigh impartially and dispassionately their ritual and theology so as to enable us to frame our own theory in regard to the relation of man with nature is what the royal prophet of the third century B. C. teaches us. How grand and convincing this message, and how indispensable even to the present times!

(No account of Aśoka's Dhaṃma can be complete unless we know with what ultimate end the

Dhaṃma was to be practised.) In other words, what is the *summum bonum* reserved for those who followed Dhaṃma? Did Aśoka believe in the future world? (This question has, of course, to be answered in the positive. He often contrasts this with the next world. Thus in Pillar Edict IV. while speaking of the Rājūkas, he says that he expects these officers to promote the *hidata* and *pālata* of the provincial people, that is, their happiness in this world and the next. Similarly, in the Dhauli and Jaugaḍā Separate Edict I., he tells us that the uppermost desire of his mind is that mankind should attain to welfare and happiness, *hida-lokika* and *pāla-lokika*, that is, pertaining both to this and the other world. But what is it in the next world that a man secures by following Dhaṃma? Aśoka replies : *svarga*, heaven. There are at least three references to *svarga* in his edicts. In Rock Edict VI. Aśoka says that whatever effort he puts forth he puts forth in order to make his people happy and in order that they may attain to *svarga* in the next world. In Minor Rock Edict I., he insists upon all officers endeavouring strenuously to make his subjects obtain *svarga*. In Rock Edict IX., however, he tells us something more. It is this edict, which, we have seen, refers to his *Dhaṃma-maṃgala*, that is, the auspicious rite which consists in the fulfilment of Dhaṃma. In two recensions of this edict he observes that the performance of Dhaṃma leads to the attainment of *svarga*. And the same thing he explains in different language in three copies of the same edict. "Every worldly rite," he remarks, "is of a dubious nature. It may or may not accomplish its object. *Dhaṃma-maṃgala*, however, is not conditioned by time, and even though it may not achieve any object here, it begets endless merit in the next world." In other words, what Aśoka means is that performance of Dhaṃma breeds much *puṇya* or merit in the next world and thus enables a man to attain to *svarga*.

The simple character of the Dhaṃma taught by Aśoka in his edicts is apparently in conflict with the fact that he was a Buddhist when he preached it and has thus much puzzled the scholars. Thus Fleet held the view that the Dhaṃma of the Rock and Pillar Edicts was not Buddhism at all but simply *rāja-dharma*, that is, a code of duties prescribed for kings.[1] But we have already shown that the Dhaṃma referred to by Aśoka even in these edicts cannot possibly be any kind of rules intended for rulers and governors to follow for good administration, but rather for the people in general to put into practice for leading righteous lives. Similarly, it has been contended by another writer that in these edicts Dhaṃma " does not stand for Buddhism, but for the simple piety which Aśoka wished all his subjects of whatever faith to practise."[2] The late Dr. V. A. Smith in one place in his *Aśoka* [3] says : " The *Dharma*, or Law of Piety, which he preached and propagated unceasingly with amazing faith in the power of sermonizing, had few· if any, distinctive features.

1 JRAS., 1908, pp. 491-7.
2 J. M. Macphail, *Aśoka*, p. 48.
3 Pp. 59-60.

The doctrine was essentially common to all Indian religions, although one sect or denomination might lay particular stress on one factor in it rather than on another." Prof. Radhakumud Mookerji follows in their footsteps. In another place[1] Smith remarks: "The *dhaṁma* of the Edicts is that Hindu *dharma* with a difference, due to a Buddhist tinge, nay, rather due to saturation with the ethical thought which lies at the basis of Buddhism, but occupies a subordinate place in Hinduism." This is something like a contradiction, because at one time he admits that there was nothing distinctively Buddhistic in Aśoka's Dhaṃma, and at another he asserts that that Dhaṃma was saturated with Buddhist ethical thought. Similarly, in a third place, Smith says that the inducements of *svarga* held out by Aśoka were hardly consistent with the Buddhist philosophy of most books," and yet in a fourth place he remarks that very probably the monarch looked forward to *nirvāṇa* although he did not express the hope.[2] Prof. F. W. Thomas says: "there is no mention of the Four Grand Truths, the Eightfold Path, the chain of causation........... the word and idea of Nirvāna fail to occur."[3] Thus there are some scholars like Smith and Thomas who have not been able to reconcile the apparently non-distinctive, non-sectarian, character of Aśoka's Dhaṃma with the fact of his being a Buddhist even at the time when he preached it. On the other hand, we have a scholar like Senart who has seen some

1 *Ibid.*, pp. 29-30.
2 *Aśoka*, pp. 64-5.
3 CHI., Vol. I, p. 505.

points of contact between Aśoka's teaching and the Buddhist *Dhaṃmapada*, and who considers Aśoka's inscriptions as representing such a whole and entire picture of Buddhism of that period as to justify the conclusion that up till the time of that monarch Buddhism was "a purely moral doctrine, paying little attention to particular dogmas or to abstract theories, little embarrassed with scholastic or monkish elements,...and as yet without a regularly defined canon."[1] The resemblances noticed by the French savant do not, however, appear to be of much importance except two. Besides, the Buddhist Dhaṃmapada possesses many texts in common with such Brahmanical works as the Mahābhārata, and it is doubtful whether the former can be regarded as an exclusively Buddhist work. And no scholar seems yet to have accepted the further statement of Senart based simply on the strength of the epigraphic records of Aśoka that up till the middle of the third century B. C., Buddhism was founded on the preference for the fulfilment of moral duties over the execution of the liturgical forms and practices. It is a mistake to suppose that Aśoka's epigraphs portray the whole of Buddhism in his time. All these scholars have apparently forgotten that Buddhism has always consisted of two parts: (1) Dhaṃma for the monks and nuns, and (2) Dhaṃma for the householders. Aśoka was a householder, at any rate he was so when he preached his Dhaṃma; and the people to whom he taught it were also householders, not men who had embraced the

[1] I.A., 1891, pp. 264-5.

monastic life. If, therefore, it is desired to find out whether his Dhaṃma was at all inspired by Buddhism, it is necessary to ascertain what scriptural texts have been reserved by that religion for the lay people to read, contemplate, and practise. The most important that has been prescribed for the Buddhist laity is the *sigālovāda-sutta* comprised in the Dīgha-Nikāya of the Buddhist scriptures. This is considered so important that it has been designated *gihi-vinaya*—' Institute for the housemen,' [1] as was first pointed out by Prof. B. M. Barua. " In this Sutta," says Buddhaghosha, " there is left nothing undescribed that constitutes the whole duty of a houseman. The Suttanta is, therefore, entitled *gihi-vinaya*—' Institute for the housemen.' Wherefore, if any person having hearkened to it, carries out what he is instructed therein, he may be expected not to decline, but to prosper." Such is the degree of importance attached to this Sutta, of course, from the laity's point of view. The gist of it is as follows: Buddha was once staying near Rājagṛiha in the Bamboo Wood; and, going out as usual for alms, observes Sigāla, a householder's son, with wet hair and garments and with clasped hands uplifted, paying worship to the several quarters of earth and sky. On Buddha asking the reason why, Sigāla says that he does this worship, holding sacred his father's word. Buddha, however, replies that in the religion of an Aryan, the six quarters should not be worshipped thus. And on being requested to explain how they should be wor-

[1] JRAS., 1915, p. 809.

shipped, Buddha points out at great length that the best way to worship the quarters is by good deeds to men around him, and sums up the whole thing in a few Gāthās, the first of which may be quoted here :[1]

> Mother and father are the Eastern view,
> And teachers are the quarters of the South,
> And wife and children are the Western view,
> And friends and kin the quarter to the North;
> Servants and working folk the nadir are,
> And overhead the Brahmin and recluse.
> These quarters should be worshipped by the man
> Who fitly ranks as houseman in his clan.

Anybody who even hurriedly considers these verses cannot fail to mark that it enumerates just those courses of conduct which Aśoka is never tired of inculcating on the minds of his people. Hearkening to parents, reverence to teachers, liberality and seemly behaviour towards friends, acquaintances, and relatives, and towards Brāhman and Śramaṇa ascetics, and seemly behaviour towards slaves and servants are the practices of Dhaṃma on which Aśoka has laid so much stress and are exactly those which Buddha emphasizes to make Sigāla a good, virtuous householder. The code of duties on which Aśoka insists may contain nothing that will not be assented to by other religious sects, such as Jainism, Ājivikism, and so forth, but most of these duties are, as it were, brought to a focus and found mentioned in this group in the Sigālovāda-Sutta,[2] a text which has been specially prescribed

[1] T. W. Rhys Davids, *Buddhism*, pp. 143-4; SBB., Vol. IV, 183 & ff.

[2] There are other Buddhist Suttas also which enumerate these ethical practices; for instance, *Aṅguttara-N.*, III, 76-8.

by Buddhism for its laity. And it is impossible to resist the conclusion that it is this religion that is the basis and the source of inspiration in regard to Aśoka's Dhaṃma. We may proceed one step further and ask whether we cannot similarly trace in Buddhist scriptures the qualities which constitute Aśoka's Dhaṃma. We have seen that they are: (1) *dayā*, (2) *dāne*, (3) *sache*, (4) *sochaye*, (5) *mādave*, and (6) *sādhave* or *kayāne*. Now, in the *Lakkhaṇa-suttanta* of the Dīgha-Nikāya we have verses [1] which set forth certain virtues which, if practised, we are told, lead to 'Heaven to share in bliss and ravishment.' [2] The verses are as follows:

> *sachche cha dhamme cha dame cha samyame*
> *socheyya-sīlālay-uposathesu cha*
> *Dāne ahimsāya asāhase rato* [3]

It will be seen that *sachcha*, *socheyya* and *dāna* are common to both the lists. And further there will be no difficulty at all in perceiving that *ahiṃsā* (*-asāhasa*), and (*dama-*) *saṃyama* of the verses must correspond to *dayā* and *mādave* of Aśoka's inscriptions. And it is not impossible that *sīla* of the verses stands for the *sādhave* or *kayāne* of the epigraphs. Here also we notice certain virtues mentioned together in the *Lakkhaṇa-suttanta* which occur together almost in that lump in Pillar Edicts II and VII of Aśoka. It is quite clear that even in the enumeration of the qualities which

[1] My attention to these verses was first drawn by Mr. Gokuldas De.

[2] SBB., IV, 140.

[3] *Dīgha-N.*, III, 147.

constitute Dhaṃma Aśoka was indebted to a Buddhist Sutta,—a scripture which speaks of Chakravartī Dhārmika Dharmarāja to whose position he was doubtless aspiring, as we will see in Chapter VII and which must have been constantly before his mind's eye.

The Buddhist Sutta, which is next in importance to the Sigālovāda-Sutta as regards lay conduct is the Mahāmaṇgala-Sutta contained in the Suttanipāta. It recommends a certain group of duties, the performance of which constitutes the greatest of *maṃgalas* to a layman. This use of the word *maṃgala* to denote righteous practices reminds us of the phrase—*Dhaṃma-maṅgala*, which Aśoka employs in Rock Edict IX to denote the *maṃgala* consisting in the performance of the ethical practices specified by him as constituting Dhaṃma. And it leaves no doubt as to his being indebted for this idea and phraseology to the Buddhist canonical text just referred to. The Sutta commends, as the greatest of *maṃgalas*, "waiting on father and mother, protecting wife and child, giving alms, taking care of relatives, abstaining from sin, intercourse with Śramaṇas, and religious conversations at due seasons."[1] Here, again, is another enumeration of most of the qualities and practices referred to by Aśoka under Dhaṃma. We have further to note that just as Aśoka compares ordinary *maṅgala* with *Dhaṃma-maṅgala* he compares ordinary *dāna*, *anugraha* and *saṃvibhāga* with *Dhaṃma-dāna* (RE., IX, & XI), *Dhaṃm-*

[1] SBE., Vol. X (Pt. II), p. 43.

ānugraha (R.E., IX) and *Dhaṃma-saṃvibhāga* (R.E., XI). Nearly thirty-five years ago, Bühler,[1] drew the attention of scholars to a passage in the *Itivuttaka* (Chat. Nip. I) which institutes exactly this comparison, leaving no doubt as to Aśoka having borrowed the idea and the phraseology from this Buddhist scripture. What is more important is that in Rock Edict IX this comparison begins with the words *asti cha pi vutaṃl sādhu dānaṃ til.* The passage from the *Itivuttaka* also commences with *vuttàm hetam Bhagavatā vuttam Arahatā ti me sutam*, showing clearly that Aśoka is here quoting the words of the Buddha as reported in the *Itivuttaka.*

If any further proof is needed to show that the Dhaṃma taught by Aśoka was inspired by Buddhism, it is furnished by what he says in Rock Edict XII. We have already seen that therein Aśoka exhorts his people not to praise one's own sect and condemn another's unduly. The whole of this edict is but a development of the theme set forth in the *Chūlaviyūha-sutta* and *Mahāviyūha-sutta* of the *Sutta-nipāta.* The following translation of some of their verses will not be out of place.

(V 891) 'Those who preach a Dhaṃma different from this, fall short of purity and are imperfect, so the Titthiyas say repeatedly ; for they are inflamed by passion for their own views.

(V 904) Their own Dhaṃma they say is perfect, another's Dhaṃma again they say is

[1] ZDMG., 48, 57 f.

wretched; so having disagreed they dispute; they each say their own opinions (are) the truth.

(V. 880) He who does not acknowledge an opponent's Dhaṃma, is a fool, a beast, one of poor understanding. All are fools with a very poor understanding; all these abide by their (own) views.

(V. 884) For the truth is one, there is not a second, about which one intelligent man might dispute with another intelligent man. (But) they themselves proclaim different truths, therefore the Samaṇas do not say one (and the same thing).

(V. 898) Those who are highest in virtue (*sīla*) say that purity *suddhi* is through restraint *Saññama*. Taking (this) vow (*vata*), they serve. Thus only let us learn purity (taught by) Him (Master).

What the above verses tell us is that different schools or sects praise themselves and stigmatise others, but that truth is one. This is exactly what Aśoka expatiates upon in Rock Edict XII and also VII. And further the verses inculcate the cultivation of *saṃyama* and *suddhi* exactly as the Buddhist king has done in these Rock Edicts. No reasonable doubt can after this be entertained as to Aśoka being indebted to a Buddhist scripture for his grand preaching that truth is one and is taught by all sects and that real purity depends upon self-restraint.

If it is once grasped that Aśoka was himself a lay follower of Buddhism and preached to the householders, and that his teaching was based on what that religion ordained for its laity, there is nothing surprising in the fact that he makes no mention of the Nirvāṇa or the *ashṭāṅgikamārga* in his edicts, but, on the contrary, speaks of *svarga* and holds it up as the reward of Dhaṃma in the next life. According to Buddhism, the doctrine of heaven and hell is especially the layman's religion, the higher attainments and the goal of Nirvāṇa being reserved for a Bhikshu. This was just the view of Buddha, who has more than once implied that a pious householder is born in the next world as a god in one of the heavens.[1] It is therefore no wonder at all, if Aśoka regards *svarga* as the *summum bonum* to be attained for leading a virtuous life on earth. The belief in *svarga* is not something peculiar to Buddhism, but was shared by many religious sects. And the question that really arises is whether Aśoka believed in *svarga* such as that described in Buddhist works. In Rock Edict IV Aśoka says: "But now in consequence of the spread of Dhaṃma by king Priyadarśin, Beloved of the gods, the sound of the drum has become the sound of Dhaṃma, after his having shown to the people spectacles of aerial chariots (*vimānas*), spectacles of elephants (*hastins*), masses of fire (*agniskandhas*), and other divine representations." What he means is that with him the drum has become the proclaimer of Dhaṃma. The sound of a drum invariably precedes either a battle, a public announcement, or the exhibition of a scene to the people. But since he entered on his career as a missionary it has

[1] *Majjhima-N.*, I, 289 & 388.

ceased to be a summons to fight, but invites people to come and witness certain spectacles; and as these spectacles are of such a character as to generate and develop Dhaṃma, the drum has thus become the proclaimer of Dhaṃma. But what spectacles did Aśoka show to his subjects? Obviously they were the *vimānas*, *hastins*, *agni-skandhas*, and so forth. The exact sense of these terms has been made clear by a work in the Pāli literature called Vimānavatthu. It describes the various rewards which are in store for a virtuous man in his next life as he becomes one kind or another of *deva* according to the degree of his merit. One of these rewards is the *vimāna* or column-supported palace which is a centre of supreme bliss and which could be moved at the will of its divine owner. Another kind of reward is the *hastin* or well-caparisoned, all-white, celestial elephant. The Vimānavatthu, again, describes most of the gods as possessed of a resplendent complexion, which is compared to lightning, star, or fire; and when therefore, Aśoka says that he exhibited *agni-skandhas* or *jyotiḥ-skandhas* to his people, what he must have done is that he showed what kinds of lustre emitted from the bodies of virtuous men when they became gods in their next birth. The lives of the Devas in heavens according to Hindu belief then as now are limited, and depend upon the merit accruing from their good acts. What the Vimānavatthu, however, does is only to describe, according to the Buddhist notion, what celestial abodes and vehicles were reserved for the pious people, and lay particular stress on them, in order to induce readers and listeners to lead good unblemished lives on earth and be zealous in the performance of religious duties. Evidently, the mention by Aśoka not only of the *vimānas* but also of *hastins* and *agni-* or *jyotiḥ-skandhas* as being the cause of the development of righteousness among his people is a clear proof of the fact that the system of *svarga* in which he believed and to which he refers in his twelfth year is that known to and evolved by Buddhism.

The above considerations are quite enough to convince anybody that Aśoka was a Buddhist, when he preached the Dhaṃma set forth in his Rock and Pillar Edicts and that there are clear traces of this Dhaṃma being inspired and inculcated by Buddhism.[1] It may, however, be now asked : was he indebted for this solely to Buddhism? Did he borrow and assimilate anything from any other religion? Aśoka himself has advised his people to listen to one another's Dhaṃma in order that they may exalt their religion and themselves

[1] It is thus difficult to see how Prof. Radhakumud Mukherji tries to distinguish Aśoka's personal religion which was Buddhism from the religion he sought to preach and introduce among people. In regard to the latter he says : "It was certainly not Buddhism" (Aśoka, p. 68), and yet he maintains that in consequence of Aśoka's foreign missions to the Western countries Buddhist thought has left its marks upon some phases of Western thought, such, e.g., as the sects of the Essenes and the Therapeutae. For he says that "it was through the instrumentality of such foreign missions from India that these results were achieved" (*Ibid.*, pp. 77-8). The Dhaṃma taught by Aśoka in the foreign land is the Dhaṃma of the Edicts which, according to Prof. Mukherji, is not Buddhism, How, therefore, Buddhism influenced the Essenes and the Therapeutae as maintained by him is far from clear.

become *bahu-śruta*, 'well-informed.' What he has exhorted others to do he must have himself done. Are there any elements in his Dhaṃma or his own conduct, which were not Buddhistic and which were adopted from other faiths? Anybody, who carefully considers the negative side of his Dhaṃma, cannot fail to be struck by the curious word *āsinava* and also the malaffections which he mentions as contributing to it. What is this word, *āsinava*? How is it to be derived? In Pillar Edict III, *āsinava* has been mentioned side by side with *pāpa*, 'sin,' and in Rock Edict X, we meet with the word *palisave* in the sense of *apuṇya*, 'demerit.' It, therefore, seems at first sight that *āsinava* of Aśoka is the same as *āsava* (=*āsrava*) of Buddhism, which has precisely the same signification. But the Buddhists have three kinds of *āsava*: (1) *kām-āsava*, 'sensual pleasure,' (2) *bhav-āsava*, 'love of existence,' and (3) *avijj-āsava*, 'defilement of ignorance.' Sometimes they add to this list a fourth one, namely, *diṭṭh-āsava*, that is, 'heresy.' Aśoka, however, mentions five ways leading to *āsinava*, which, again, are of an entirely different nature. They are, as we have seen, *chaṃḍiye*, 'violence,' *niṭhuliye*, 'cruelty,' *kodhe*, 'anger,' *māne*, 'conceit,' and *isyā*, 'envy.' The conclusion is irresistible that, curiously enough. Aśoka, although he was a Buddhist, did not adopt the *āsava* of Buddhism, supposing *āsava* is the same as *āsinava*. From where could he then have borrowed his *āsinavas*? Bühler notes that "the Jainas possess a term *aṇhaya*, which exactly corresponds to *āsinava*, and is derived, like the latter, from *ā-snu.*'"[1] *Aṇhaya* we find used, *e.g.*, in the well-known Jaina work *Āyāraṁga-sutta*[2] and translated as 'sins' by Prof. Jacobi.[3] This suits here excellently, because in Pillar Edict III *āsinava* (=*aṇhaya*) has been placed side by side with *pāpa*. The former could not have been exactly identical with the latter in meaning, and we shall not be far from right if we take *āsinava* (*aṇhaya*) to signify 'depravity, defilement.' This also seems to be the meaning of *parisava* used by Aśoka in Rock Edict X, where he equates it with *apuṇya* (demerit).

Now Jainism specifies eighteen kinds of *pāpa* or sin and forty-two kinds of *āsravas*.[4] These two lists have four malevolent affections in common, called *kashāyas*. Two of these are *krodha* and *māna*,[5] exactly two of the passions named by Aśoka. The *isyā* of Aśoka, again, is to be found in the Jaina list of the *pāpas* as *īrshyā* or *dvesha*. *Chaṃḍiye* and *niṭhuliye* are alone not traceable, though they are no doubt covered by the malaffection *hiṃsā* mentioned under *āsrava*. Thus the use of the term *āsinava* (*aṇhaya*),[6] distinction between it and *pāpa*,

[1] EI., Vol. II, p. 250.

[2] (PTS.), p. 92.

[3] SBE., Vol. XXII, p. 151.

[4] Mrs. Stevenson, *Heart of Jainism*, pp. 302 & ff. and pp. 305 & ff. Such comparative enumerations of *pāpa* and *āsava* do not seem to be known to the Buddhist scriptures.

[5] Some of these malaffections are no doubt mentioned by the Buddhists but they are classed under *kilesa*, not under *āsava* or *pāpa*.

[6] It deserves to be noticed that the word *aṇhaya* alone does not occur in the early Jaina scriptures, but that the terms *āsava* and *parissava* are also met with—in different senses (*Āyāraṃga-sutta*, p. 18). *Āsava* is that by means of which *karman* takes effect upon the soul; *parissava*, that (*nijjarā*) by which the influence of *karman* is counter-

and the inclusion of at least three passions of the Jaina lists are enough to convince anybody that, in all likelihood, Aśoka has here adopted and assimilated some psychological concepts of Jainism. We thus see that although Aśoka was an ardent follower of Buddhism, he was yet Catholic enough to study other faiths such as Jainism, and adopt such features of the latter as commended themselves to him. The same conclusion is pointed to by the terminology he employs when he speaks of the various kinds of life. He uses such words as *jīva*, *pāṇa*, *bhūta* and *jāta*. Does this not remind us of the phraseology, *pāṇā bhūyā jīvā sattā*, which is employed, for instance, in the Āyārañga Sutta of the Jainas?[1] Of course, it is possible to contend that he never uses all of these words together, and may not have therefore, intended to distinguish between them. But it cannot be denied that at least *bhūta* Āśoka does contrast from *prāṇa*, when he enumerates his ethical practices, as in *anāraṃbho prāṇānaṃ, avihisā bhūtānaṃ*. Buddhist literature nowhere distinguishes between *prāṇa* and *bhūta*, whereas Jaina scriptures not only distinguish them one from the other but also both from *jīva* and *satta*.

This leads to the question : what was Aśoka's attitude towards other religious sects? We have seen that in Rock Edict VII he admits that all sects aim at self-restraint and purification of heart,

acted (SBE., Vol. XXII, p. 37, n. 1.). It will be seen that *Āsinava* (=*Aṇhaya*=depravity) may be the same as *āsava*, Buddhist or Jaina, but that Aśoka's *parisava* (=*apuṇya*) is exactly the opposite of the Jaina *parissava*.

[1] SBE., Vol. XXII, p. 36, & n. 1.

and desires that they may dwell at any place in his empire. This point he has made clear in Rock Edict XIII by saying that the practices of Dhaṃma which he is preaching are practically the same as those inculcated by these sects. And he takes us one step further by remarking in Rock Edict XII that all people should love to listen to one another's Dhaṃma and thus augment its essence (*sāra*). That Aśoka really meant what he has said is clear from the fact that his Dhaṃma, though it is Buddhism in the main, contains elements borrowed from other religions, such as Jainism, as we have just shown. When such is his mental attitude towards the various sects, one can well believe him when he tells us that he lavished gifts and honours on members of all sects, without any distinction, whether they were recluses or householders. And this belief is strengthened when we note that he regarded, as one of the constituents of Dhaṃma, respect and liberality towards Brāhmaṇs and Śramaṇas, that is, not only towards the non-Brahmanical sects other than Buddhism but also towards all Brahmanical sects. The Dharma-Mahāmātras also were ordered to promote the temporal and spiritual weal of *all* sects, not only of the Buddhist Saṃgha but also of the Nirgranthas, Brahmanical Ājīvikas, and so forth. The only action of his that is apparently inconsistent with his extremely tolerant attitude towards all religions is the prohibition of animal sacrifices to which he has referred in Rock Edict I. This, it is contended, was directed against the Brāhmaṇs and receives confirmation from a passage in Minor Rock Edict I.

The passage, however, is no longer interpreted by any scholar of repute as showing hostility to Brahmanism. And in regard to Rock Edict I, it is admitted that it does speak of Aśoka having prohibited sacrifices, but it is by no means clear that this prohibition was meant to be universal and not confined merely to his royal household. And even supposing for the moment that he prohibited sacrifices all over his kingdom, it does not necessarily imply any antagonism to Brahmanism as some of the Upanishads,[1] which are *śrutis* to a Brāhmaṇ, have declared themselves in no uncertain terms against animal sacrifices and in favour of *ahiṃsā*.

CHAPTER V

Aśoka as a Missionary

We have seen that Aśoka was a Buddhist and also that the Dhaṃma he preached was not simple piety common to all religions but the code of righteous practices laid down for a lay follower by Buddhism. Let us now find out what means he adopted for the promotion and propagation of Dhaṃma. Let us discuss what kind and degree of activity he displayed as a religious propagandist.

We have already seen that Aśoka embraced Buddhism in the ninth year of his reign. For one year, he did not show himself to be a zealot. But thereafter a change came over him, and about the middle of his tenth year he began to live with the Saṃgha and visited the Bodhi Tree. This was life turning a new leaf in the book of his life. He suddenly developed his missionary activity, and exerted himself to such an extent that although it was scarcely more than a year that he was with the Saṃgha, he felt himself justified in giving a glowing description of it. This he has done in two places, once in Minor Rock Edict I, and another time in Rock Edict IV. In the first of these records which is addressed to his officers, Aśoka says: "During this period (that is, the period that he was with the Saṃgha), human beings who were unmixed were caused to be mixed with gods throughout Jambudvīpa. This is the fruit of exertion. This is possible not only for the superior (official) to achieve, but, indeed, it is possible for a subordinate one also, if he exerts himself, to cause people to attain to much heavenly bliss." In this edict Aśoka has described the result of his missionary work in a twofold manner, first by saying that he has made gods and men one another's associates and next by saying that there was attainment of heavenly felicity. The commingling of men and gods must therefore be so explained as to show that it was tantamount to the achievement of heaven. This is possible only if we say that by following Aśoka's Dhaṃma men became so virtuous that they attained to heaven and were associated with gods. The idea that in the days of yore men and gods lived together is known to Brahmanical literature also. Thus the Dharmasūtra of the Āpastamba [1] has the following: "Formerly men and gods lived together in this world. Then the gods through *karman* went to heaven; men were left behind. Whosoever perform the *karman* of those (gods) in the same manner dwell (after death) with the gods and Brahmā in the other world." [2] From this it is clear that what Aśoka means is that he led men in the path of Dhaṃma and induced them to perform virtuous courses to such an extent that they became fit to be commingled with gods, not simply in the next, but rather in this, world. Instances are not wanting, in early Buddhist works, of men being worshipped by Brahmā and his gods in this world as soon as their spiritual elevation was complete.

[1] II, 7, 161.

[2] SBE., II, 140.

Knowing, as we do, how miracles come to spring into existence and cluster round the name of a saint in his life time even in India of the modern day, it is not unreasonable to suppose that in Aśoka's time those men from Jambudvīpa who followed Dhaṃma and led a pure noble life came soon to be looked upon as saints and that they were believed to be associated with gods.[1]

By what measures, it may now be asked, was Aśoka able to accomplish such a phenomenal result during the short space of a year or so? The reply is furnished by Rock Edict IV, where also the king gives a glowing account of his achievement. In this record, as we have seen from the last chapter, Aśoka informs us that he fostered and propagated Dhaṃma among his subjects by showing them spectacles of the *vimānas*, *hastins*, and *agni* or *jyotiḥ-skandhas*. These represent the kinds of heavenly bliss that are in store for the good virtuous people in their next birth when they become gods. We have thus to take note of this important fact, that is, of the first measure which Aśoka adopted for generating and developing his Dhaṃma. He showed to the people spectacles of the various classes of gods and of the various kinds of felicity they rolled in. In the last chapter it has been suggested that he must have exhibited these spectacles in the Samājas, not the Samājas or feasts where the people were treated to meat and drink and which Aśoka condemned, but the Samājas or amphitheatres where the people were entertained with shows,

[1] ABORI., X, 254-58.

music and dancing and which he looked upon favourably. Perhaps the first step then which Aśoka adopted when he started his missionary career was the exhibition of the different orders of gods, their resplendent complexions, their heavenly palaces, celestial elephants and so forth, which constituted their pomp and glory. How long he continued the exhibition of such spectacles we do not know. Probably he was showing them the whole period of his reign, as it most effectively served two purposes, namely, that of amusing the people and also of inducing them to live a life of piety. But certain it is that he persisted in it for over a year that he was with the Saṃgha, and that although this period was not a big one, Aśoka thought that by this means there was much growth of Dhaṃma, to such an extent, indeed, that it had never been developed to this degree ever before.

We have already seen that the celestial booms referred to by Aśoka have been graphically described in a Pāli work called *Vimānavatthu*. It is with much forethought that stress is laid upon their descriptions in this work, the object evidently being to induce the people to lead holy and pious lives. In this connection it is desirable to note a story narrated in Buddhist works [1] about Moggalāna, the right-hand disciple of Buddha, who was also a unique missionary. He succeeded in attracting such a number of followers to Buddhism that the preachers of other religions

[1] *Commentary on the Dhaṁmapada*, III, 65 (P.T.S.); *Intro.* to Jat., p. 522.

became jealous of him, and hired assassins to put him to death. (But what was the secret of his missionary activity ? By means of his perfection in supernatural powers, we are told, he used to go to heavens, meet the gods, and interrogate every one of them as to how he contrived to rise to the position of a god. And they used to tell him by performing what acts they became what kind of gods. Similarly, he used to go to the world of Hell and ask its unfortunate inmates the story of their sufferings. Moggalāna thereafter used to return to the earth and inform the people. This produced such a deep impression on the minds of the people that they used to flock to him in masses and get themselves converted to Buddhism. Most probably this story of Moggalāna was known to Aśoka. But even supposing for the moment that it was not, it does not require much stretch of imagination on the part of a thoughtful and enthusiastic propagandist, such as Aśoka doubtless was, to bring into requisition the graphic descriptions of the various types of celestial felicity depicted in the *Vimānavatthu* and such works, and give it a practical turn by preparing actual representations of the *vimānas, hastins*, and so forth and exhibiting them to the people on such occasions as those of the Samājas where they must naturally gather in large masses. And if Moggalāna could secure a large number of followers by merely intimating orally what virtue ensured what heaven and what unrighteousness what hell, in what terrific numbers must the people have rushed to the faith of Aśoka when not mere verbal descriptions but actual representations of the heavens and the varieties of supreme bliss to be enjoyed there were placed by him before them. There is nothing at all surprising if even in such a short space of time as one year or so, such a well-conceived, well-planned and well-carried-out propaganda work, as might be expected of Aśoka, gave him such wonderful results, —wonderful beyond all expectations.

There were other measures also which Aśoka adopted for the furtherance of his object. The beginning of his strenuous career, we have seen, synchronised with the formulation of another scheme, upon which he embarked. Rock Edict VIII says:

"For a long time past kings used to go out on tours of pleasure (*vihāra-yātrā*). Here there were chase and other similar diversions. Now king Priyadarśin, Beloved of the gods, repaired to Saṃbodhi (Bodhi Tree), when he had been consecrated ten years. Hence these tourings for Dhaṃma. Here this happens, namely, visits and gifts to the Brāhman and Śramaṇa ascetics, visits and largesses of gold to the aged, and visits and instructions in and enquiries about Dhaṃma of the provincials."

Here Aśoka tells us that up till the tenth year of his reign he like the previous kings used to find relaxation in *vihāra-yātrās* or tours of pleasure, where he indulged in hunting and other sports. In that year he gave up the idea of ever going on *vihāra-yātrās*, and started instead the *Dharma-yātrās* where he now found his relaxation. The latter fulfilled the object that was uppermost in his mind, namely, the fostering of Dhaṃma. He developed Dhaṃma in himself by visiting and giving gifts to the recluses and mendicants of both the Brāhmaṇ and Śramaṇa sects. During these visits he must have listened to and studied the Dhaṃma of every sect and assimilated its essential features, thus making himself *bahuśruta*. As regards the people, he propagated Dhaṃma among them by coming into their personal contact, preaching righteousness, and enquiring about their spiritual progress. In other words, Aśoka turned a missionary in the real sense of the term. (But when and how did the event happen? In the tenth year of his reign, when he paid a visit to the Bodhi Tree. In fact, his visit to the Bodhi Tree, as we have seen, was the first of his Dharma-yātrās, which he undertook along with a Saṃgha of Bhikshus, and the manifold spiritual benefits accruing not only to himself but also to his people induced him to repeat it so as to make it a permanent feature of his missionary programme. We may, therefore, safely say that side by side with the exhibition of the heavens and the blisses associated therewith, Aśoka undertook the work of personally preaching to his people, of course, with the same object in view, that is, for the dissemination of Dhaṃma.

The king actually taking upon himself the duty of preaching to his subjects must have produced a profound impression on their mind and must have been a most potent cause of the promotion of Dhaṃma all round. But the king, after all, was a single individual, and it was not possible for him to approach all people. Aśoka therefore thought it necessary to order his representatives, his officers, to follow in his footsteps and help him in the completion of the work personally started by him. This is clear from what he says in Pillar Edict VII, which, being a résumé of the whole work achieved by him up till the twenty-seventh year of his reign, naturally describes the various measures devised and adopted by him for the realisation of his object. The edict itself begins with a vivid expression of his extreme and genuine solicitude for the spread of Dhaṃma among his subjects. The words he uses are so instinct with sincerity that they are worth quoting :

"This occurred to me :—In times past kings had wished that men should grow with a befitting growth of Dhaṃma. But men did not grow with a befitting growth of Dhaṃma. How then may men be moved to conform (to Dhaṃma)? How may men grow with a befitting growth of Dhaṃma? How may I uplift some of them with a growth of Dhaṃma? "

It is quite clear from the above passage that the question of the propagation of Dhaṃma Aśoka was for a long time revolving in his mind in all seriousness and with much careful thought. He is frank enough to admit that he was not the first king who thought of spreading Dhaṃma. But the efforts of the previous kings were not crowned with any success worth mentioning. He, however, appears to have much pondered over the problem and finally hit upon a line of action which he now resolved to carry into effect for the attainment of his object. And most of the means he so adopted he mentions in this edict: "The same (object) being in view," says he in this edict, "I have set up Dharma-stambhas, appointed Dharma-Mahāmātras, and made Dharma-śrāvaṇas." And he then proceeds to explain what he understood by each one of these measures. The first of these, namely, Dharma-stambhas do not denote any material pillars as one is apt to suppose, but rather his works of charity which he forthwith goes on to describe thus :

"On the roads I have planted the banyan trees. They will offer shade to man and beast. I have grown mango orchards. I have caused wells to be dug at every eight *koses*, and I have had rest-houses. I have made many watering sheds at different places for the enjoyment of man and beast. This (provision) of enjoyment, however, is indeed a trifle, because mankind has been blessed with many blessings by the previous kings as by me. *But I have done this with the intent that men may follow the practices of Dhaṃma.*" It is these works of public benevolence that are to be understood by the Dharma-stambhas specified by him in Pillar Edict VII. Aśoka here candidly confesses that the provision of the various kinds of enjoyment which he has made for man and beast is not something which he alone has done, but is a duty which even kings preceding him have performed. Why then, it may be asked, does he notify his works of charity? He himself has given the reply to it. He says, he has done so, because others may follow his example. There can be no doubt that this was the real motive of Aśoka. For a little further on in the same edict he says precisely the same thing. "Whatever charitable works I have performed," says he, "these have been conformed to among men, and these they will perform (in future)." It looks singular that Aśoka should attach so much importance to the performance of charitable works. And it may naturally be asked whether Buddhism lays any stress on any works of public benevolence such as those referred to by Aśoka. The following text from the Saṃyutta-Nikāya [1] will clear up the point:

Planters of Groves.

Say of what folk by day and night
For ever doth the merit grow?
In righteousness and virtuous might
What folk from earth to heaven go?
Planters of groves and fruitful trees,
And they who build causeway and dam,
And wells construct and watering-sheds
And (to the homeless) shelter give:—
Of such as these by day and night
For ever doth the merit grow.
In righteousness and virtue's might
Such folk from earth to heaven go.[2]

[1] I. 5. 7; also Eng. trans. by Mrs. Rhys Davids, pp. 45-6.

[2] If these works of charity can lead people from earth to heaven, they can very well be described as *Dharma-stambhas.* A not unsimilar phrase is *Dharma-setu* which is used in a Nāsik cave inscription (*Ep. Ind.*, Vol. VIII, p. 60, l. 11) to describe the gift of this cave by Gautamī. *Dharma-setu* means 'a bridge or dam of merit' which enables a pious individual to cross the ocean of *saṃsāra. Dharma-stambha* must similarly mean 'a pillar or support of merit' propping up a virtuous man from earth to heaven. The pillar erected by Yaśodharman is thus described in a Mandasor inscription:

The second measure which Aśoka took for promoting Dhaṃma was the creation of Dharma-Mahāmātras. These officers, as we have seen, had to look to the spiritual as well as to the temporal good of the people. How they were to discharge the latter duty has been shown in Chapter II. Here we have to see how Aśoka used them for the promotion of Dhaṃma. It has been pointed out in the last chapter that there does not seem to have been much of good will and amity between one sect and another in his time. The teaching of the sects was practically identical in regard to the essentials, but there was much divergence on doctrinal matters. They ignored the points of agreement though they were the pith of religion and wrangled with one another about discrepant matters, though they were the unimportant features of it. It was therefore absolutely necessary to direct their attention to what was essential in a religion and put an end to all acrimony and animosity. This work Aśoka entrusted to the Dharma-Mahāmātras, who were occupied with all sects that flourished in his wide empire, above all, the Buddhists, the Ājīvikas and the Nirgranthas. Thereby Aśoka hoped that every sect would exalt itself and that Dhaṃma would shine more brightly. This was one of the most important duties which the Dharma-Mahāmātras were commissioned to discharge in connection with Dhaṃma. There was also another duty assigned to them. It was connected with the organisation

nirdeshṭuṃ mārgam-uchchair-diva iva sukṛit-opārjityāyāḥ sva-kīrtteḥ, '(erected) as if to point the path, to heaven above, to his fame acquired through good works' (Fleet's *Gupta Inscr.*, p. 147, l. 7).

of charities just mentioned. He wished that in his philanthropic activity the members of his royal family should associate themselves and heartily co-operate. And he, therefore, instructed the Dharma-Mahāmātras and other head officers to approach them and elicit money grants for charitable purposes. "These (that is, the Dharma-Mahāmātras) and many other head officials are employed in the distribution of bounties, both my own and those of the Queens; and all my gynæceum...........And I have arranged that they shall be occupied with the distribution of the bounties of my sons and other sons of queens." It will thus be seen that Aśoka was not content with the philanthropic activity he personally displayed, but made every endeavour through the Dharma-Mahāmātras and other officials to induce his near relatives also to follow in his footsteps. Who the 'other head officials' were we do not know. But certain it is that the Dharma-Mahāmātras were entrusted with the mission of educing charities not only from the king's relatives but also from other people. For Rock Edict V not only repeats what Pillar Edict VII states about the duty of the Dharma-Mahāmātras in connection with the members of the royal household, but also adds that they were to concern themselves with everybody, in fact, that may be found to be "leaning on Dhaṃma, to be an abode of Dhaṃma or to be given up to alms-giving." It no doubt looks singular that Aśoka should lay so much stress on the performance of charities by all people, big or small, rich or poor. Of course, as king it was his duty to institute works of public weal and utility. But he unmistakably gives us to understand that he did it all in order that the people might follow his example. He is also anxious that his relatives should similarly perform acts of charity apparently with the object of not only incurring spiritual merit but also setting an example to the people in general.

The third measure which Aśoka adopted for the propagation of Dhamma is *Dhaṃma-sāvana* and *Dhammānusathi* which are two aspects of one and the same thing. Here too he enumerates what virtues and practices constitute Dhaṃma exactly as he does in Pillar Edict II and the Rock Edicts. But how were they to be inculcated on the minds of the people? The idea that struck him in this connection he also dwells upon in Pillar Edict VII. Here he tells us that he ordered his officers, the Purushas and the Rājukas, to preach to the people. In Rock Edict III, however, he gives us somewhat more detailed information. There he tells us that in the twelfth year of his reign he commanded not only the Rājukas but also the Prādeśikas and the Yuktas, to go out on circuit tour every five years, to deliver instructions in Dhaṃma to the people as well as for the discharge of their office duties. And what are these instructions in Dhaṃma which they are to impress on the people? These are, of course, the ethical practices which make up his Dhaṃma, and it is these which are to be *Dhaṃma-sāvanas* and caused to be heard by the people. We have seen above that the Rājukas, Prādeśikas and Yuktas were, all of them, mufassil officials of the highest grade and charged with duties which required them to tour in districts or divisions. And over and above this office work they had to discharge in their periodical visits, they were now commissioned by Aśoka to perform like himself the duties of a missionary and preach Dhaṃma to the provincials. His district officers of the superior rank were thus not only officers but also teachers. Aśoka doubtless hit upon a novel and ingenious mode of propagating Dhaṃma. Certainly it was his own idea. It was not known to have been practised by any king prior to him, and even in later times the principle was observed only in the palmy days of the Portuguese rule in India when the highest officials at least combined the work of preachers with their ordinary duties.[1]

We can never be in a position to form an accurate estimate of Aśoka's work as a missionary unless we also take into account what he did for the weal and happiness of the animate world. It deserves to be noticed that as king Aśoka thought he had a duty to perform not simply to human beings but also to creatures in general. And it is therefore necessary to see what measures he adopted to preserve their life and promote their happiness. His work under this head falls into two sections: (1) the means he took to prevent not only injury to, but also killing of, living beings, and (2) the steps he adopted to increase their physical happiness. In regard to the first matter, Pillar Edict V gives us much information. There Aśoka tells us what restrictions he had imposed upon the infliction of

[1] J. M. Macphail's *Aśoka*, p. 48.

injury and destruction of life. In the first place, he lays an embargo on the killing of any living being that is neither eaten nor required for any decorative or medicinal purpose. In other words, he puts a stop to wanton destruction of life, and goes even to the length of ordering that chaff containing life shall not be burnt. In the case of animals that serve as food or are used for domestic and other purposes, he lays down that they shall not be killed, and shall not be injured by branding or castration on certain auspicious days that he specifies. At first sight, it no doubt appears that these restrictions were of Aśoka's creation. But similar restrictions have been recommended in Kauṭilya's Arthaśāstra. Thus Chapter XLIII [1] of this work lays down that all fish and birds which are not killed for food and all *vihāra* or pleasaunce birds and all auspicious creatures, whether birds or beasts, shall be protected from destruction or molestation. The list of the garden birds given there includes at least four of those mentioned by Aśoka as unworthy of being killed. Again, Chapter CLXXII of this work [2] says that the king shall order non-slaughter of animals and prohibit castration and destruction of fœtus in the womb on certain auspicious days which practically agree with those mentioned by Aśoka. Similarly, Manu lays an embargo on the wanton salughter of certain creatures, which have been specified in Chapter XI,

[1] *Arthaśāstra*, p. 122. The expression *apravṛittavadhānāṃ* occurring in this chapter has been misunderstood. It means literally "those whose killing (for food, &c.) is not in vogue."

[2] *Ibid.*, p. 407.

vs. 133-8. His list includes many of the species mentioned in Pillar Edict V., and one commentator actually remarks that these are the creatures whose killing is not sanctioned by the Sacred Law. These restrictions did not therefore originate with Aśoka, but he was simply giving effect to those comprised in the Artha- and Dharma-śāstra. And all that we can here say is that he must have spared no pains to carry them out thoroughly. But howsoever thoroughly he may have carried out the measures, they could not have amounted to much. Aśoka himself admits that in Pillar Edict VII. he says that he was not able to produce much beneficial result by imposing such restrictions and declaring certain species of creatures exempt from butchery, but that he gained his object by *nijhati*, that is, through exhortations. With this object in view he commanded his missionary officers, while preaching Dhaṃma to the people, to impress on their mind the necessity of *anārambho prāṇānam* and *avihisā bhūtānam*. Aśoka has thus proceeded one step further, as he wants now not merely to curtail injury and slaughter of life but to prevent it altogether, if he can. And, as might be expected of him, he himself sets an example to the people in this respect. The first chapter describes the course of conduct which he was pursuing, like most kings prior to him, to make himself popular with the people. We know that he was in the habit of celebrating Samājas, some of which entertained them with shows, music and dancing, and some regaled them with meat and drink. In Samājas of the second kind, many animals must have been killed to serve meat to the large masses that came for the feast. Aśoka was also observing, as we have seen, the time-honoured custom of doling out meat to the people every day in his palace, for which, he tells us, hundreds of thousands of animals had to be slain every day in the royal kitchen. Animals required for the Samāja or for charity were doubtless butchered for the purposes of eating, and their slaughter could not be prohibited by any of the restrictions specified in Pillar Edict V. But when Aśoka embarked on the programme of *nijhati*, he was not satisfied with merely preaching it to the people but set them an example by himself putting it into practice so far as his royal household was concerned. But he did not stop there. For he did not spare even himself, and we are aware of what restrictions he placed on the meat served for his own table and how finally he gave up eating meat altogether, even the flesh of a pea-fowl which was considered to be such a delicacy by the people of the Middle Country.

The measures detailed above were intended to prevent injury and slaughter of creatures in general, not to promote their physical happiness. This second object he endeavoured to realise by other means. These were the measures he adopted for the enjoyment of life not by man only but also by beast, and constitute the charitable works executed by the king. They have been described in Pillar Edict VII., and we have seen what they are. Practically the same philanthropic works have been enumerated in Rock Edict II. But the latter mentions one work which is of great importance and which is not referred to in the former. Here Aśoka says that he has established two kinds of *chikitsā* or curative arrangements, one relating to men and the other to animals. How he carried out this object he describes as follows: "Where medicinal herbs, wholesome for men and wholesome for animals, are not found, they have everywhere been imported and planted. Roots and fruits, wherever they are not found, have been imported and planted." What causes our extreme admiration for the king is that he carried out this work not only in his dominions but also those of the neighbouring and distant kings, who are mentioned in Rock Edict XIII. We have seen who they were.

What was the upshot of Aśoka's missionary activity? It was not simply within the boundaries of his own empire, extensive as it was, but also in the realms of the independent kings near and far, that Aśoka claims to have spread his Dhaṃma. In Rock Edict XIII. where he addresses himself to his sons and grandsons, the Buddhist monarch says: "But this conquest is considered to be the chiefest by the Beloved of the gods, which is conquest through Dhaṃma. And that, again, has been achieved by the Beloved of the gods here and in the bordering dominions, even as far as six hundred yojanas." Aśoka thus clearly tells us that conquests by Dhaṃma he effected not only in his empire but also in the adjoining kingdoms. In regard to the former he specifies the different frontier countries which were incorporated in his empire. In regard to the foreign dominions he mentions not only the independent kingdoms in the southernmost part of

India but also those of the five Greek kings. We have thus to note here the wide range over which Aśoka's missionary activity had spread. It had been disseminated not only over the whole of India and Ceylon but also over those parts of Syria, Egypt, Macedonia, Epirus and Cyrene, which were subject to the Greek rulers. But this was not all. For in the same edict the king further tells us: "Even where the envoys of the Beloved of the gods do not go, they, having heard the utterances of Dhaṃma, the ordinances, and the teaching of Dhaṃma by the Beloved of the gods, practise Dhaṃma and will so practise." This may refer to his religious propaganda in China and Burma.

If we take into consideration the well-planned programme and the systematic efforts which Aśoka put forth to carry it through, the statements contained in Rock Edict XIII. in respect of the extent of his missionary operations are by no means unworthy of credence. Some scholars, however, are prone to cast a doubt on them and hold that Buddhism in Aśoka's time had not gone beyond the confines of India. The most pre-eminent of them is the late Prof. T. W. Rhys Davids. In regard to the propagation of Dhaṃma mentioned by Aśoka in this edict, the Pāli scholar says: "It is difficult to say how much of this is mere royal rhodomontade. It is quite likely that the Greek kings are only thrown in by way of make-weight, as it were; and that no emissary had actually been sent there at all. Even had they been sent, there is little reason to believe that the Greek self-complacency would have been much disturbed. Aśoka's estimation of the results obtained is better evidence of his own vanity than it is of Greek docility. We may imagine the Greek amusement at the absurd idea of a 'barbarian' teaching them their duty; but we can scarcely imagine them discarding their gods and their superstitions at the bidding of an alien king.'"[1] Here Rhys Davids implies that Aśoka sent envoys to the Greek kings in order to spread Buddhism. But this is a mere assumption. What we have really to understand from Rock Edict XIII is that Aśoka was already in the habit of sending ambassadors to the Greek courts, but that he now thought of propagating his faith through these his own officers in the Greek kingdoms just as he did in his own empire through his other officers. The Seleukidan monarchy, we know, sent two ambassadors one after another to the Mauryan court. Ptolemy Philadelphos, the ruler of Egypt, also dispatched an envoy to this Indian court. This shows clearly that the Mauryan monarchy also must have sent emissaries in return to the Greek courts since the time of Chandragupta. And as one of the most effective methods adopted by Aśoka for the dissemination of Buddhism was the employment of the higher order of his officials, it is but natural to expect him to follow precisely the same method for the same work even in regard to the Greek dominions, where also he had his officials, namely, the emissaries. Rhys Davids further thinks that even supposing for the moment that

[1] *Buddhist India*, pp. 298-9.

Aśoka's ambassadors undertook the mission work also, they could not have secured many converts from among the Greeks, because the Greeks were too self-complacent to give much heed to the preachings of the 'barbarians' and discard their gods and superstitions. Here the Pāli scholar assumes that Aśoka made converts only among the Greeks. All that the Buddhist king says is that he propagated his religion in the Greek kingdoms, the people of which must have consisted of many men who were not Greeks. Why, again, this incapacity of the Greeks to adopt other religions? Their attitude towards the faiths of the 'barbarians' inferior to them in civilisation, is, of course, intelligible enough. But why suppose that they were intellectually perverse and impervious to the religious influences of a people by no means their inferiors in culture? Do we not for instance know that the Greeks or Yavanas, who came in contact with Indian civilisation had become converts to Buddhism and other Indian faiths?[1] There are many references to them in literature and epigraphic records. Again, Ptolemy Philadelphos of Egypt was the founder or expander of the Alexandrian Library, and we know on the authority of Epiphanius [2] that his librarian was anxious to translate the books of the Hindus. The Greeks were certainly not such cultural obstinates, as some of their modern admirers take them to be.

[1] IA., 1911, pp. 11-3.

[2] Epiphan. *de Nens. et Pond* 8.

Rhys Davids thinks that the story of the spread of Buddhism in Aśoka's time is better preserved in the Sinhalese chronicles than in his edicts. The former give an account of the missions sent out by Tissa, son of Moggali, to the various parts of India. Each mission consisted of a leader and his four assistants. "And when we find," says the Pāli scholar, "that they ascribe the sending out of the missionaries, not to Aśoka, but to the leaders of the Order, and that they make no mention of any such missions to the Greek kingdoms in the West, it is at least probable that the view they take is more accurate, in these respects, than the official proclamation."[1] In other works, what Rhys Davids means is that Buddhism could not have extended to the Greek dominions on account of the self-complacent, self-opinionative cast of the Greek mind, and that as the Sinhalese chronicles speak of the Buddhist faith being preached in Aśoka's time only in the bordering regions of India, that must be accepted as more probable and more accurate. And as the chronicles, again, attribute the dispatch of the missionaries, not to Aśoka, but to the leader of the Buddhist Order, the assertion of Aśoka that he disseminated Buddhism in the allied kingdoms of the Greeks or even that he was successful in spreading it in India at all is pure royal rhodomontade and must be ascribed to his vanity. The implicit faith that he reposes in the Sinhalese chronicles, he thinks, is warranted by the genuine scraps of history pre-

[1] *Buddhist India*, pp. 301-2; JRAS., 1905, p. 681 & ff.

served and put down for us by the Ceylon monks. And the late Professor tries to show how this remark holds good, in particular, in the case of the tradition chronicled by them in respect of these missions. He says that three of the missionaries sent to the Himālayan region to teach the doctrine were Majjhima, Kassapa-gotta and Dundubhissara. Who would not have supposed that the chronicles had drawn upon their imagination for this detail? Yet, in the Topes opened by Cunningham at and near Sāñchi, he found some relic caskets with inscriptions on them containing these names and informing us that the last two of these monks were connected with the Himālayan missions. This is a clear proof, the Pāli scholar thinks, that the Sinhalese monks had correctly handed down, in unbroken tradition, what had happened in Aśoka's time in regard to the propagation of Buddhism. Now, the Dīpavaṃsa (VIII. 10) gives in this connection five names including that of Majjhima, and the Mahāvaṃsa (XII. 41) adds that the mission was headed by Majjhima. In the inscriptions on the Sāñchi relic caskets, the name of Majjhima, no doubt, occurs [1] but the person who is spoken of as the teacher of the Himālayan countries is not Majjhima at all but Gotiputa Kasapa-gota.[2] These inscriptions, again, associate no less than nine monks with Kasapa-gota, the Himālayan teacher, two of whom alone

1 Lüders' *List of Brāhmī Inscriptions*, No. 157.

2 Ibid., No. 156 & 158.

agree with those given by the Dīpavaṃsa.[1] Why do the Sānchi inscriptions omit the other two mentioned by the Dīpavaṃsa, or why does the latter ignore seven of those named by the former? How therefore the Ceylon Chronicles can be credited with historical fidelity and accuracy so far as this account of the mission is concerned is by no means clear to us. Can the remaining part of this account, again, stand the test of critical reasoning? The Chronicles tell us that four of the apostles sent were Rakkhita, Dhaṃmarakkhita, Mahādhaṃmarakkhita, and Mahārakkhita. Is not this similarity of name in the case of no less than four persons enough to cast a strong suspicion on the account? Similarity of name is perceptible also in the case of the two monks, Majjhima and Majjhantika. Again, the duumvirate, Sona and Uttara, who went to Suvarṇabhūmi on mission, are believed by scholars to represent one single individual. It has thus been rightly thought[2] that as a historical document this account must be handled with great caution. Under such circumstances to maintain that the Sinhalese Chronicles have preserved a more reliable account of the Buddhist missions than the Aśoka edicts is "a speculation too bold to follow."

It is not in one place only that Aśoka refers to the dominions of the Greek kings. It is not

[1] All these names are engraved on the steatite box exhumed from Sānchi Stupa No. II. (Cunningham's *Bhilsa Topes*, pl. XX.; Lüders' *List*, No. 655 & ff.).

[2] Kern, *Manual of Indian Buddhism*, p. 117.

simply in the account of his religious propaganda to the distant countries that he speaks of them. These princes have also been referred to by him in another place, namely, in Rock Edict II, where he adverts to the curative arrangements established by him for the good of the man and the beast and the consequent importation and plantation of medicinal herbs at places where they were unknown. This philanthropic work, he says, he carried out not only in India and Ceylon but also in the Greek kingdoms. Are we therefore to say that in both the cases Aśoka has stated what was never a fact? This would be charging him with downright fabrications,—a conclusion which no sane person will accept. What is, however, possible is that he may have exaggerated the results actually achieved. But no unbiassed person can reasonably doubt, when he tells us, that he carried on his propaganda work through his own officials and that he did so not only in his own territory but also in the foreign countries. It may however be asked and rightly asked whether his missionary activities had produced any lasting effect in those quarters. We have therefore to consider how far Aśoka's mission was successful in the Greek territories.

It is a noteworthy fact that Buddhism and Christianity possess many important features in common, and that their agreement cannot be ascribed to mere chance. Here we cannot do better than summarise the contents of an illuminating lecture delivered by F. Max Müller nearly twenty-five years ago. He said that two Roman

Catholic missionaries travelling in Tibet were startled at the coincidence between their own ritual and that of the Buddhist priesthood. They attributed the coincidence to the Devil. But if a coincidence can be produced by natural causes, no other explanation need be sought. And it was an historical fact that Christian missionaries were active in China from the middle of the seventh to the end of the eighth century. Here then was the coincidence explained in a fairly satisfactory manner. There were other coincidences, however, between Buddhism and Christianity which belong to the ancient period of the former. They included confessions, fasting, celibacy of the priesthood, and even rosaries. And, above all, there was Māra the tempter, who was to Buddha what Satan was to Christ. And, as they were honoured or known in India before the beginning of the Christian era, it followed that if they had been borrowed, the borrowers were the Christians. If such coincidences [1] could be accounted for by reference to the tendency of our common humanity, let analogous cases be produced. If they were set down as merely accidental, let similar cases be brought from the chapter of accidents. Max Müller's own opinion was that at least they were too numerous and complex to be attributed to the latter cause.[2] How, it may be

[1] These coincidences and also what has been set forth by me in the next para. are unfortunately blinked by Prof. Charpentier (JRAS., 1925, p. 806). And he has the temerity to remark that I do not tell 'on which points' Buddhism has influenced Christianity. It is, however, doubtful whether he had perused the whole of my book when he reviewed it (see the Preface of the second edition).

[2] *Jour. Maha-Bodhi Soc.*, V. 4.

asked, had knowledge of these things been spread? Of course, Indian influences had long been suspected in the Æsopian fables and some parts of the Bible. When this exchange of thought was going on between the east and west from times immemorial, are we to suppose that the main ideas of Buddha's religion alone should remain unknown in the west? The Buddhist books, however, nowhere say that Buddhism was preached by the monks in those regions. On the other hand, we know, as Aśoka distinctly tells us, that he had employed his official legations to the courts of his contemporary Greek princes as much to propagate Buddha's Dhaṃma as to carry out his humanitarian purposes. Can there be the slightest doubt that the spread of Buddhism to western Asia was due to Aśoka's missionary activities? Because Buddhism has thus influenced Christianity, it does not, however, follow that the latter is only a deteriorated form of the former. This by no means deprives Christianity of its claim to originality, beauty and truth. As Dr. Paul Carus tells us, "none of the elements of Christianity is radically new, nevertheless, the whole in its peculiar combination is decidedly original and marks the beginning of an era which, at least in the west, stands in strong contrast to all the ages past." [1]

Christianity, again, was perhaps not the only religion, though that was the most important one in Western Asia, on which the influence of Buddhism was incontrovertible. There must have been some

[1] *Buddhism and its Christian Critics*, pp. 215-16.

other religious sects which were similarly influenced. One such sect is that of the Essenes, whose clergy formed a small monastic Jewish order with their quaint semi-ascetic practices and lived on the shores of the Dead Sea. And it has long since been admitted by scholars that they were indebted to Buddhism for some of their important characteristics.[1] It has also been admitted that the Essenes were in existence even before the rise of Christianity. A similar religious confraternity is the Therapeutæ who were residing in the neighbourhood of Alexandria and formed another order of the pre-Christian Judaism. Even here the influence of Buddhism has been recognised in their precepts and modes of life.[2] The Buddhist influence on the religious condition of Western Asia is thus traceable prior to the first century A.D., and must undoubtedly have been caused by the missionary zeal and activity of Aśoka in those regions.

Of course, when we say that Aśoka propagated Dhaṃma through his officials both in his empire and outside, both in India and Western Asia, that does not mean that the Buddhist monks themselves did nothing for the spread of their religion. As both the Dīpavaṃsa and Mahāvaṃsa inform us that Moggaliputta Tissa dispatched missionary monks to the different parts of India, we have to take it that the Buddhist clergy also in Aśoka's time adopted some measures of their own for the dissemination of their faith. But as

1 ERE., V. 401.

2 *Ibid.*, XII. 318-9.

we have seen, we have to use their account with caution. What, in all likelihood, the clergy did was that they dispatched at least two parties, one to the Himālayan regions and the other to West India. The first party was headed not by Majjhima, but by Gotiputa Kasapa-gota. And these Himālayan regions included Kashmir and Gandhāra. Thus Majjhantika, said to have been dispatched separately to these provinces, becomes identical with Majjhima. What probably happened was that the party headed by Gotiputa Kasapa-gota included Majjhima and that the former put the latter in charge of these two provinces for missionary purposes. Similarly, Rakkhita, Dhaṃmarakkhita, Mahādhaṃmarakkhita, and Mahārakkhita are not four separate names, as the Sinhalese chronicles lead us to infer. They, in all likelihood, denoted one individual, who was dispatched to Western India, comprising Vanavāsī, Aparānta, Mahāraṭṭha and Yonaloka. Two more missions seem to have been similarly sent out,—one to Suvarṇabhūmi and the other to Laṅkā or Ceylon. For these missions Moggaliputta Tissa was perhaps responsible, but they had nothing to do with the measures which Aśoka adopted with the same object in view. The latter had the whole machinery and finances of his imperial government to help him to push forward his Dhaṃma ; and when, as we find, he hit upon the novel but effective method of requisitioning the whole higher hierarchy of officials as his proselytising agents, naturally we must expect far more real, rapid and extensive results. And if we bear in mind that the Buddhist clergy also put forth effort more or less strenuously in the same direction, it is no wonder if the convergent activities of both were crowned with phenomenal success. For do we not find Buddhism suddenly spread over a very wide area from about the middle of the third century B.C. onwards and studding the various parts of India and Afghanistan with religious edifices, such as *Stūpas*, monasteries, and caves? The Buddhist faith occupies such a preponderant position during this period that it practically puts all other religions in the background, very few vestiges of which are found, pertaining to architecture or literature. But by far the greater portion of the credit must go to the Buddhist Emperor, the Chakravartī Dharmarāja, of the third century B.C.

CHAPTER VI

Social and Religious Life from Aśokan Monuments

It is not possible to obtain a clear picture of Aśoka and his achievements unless we consider the social and religious environments in which he worked. Here too it must be borne in mind that this chapter cannot give the whole picture. Our object is merely to show what light is thrown upon this subject by the lithic records of Aśoka and make it clearer and brighter with the help of extraneous sources only where this is absolutely necessary.

We will first make an attempt to glean whatever information we can of the religious life of India. We have seen that among the practices of Dhaṃma which Aśoka inculcates on the minds of his people, he makes mention of the seemly behaviour to be shown towards 'Brāhmans and Śramaṇas.' The meaning of this expression has not been clearly understood. It has been taken to denote vaguely 'the Brāhmaṇas and the ascetics' or 'the Brāhmaṇas and the recluses.' The same phrase occurs in the Pāli literature, for instance, in the *Mahā-parinibbānasutta*, where Prof. Rhys Davids translates it by "the Brāhmaṇs by saintliness of life."[1] It is, however, a *Dvandva* and not a *Karmadhāraya* compound, and must be taken to denote "the Brāhmaṇas and the Śramaṇas." In

[1] SBE., XI, 105, n. 1.

all the Pāli scriptures of the Buddhists, wherever Brāhmaṇs are mentioned side by side with the Śramaṇas, both are held up as objects of the highest but equal sanctification and veneration.[1] They therefore denote two orders of religieux but of opposite character. The Brāhmaṇs seem to be recluses and mendicants [2] whose speculations and disciplines were in conformity with the Vedas; and Śramaṇas, those whose doctrines and practices were opposed to these Brahmanic scriptures. Members of both the orders, in spite of their divergent tenets and disciplines, might lead equally holy lives and might thus be entitled to equal reverence from the people in general. This is just the reason why the Brāhmaṇ religieux were shown as much respect as the Śramaṇas in Buddha's time, and this is also the reason why Aśoka himself shows the same degree of reverence to both and insists upon his people also doing the same.

Pillar Edict VII specifies three religious sects, namely the Saṃgha, the Brāhmaṇa-Ājīvikas, and the Nigaṃṭhas. It is worthy of note in this connection that Aśoka says that there were other sects besides these, but as he does not mention them and names these three, it is plain that in his time those were the only sects that were considered most important. Of the three mentioned by him, Saṃgha, of course, must here denote the Buddhist fraternity, and as Aśoka was himself a follower of their religion, he naturally makes mention of it

[1] IA., 1891, p. 263.

[2] For some kinds of Brāhmaṇ ascetics specified by Buddhaghosha, see JPTS., 1891, pp. 34ff.

first and also by this name. We know nothing of the special features, except one, of the Buddhism which was prevalent in Aśoka's time, namely, the mention of Konākamana Buddha in the Niglīva Pillar Inscription. In this record Aśoka says that he enlarged the *Stūpa* of this Buddha for the second time when he visited the place in person in the twentieth year of his reign. It is clear from this that already in Aśoka's time the cult of the former Buddhas had come to be foisted on the religion of Gautama.

It also deserves to be noticed that there is no actual image of Buddha found, connected with Aśoka's monuments or even of his time. On the north face of the Kālsī rock is the figure of an elephant traced in outline, with the label *gajatame*, 'the superlative elephant,' engraved below. Similarly, immediately above the Inscription of the edicts at Dhauli is the fore half of an elephant hewn out of the solid rock. It is true that there is no label incised below this figure, but at the end of Rock Edict VI, at this place we have the word *Seto*, 'the white one'. A welcome light on the meaning of these names is shed by the partially preserved line below Rock Edict XIII at Girnār. This line reads *(sa)rva-sveto hasti sarva-loka-sukh-āharo nāma*, "the All-white Elephant named 'Bringer of Happiness to the Whole World'." It seems that the Girnār rock also bore the representation of an elephant. That here Śākya Buddha is implied there can be no doubt, for the legend says that the Bodhisattva, the future Buddha, left the Tushita Heaven to bring happiness to men and entered his mother's womb as a white elephant.[1] It will thus be seen that although there was no icon of Buddha, he was represented at least by the elephant symbol in Aśoka's time.

Nigaṃṭhas are the same as the Nirgranthas the followers of Mahāvīra, that is, the members of the Jaina order. There thus remain the Ājīvikas,[2] who curiously enough have been called Brāhmaṇ. What that exactly means we do not know. What, however, appears to be the case is that there were two orders of Ājīvikas, one Brahmanical,[3] and the other non-Brahmanical. The non-Brahmanical Ājīvikas were probably those who were associated and even connected with the Jainas, and the other order was probably represented by the Maskarins or parivrājakas referred to by Pāṇini and Patañjali. It may be interesting to see whether these two fraternities of the Ājīvikas can be distinguished one from the other in regard to their doctrines and practices which at present seem to have been hopelessly mixed up. To take only one instance, one Buddhist authority says that the Ājīvikas ate fish, but this does not agree with the extreme solicitude for life with which they are credited by another Buddhist text. If again, they did not believe in the efficacy of *kaṃma* as some Buddhist Suttas tell us, how could they bring themselves to practise religious

1 IA., V. 257-58.

2 JDL., II. 180 comprises a learned article on the *Ājīvikas* by Dr. Benimadhav Barua, which contains all that is known about them from the various sources. The inference, however, that there were at least two sects of the Ājīvikas is entirely mine, and is stated in this chapter for what it is worth.

3 See n. 5 on PE. VII, below.

austerities of the most rigorous type as other Suttas report about them? There is thus a curious medley of contrary doctrines and practices here which can clear themselves up only if an attempt is made to assort them to the proper Ājīvika orders. What we have to note here is that if there were two Ājīvika sects, the Ājīvikas of the Brāhmaṇ order were more important than the other, and represent probably the Ājīvikas for whom Aśoka excavated the rock caves at Barābar.[1] Another point to note is that here Aśoka himself is telling us what he meant by the phrase *Brāhmaṇa-śramaṇa* referred to above. The Saṃgha of Aśoka and the Nirgranthas represented the Śramaṇa, and the Ājīvikas the Brāhmaṇ, order of the religieux.

The word used by Aśoka to denote these religious orders is *pāsaṃḍa*. This has been taken to be equivalent to the Sanskrit *pāshaṇḍa*, which, even in his time as is evident from Kautilya's Arthaśāstra, denoted 'a heretic'. This is not, however, the sense in which Aśoka employs the word, for even his own Saṃgha is called *pāsaṃḍa* by him. It must also be remembered that in the Rock Edicts where this term is found the Shāhbāzgarhi and Mānsherā versions give almost invariably *parshaḍa* or *prashaṃḍa* for *pāsaṃḍa* of the other copies. This points to a Sanskrit equivalent different from *pāshaṇḍa*, and corresponding rather to *pārshaṃḍa*, which does not exist in later Classical Sanskrit but may have existed in the

[1] There is no harm in supposing that the Brahmanical and non-Brahmanical Ājīvikas lived side by side at Barābar, just as the Buddhists, Brāhmanists and Jainas did, *e.g.*, in caves at Ellora.

language (*bhāshā*) in Aśoka's time. The *pāsaṃḍas* were divided into three classes: (1) Brāhmanic, (2) Śramanic and (3) those which were neither Brāhmanic nor Śramanic. What sects exactly were included in this third class are not known, but that there was such a class is clear from R.E. XIII, which speaks of *pāsaṃḍas* other (anye) than the Brāhmaṇas and Śramaṇas. Possibly they denoted some forms of non-Aryan faith. Then again we have to note that *pāsaṃḍas* have been distinguished from both *pravrajitas* and *gṛihasthas* in R.E. XII and P.E. VII. This shows that every *gṛihastha* or every *pravrajita* did not attach himself to a *pāsaṃḍa* and that a man could turn a recluse or remain a householder without being an actual member of a *pāsaṃḍa*.[1]

Connected with the Pāsaṃḍas is the term *Dhaṃma*, which it is impossible to translate by one English word. We have seen what Aśoka understood by Dhaṃma. It denoted with him a code of moral duties, and, as he was a Buddhist layman, naturally it consisted just of those duties which Buddhism has prescribed for a householder. It must, however, be borne in mind that he was not at all unaware that practically the same duties were inculcated by other Pāsaṃḍas also. It has been shown above that in Rock Edict XIII, Aśoka admits that the ethical practices on which he insists under the name Dhamma are something which all Pāsaṃḍas, whether of the Brāhmaṇ or the Śramaṇa order, teach in common. In other words,

[1] Compare *Gahaṭṭha-muni* of the Mahāniddesa.

practically the same Dhaṃma is attributed by him to all sects. And this is just the reason why in Rock Edict VII he says that "all sects may dwell at all places (in his kingdom), because they all aim at self-restraint and purification of heart," and in Rock Edict XII, that people should hear Dhaṃma from one another's mouth in order that its *sāra* or essence may grow. What deserves to be noticed here is that certain righteous qualities and practices were preached by all sects in common and constituted Dhaṃma according to them. The words of Prof. Rhys Davids are worth quoting in this connection. "Dhaṁma has been rendered Law. But it never has any one of the various senses attached to the word 'law' in English. It means rather, when used in this connection, that which it is 'good form' to do in accord with established custom. So it never means exactly religion, but rather, when used in that connection, what it behoves a man of right feeling to do—or, on the other hand, what a man of sense will naturally hold. It lies quite apart from all questions either of ritual or theology."[1] This is the reason why in Minor Rock Edict II where Aśoka specifies his moral qualities as elsewhere, he winds up by saying that they form *porāṇā pakiti dighāvuse*, 'the nature (of man) which is ancient and long-enduring'. Prof. Jolly takes us one step further when he says that Dharma "is one of the most comprehensive and important terms in the whole range of Sanskrit literature. Indian commentators have explained it as denoting an act which produces the quality of the

[1] *Buddhist India*, 292.

soul called *apūrva*, the cause of heavenly bliss and of final liberation."[1] Dhaṃma thus denotes any act in accord with established duty, which a man of right feeling will naturally do and which, further is the cause of heavenly bliss. This is also just what Aśoka means, for in Rock Edict IX he clearly says: "Every worldly rite is of a dubious nature. It may or may not accomplish its object. *Dhaṃma-maṃgala*, however, is not conditioned by time; and even though it may not achieve any object here, it begets endless merit (*puṇya*) in the next world."

The above connotation of the word *dhaṃma* gives rise to a big question. For it means that a righteous act, if efficacious in itself, is capable of giving heavenly felicity without the intervention or mediation of any god. This is just the reason why Smith describes Aśoka's Dhaṃma as a system of theocracy without a god.[2] But what he has said holds good not only in the case of Aśoka's Dhaṃma but also of the Dhaṃma of most of the Pāshaṃḍas of his period. Up till the time of that monarch, belief in the doctrine of *karma* was rampant. The ordinary people were content with the performance of virtuous deeds and with the hope of being born one god or another in their next life as the effect of their *karma*, as the reward of their righteous practices in this world. The destruction of *karma* and of the consequent re-birth was reserved for and attempted by recluses and mendicants, whether Brāhmaṇs or Śramaṇas. And consequently there was no necessity of any belief in a living, personal

[1] ERE, IV, 702.

[2] *Aśoka*, pp. 33-4.

god. From the fifth century B.C. onwards to the time of Aśoka, school after school and sect after sect arose with its peculiar doctrine about the emancipation of the individual soul. But all except one or two were taken away by the fascinating theory of *karma* and maintained that action alone led to the individual beatitude. Such was Buddhism, such was Ājīvikism, such was Jainism, such was, in fact, every sect except the Bhakti-mārga, which however was not obsessed by the doctrine of *karma* to any large extent and laid down that devotion to the supreme soul alone could give salvation. The Bhakti sect however was not much in prominence up to this time and began to preponderate only after Aśoka. As a matter of fact, it then came so much to the forefront that it left an impress of *bhakti* on that very Buddhism which was so much and so long in the ascendant.

There is yet another element of the popular faith to which Aśoka refers in one of his Rock Edicts. It is true that the Hindu Society was so much permeated by the doctrine of *karma* that the performance of action alone was considered to be important and efficacious and that very little thought was given to the worship of, and communion with, a personal god. But this was true only so far as the future life was concerned. What about the present life? It is inconceivable that the people of ancient India could be so philosophic and unworldly as not to care for earthly pleasures and joys. In Rock Edict IX, Aśoka says: "People perform various (lucky) rites in sicknesses, at marriages, on the birth of sons, and on journey. On these and other similar occasions people perform various rites. In this matter, however, womankind performs much, manifold, (but) trivial, useless rite." This throws light on another phase of popular belief in Aśoka's time and points to the continuance of the worship of Yakshas, Chaityas, Gandharvas, Nāgas and so forth about which we read so much in the Buddhist Pāli scriptures. And further it may not be impossible to prove from these Buddhist texts that Aśoka is right in saying that such auspicious rites womanfolk was inordinately fond of performing. Aśoka's attitude towards this trait of popular faith was by no means hostile. "Lucky rites," says he, "should undoubtedly be performed. But a rite of this kind bears little fruit." And it is in this connection that he compares such rites to the *Dhaṃma-maṅgala*, and says that whereas the former are of dubious efficacy even so far as this world is concerned, the latter is unconditioned by time and unerringly engenders infinite merit (*puṇya*) at least in the next world.

About social life also interesting information can be gleaned from Aśoka's inscriptions. One of the most important items connected with the Hindu social life is the consideration of the food allowed or disallowed by the Śāstras. We know that in Pillar Edict V, Aśoka specifies some classes of animals, birds, and fishes whose slaughter he prohibits. Some of the names mentioned there cannot be identified, but a good many of them are known. In regard to them Aśoka expressly says that they are the creatures which are neither eaten nor put to any use. What he exactly means by the second part of his statement is not quite clear. But there can be little doubt that he is here referring to those creatures, which, though they are not required for food, have yet to be killed for medicinal and decorative purposes. Now, if we compare Aśoka's list of such creatures, with those which the Dharma-sūtras or Dharma-saṁhitās sanction or forbid for food or killing, we obtain most curious results. Of course, we do find some which are tabooed both by Aśoka and the Dharma-śāstras. Such are the *śuka* (parrots), *sārikā* (starlings), *chakravāka* (Brahmani ducks), and *haṃsa* (geese).[1] But there are others which were forbidden in Aśoka's time but allowed by the Smṛiti authors. Here again we have to distinguish between two classes according as they are allowed by all or some Smṛitikāras. Of the former class are *kaphaṭa* and *duḍi* or male and female tortoises and *ṣayaka* or porcupine which have been permitted by all Smṛitis but tabooed by Aśoka. Of the latter class only one instance is furnished, namely, *palasate* or rhinoceros, which is forbidden by Aśoka but allowed by Yājñavalkya, Gautama, Manu and Āpastamba, and disputed as food by Vasishṭha and Baudhāyana. What we have so far considered is a list of creatures which are altogether exempted by Aśoka from slaughter but which have been allowed by some or all the Smṛitis for food. But there is one bird which has been forbidden by most of the Smṛitis but served as an article of food in the time of Aśoka. This,

[1] See in this connection the most scholarly monograph of Monomohan Chakravarti on *Animals in the Inscriptions of Piyadasi* (MASB., Vol. I, No. 17).

of course, is the *mora* or peacock whose flesh was much relished by the people of the Madhyadeśa and which continued to be killed for the royal table for a long time though Aśoka had already embarked himself on the practical programme of preserving all animate beings.[1] But all the Dharma-śāstras except two lay down a penance for the killing of a peacock.

The object of this chapter is not to enter into any discussion about the age and the structure of the different Dharma-śāstras. But as Aśoka's pillars which contain the edict have all been found in Madhyadeśa, it follows that the items it supplies in regard to food allowed or forbidden must be taken as applying to that country. Of the Dharma-sūtras, Baudhāyana and Vasisṭha are looked upon as embodying the practices of Āryāvarta or Madhyadeśa. But while the former[2] lays down that the customs of the North should be followed in North India and those of the South in South India, the latter[3] insists upon the practices approved of in the Āryāvarta being everywhere acknowledged as authoritative. This agrees with the fact that the flesh of the peacock was disapproved by all Smritis, but not by Baudhāyana and Vasishṭha and that they therefore pertained to the Madhyadeśa. Now, what we have to note about India is that owing to the ever-increasing influence of Buddhism and Jainism there was an ever-growing tendency toward vegetarianism and that consequently foods originally permitted might in a succeeding age be

[1] *Above*, p. 16.
[2] I. 1. 2. 1-6.
[3] I. 10.

disallowed, but those originally tabooed could not subsequently be allowed. Both Baudhāyana and Vasishṭha allow the eating of the five-toed animals, the porcupine and the tortoise, but say that there is some doubt about the rhinoceros. But in Aśoka's time not only the rhinoceros has been tabooed but also the porcupine and the tortoise. So far as at least these grounds are concerned, we must place the composition of these Dharma-sūtras anterior to Aśoka's reign.

Another item of interest connected with social life is the condition of woman. The general belief is that the seclusion of woman was unknown to ancient India and that the Purdah system was introduced into the country by the Muhammadans. But nothing is more erroneous. A study of the dramas of Bhāsa and Kālidāsa leaves no doubt as to Purdah being practised in their time. This is more than confirmed by the *Kāmasūtra* of Vātsyāyana who flourished in the third century A. D.[1] But the practice can be traced back to a time long before Christ. Aśoka, we have seen, speaks of his *avarodhana*, which means inner closed female apartments. And quite in consonance with it is the mention of *antaḥpura* or harem in the *Artha-śāstra*,[2] where Kauṭilya gives directions not only how to build it but also how to guard it against outsiders. The Rāmāyaṇa, again, contains several allusions to this custom of secluding women. But

[1] SAMSJ., Vol. III, pt. I, pp. 537 and 355-60.

[2] P. 40 and ff.

the earliest known reference to it is Pāṇini, III. 2.36, which yields the term *asūryaṁpaśyā* and has been explained in the *Kāśikā* as *asūryaṁpaśyā rāja-dārāḥ*, " those who do not see the sun, that is, the wives of a king." [1] If the *Kāśikā* has given this as an example traditionally handed down, that means that the queens of a king were so rigorously shut up in the harem in Pāṇini's time that they had no opportunity of seeing the sun even.

Again, in Rock Edict IX where Aśoka speaks of *maṅgalas* or lucky rites observed in times of sickness, marriage, son's birth, journey and so forth, the king remarks that in that respect "womankind performs much, manifold (but) trivial, useless rite." The trait has been preserved almost intact by the Hindu orthodox women of the modern day, and reminds us of Bentham's observation that " the religion of a woman more easily deviates towards superstition; that is, towards minute observances." [2]

What the exact structure of society was in Aśoka's time we do not know. But a few and partial glimpses are afforded by two or three statements in his edicts. Thus in Rock Edict V we are told that the Dharma-Mahāmātras were to concern themselves with those Brāhmaṇs and Ibhyas who were hirelings. The Brāhmaṇs here are of course, the worldly Brāhmaṇs, and not the Brāhmaṇ recluses and mendicants who are associated with

[1] The term *asūryampaśyā* we find actually used with reference to a princess in the historical drama *Kaumudī-mahotsava*, II. 4.

[2] *Theory of Legislation* (Paternoster Library, 1896), p. 39.

the Śramaṇas. The term *ibhya* is a curious one. It occurs once in the Upanishads and is not unknown to the Pāli literature. It is, for instance, found used in the Mahānārada-Kassapa Jātaka, where the commentator explains it by Gahapati (Gṛihapati).[1] Gṛihapati has been commonly taken to stand for the third class, Vaiśyas, of the Brahmanical system. But the term Vessa (Vaiśya) is met with in Pāli texts only in connection with theoretical discussions, but they contain no indication that the Vaiśyas formed one distinct caste or class.[2] The Ibhyas or Gṛihapatis, on the other hand, formed a definite social group, an aristocratic class always ranking after the Kshatriyas and the Brāhmaṇas. It may appear somewhat singular that the Aśoka inscriptions do not contain a single reference to the Kshatriyas. But we have to bear in mind that like the Vaiśyas the Kshatriyas also, in the sense of the warrior caste, had no existence. Kshatriyas then denoted the ruling class, which in Aśoka's time comprised his relatives, his feudatories and the Anta or bordering kings in South India. And these, we know, have been referred to by Aśoka in his edicts. Like the Kshatriya or warrior caste the Śūdras also were known to theoretical discussions only, but had no real existence as a caste or a single class, and the lower strata of society in Aśoka's time are represented by Bhṛitakas or hired labourers and Dāsas

1 According to Patañjali, however, *ibhya* means *Kshatriya*. See below, n. 5 to the translation of RE. V.

2 Fick's *Social Organisation, etc.*, (trans.), pp. 251 and ff.

or bondsmen, kindness and mercy to whom are specially inculcated by the king and form part of the code of moral duties that according to him fall under Dhaṃma. The Bhṛitakas and Dāsas [1] were essentially distinct social groups at a time when the caste system, as we understand it, had not arisen. The system of slavery no longer exists in India now, and although hired labourers are by no means unknown, they come from various castes ; and caste, and not class, forms the characteristic feature of the modern social hierarchy.

Another point connected with the social life of India in Aśoka's time is hinted by his Rock Edict II. There the king tells us that in his own dominions as well as those of the neighbouring potentates he established two kinds of medical treatment, one relating to the man and the other to the animal. And he further informs us that medicinal herbs, roots, and fruits, wherever they are not to be found, have everywhere been imported and planted. What we are to understand by this record is that Aśoka opened dispensaries for men and *pinjrapols* for animals. It is difficult to say whether the practice of establishing charitable institutions existed in any other part of India, but certainly it was not unknown in the Bombay Presidency. Thus, from the records of the eighteenth century it is quite clear that in both Mahārāshṭra and Gujarāt, kings and chiefs frequently arranged for free medical help being given to the needy and

[1] For the condition of labourers and slaves in the Mauryan period, see MCNL., p. 189.

indigent, that, as a consequence, the physician was often rewarded with grants of rent-free land of village, and that in some cases the purpose of these grants is expressly stated to be the growing of medicinal herbs on those plots of land.[1] As regards the *pinjrapols* or animal hospitals, they are found to this day in Western India. The earliest description of a *pinjrapol* is that furnished by Hamilton and is of one that was maintained at Surat late in the eighteenth century.[2] Any animal with a broken limb or otherwise disabled is admitted without any regard to the caste or nationality of its master. This suits here excellently. For, when Aśoka says that he organised medical treatment for both man and animal, what he means is that in the case of the former he established charitable dispensaries for distributing medicine gratis and in the case of the latter something like a *pinjrapol*. When again he says that medicinal herbs, roots and fruits were imported and planted where they did not exist previously, we are to understand that he established farms attached to those institutions so that all medicines might be there for ready use. It is indeed curious to find that the custom of giving free medical relief to the diseased man or animal which was in existence in West India in the eighteenth century was prevalent

[1] *Selections from the Satara Rajas' and the Peshwas' Diaries*, Vol. VIII, pp. 221-3; S. H. Hodivala's *Studies in Parsi History*, pp. 186-8. I am indebted to Dr. Surendranath Sen for both these references.

[2] Hamilton's *Description of Hindostan* (1820), Vol. I, p. 718, 4th ed.

as early as the third century B.C.,[1] and that it was introduced at that early period by Aśoka into Western Asia and Europe, where medical knowledge and treatment had certainly developed but where charitable dispensaries for man and beast were perhaps unknown. And what is still further noteworthy is that through the philanthropic activity of Aśoka all the drugs then known were made available to the world.

No account of the social life of this period can be complete without a consideration of its cultural side. This we will now attempt as briefly as possible. Here too it must be remembered that the Aśoka inscriptions tell us little about the cultural development, as such, of the period. They, however, shed much light upon the vehicles of culture, namely, writing or alphabet and speech or language. The records of Aśoka, it will be seen, have been engraved in two *lipis* or scripts ; (1) Brāhmī and (2) Kharoshṭhī. Those incised in Kharoshṭhī are the Fourteen Rock Edicts found at Shāhbāzgaṛhī and Mānsherā. All his other inscriptions are in Brāhmī. Bühler, relying on one Chinese authority, gives Kharoshṭhī as the true form and derives it from Kharoshṭha (Ass-lip), the name of a sage who invented it. Dr. Sylvain Lévi, however, relying on another Chinese authority, calls it Kharoshṭrī and traces it to Kharoshṭra,

[1] The subject requires a careful investigation; but, in the meanwhile see *The Surgical Instruments of the Hindus*, by G. N. Mukhopādhyāya, Vol. I, pp. 34 and ff., and pp. 48 and ff.

the name of the country near but outside India. The other script was called Brāhmī, because it is believed to have emanated from the god Brahmā. The former was written from right to left like Persian, Arabic and Urdū, and the latter from left to right like all Hindu scripts of the modern day. The former flourished in the north-west part of India and the neighbouring foreign countries as far as Chinese Turkestan, and the latter was in vogue all over India comprising even the regions where the Kharoshṭhī was written. The Kharoshṭhī died a natural death about the fifth century A.D., whereas the Brāhmī has been recognised to be the parent of all the scripts indigenous not only to India but also to Ceylon, Burma and Tibet. The fact that Kharoshṭhī was written from right to left points to its Semitic origin. It is derived from the Aramaic script which was widely spread, from Egypt to Persia, during the rule of the Achæmenians. The theory that they, after their conquest of Gandhāra, imported the Arameans for the purpose of government and thereby made the people of India acquainted with the Aramaic language and alphabet has been proved by the recent discovery of an Aramaic inscription at Taxila.[2] The Persian influence on the protocol and royal chancery of the Mauryan administration we have already

[1] Dr. Przyluski, however, traces the word to *kharaposta* (=the hide of the donkey), on which the documents in Kharoshṭhī were originally written but which afterwards became the name of the saint to whom its invention was attributed (I.A., 1931, pp. 150-1).

[2] See *E.I.*, Vol. XIX, pp. 251-3, where Dr. Herzfeld ascribes the record to Aśoka himself.

noticed, and we have stated that it was due to Achæmenian occupation of north-west India.[1] Numerous and diverse are the views regarding the origin of the Brāhmī alphabet. They may, however, be reduced to two main theories. The first of these regards Brāhmī as of indigenous origin. It was first suggested by Lassen and afterwards supported by Sir Alexander Cunningham. The second theory is that of the Semitic origin. This theory is of two kinds, and of these the view which is now accepted by all European experts in Indian palæography is that of Weber and Bühler who maintain that Brāhmī is derived from the script of the Northern Semites, the earliest Phœnician alphabet known to us and supposed to be of about B. C. 850. One of the strongest arguments urged by Cunningham in rejecting the Semitic origin was that Brāhmī ran from left to right, and not from right to left as Semitic scripts do. But Bühler has conclusively shown that even Brāhmī was originally written from right to left. Reminiscences of such a practice are traceable in Aśoka inscriptions. One such may be detected in the reversed forms of single letters like *dh*, *t* and *o* which are met with in these records. Conjunct consonants also are sometimes written in a reversed manner in these inscriptions. Thus *tpa*, *sta* and *vya* are engraved as if they were *pta*, *tsa* and *yva*. This is another reminiscence of the original writing

[1] Bühler's *Indian Palæography* (trans.), pp. 24 and ff.; I.A., 1904, pp. 79, and ff. ; *ibid*, 1905, pp. 21 and ff., and pp. 41 and ff. ; *ibid*, 1906, pp. 4 and ff. ; *Cambridge History of India*, Vol. I, pp. 62 and 657.

of Brāhmī from right to left. The triumph of the Semitic theory was thus complete until six years ago when the prehistoric cairns in the Nizam's Dominions were excavated and the marks on their pottery studied. At least five of these marks are identical with the letters of the Aśokan alphabet. Again, there is one neolith in the Indian Museum containing three contiguous marks which apparently form a writing and which bear a fairly close resemblance to three Aśokan letters. Thus the discussion about the origin of the Brāhmī alphabet is transferred from the historic to the prehistoric sphere. This is just as it should be, for even in Europe all Semitic and other alphabets are now being traced to the prehistoric times, and the view is gradually gaining strength that alphabet originated with the prehistoric man. And consequently when as many as eight symbols on prehistoric artifacts in India are found closely to correspond to the alphabetic characters of the Aśoka period, it is more reasonable to suppose that Brāhmī has an indigenous though prehistoric origin than connect it with a Semitic alphabet of 800 B.C.[1]

The question that we have to consider now is the condition of language in Aśoka's time. Before we proceed to discuss this problem, we have to take note of two orthographic peculiarities evidenced by the inscriptions; otherwise they are likely to be confounded with dialectic characteristics.

[1] SAMAJ., Vol. III, pt. I., pp. 493 and ff. ; I.A., 1919, pp. 57 and ff. JASB., 1921, pp. 209 and ff. ; *Calcutta Review*, 1923, July-September, pp. 358 and ff.

In the first place, we have to notice that homogeneous consonants are nowhere doubled in Aśokan records. Thus instead of *atthi* (Sk. *asti*) or *savva* (Sk. *sarva*) we find simply *athi* and *sava*. But this is not a peculiarity of these inscriptions only. For up till the fourth century A.D., there is hardly any epigraph,[1] written in monumental Prākṛit, where this doubling of consonants caused by assimilation is graphically shown. Secondly, in the case of the Shāhbāzgaṛhi and Mānsherā versions of the Fourteen Rock Edicts we find that the long and the short vowels have not been graphically distinguished. This also is not an orthographic feature which is peculiar to the Aśokan records, but is found exhibited by all the Kharoshṭhī inscriptions of the later periods. These are the only two points which can legitimately be explained away as orthographic modes, but in all other matters the inscriptions may safely be taken as representing the actual pronunciation.

Now, what are the dialectic characteristics revealed by our records? Is there any evidence of the existence of dialects in Aśoka's time? This is the point we will now discuss. If we take the Seven Pillar Edicts of this king, we cannot fail to note that they have all been couched in practically one dialect, with distinctive characteristics uniformly exhibited by them all. These have been ably described by M. Senart.[2] Here we have no cerebral *n*, no palatal *ñ* but invariably the dental *n*.

1 Except in records printed, *e.g.*, in El., VIII, 144; IX, 57.
2 I.A., 1892, pp. 171 and ff.

The initial *y* is elided, so that we have for instance *athā* instead of *yathā*. *L* is always substituted for *r* (*lājā* for *rājā*). The nominative singular of masculine and usually of neuter, end in *e*, as in *samāje* for *samājo* and *dāne* for *dānaṁ*. The conjunct consonant with an uninitial *y*, as a rule, avoids assimilation by the insertion of an *i*—as in *avadhiyāni* for *avadhyāni*. An uninitial *r*, again, is invariably elided, as in *piya* for *priya*. When we come to the Fourteen Rock Edicts, we find that this dialect of the Seven Pillar Edicts is exhibited fully by the Dhauli and Jaugaḍā versions and almost fully by the Kālsī copy. But when we take into consideration the remaining versions, we note that the Shāhbāzgaṛhī, Mānsherā and Girnār edicts, although they contain many characteristics of the P.E. dialect, yet exhibit not a few peculiarities of their own which are tantamount to dialectic differences; and if we further investigate the case, we find that they constitute two different dialects, one represented by the Shāhbāzgaṛhī and Mānsherā and the other by the Girnār copy.

It will be seen that the dialect of the Pillar Edicts was spread over a very large area, embracing not only Madhyadeśa but also provinces conterminous such as those represented by the present Behār, Orissā and Dehra Dun. It would be preposterous to suppose that there was only one vernacular spoken over such a wide region. What seems all but certain is that the dialect of the pillar inscriptions was an official language developed at the royal court of Pāṭaliputra and based upon the vernacular of Magadha. The peculiarities of the

Māgadhī, such as are noted by the Prākṛit grammarians, are all except one to be found in the dialect of these records. The change of *r* to *l* and of *o* to *e*, so peculiar to Māgadhī, are noticeable in the language of these inscriptions, the only exception being in regard to the use of palatal *ś* for dental *s*. All these Magadhisms are traceable in an inscription of the third century B.C. and engraved in the Jogimārā Cave on Rāmgaṛh Hill, which, being situated in Behār, must have been originally in Magadha. Why the use of *ś* for *s* alone is not noticeable in the Aśokan Pillar records is not quite clear.[1] When an order was issued from the Secretariat of Pāṭaliputra, copies of a draft must have been despatched to every provincial government. And as practically one and the same draft we find incised in the Seven Pillar Edicts at six different places and also in the Fourteen Rock Edicts at Kālsī, Dhauli and Jaugaḍā, it seems that the Magadha court language, owing to the imperial capital being stationed at Pāṭaliputra, was completely foisted on Madhyadeśa and Kaliṅga, and became a sort of *lingua franca* over that wide area.

Shāhbāzgaṛhī and Mānsherā, however, are comprised in Uttarāpatha, and Girnār in Dakshiṇāpatha.[2] They had their own dialects, and here although every attempt was made to impose the Magadha draft upon them, that could not prevent

[1] It is quite possible that this peculiarity was confined to the lower classes.

[2] Cl., 1918, pp. 44 and fol.

the provincial dialectic peculiarities from creeping in.[1] It thus seems that the influence of the Magadha language was not so deep and thorough over the remote countries of Uttarāpatha and Dakshiṇāpatha and that consequently the official draft of the Pāṭaliputra court was not adopted wholesale as it was done in Madhyadeśa and Kaliṅga. Now, what are the dialectic characteristics which were peculiar to Uttarāpatha on the one hand and Dakshiṇāpatha on the other? That these dialects were different from that of Madhyadeśa is indicated by the fact that the characteristics of the Madhyadeśa dialect are all conspicuous by their absence. Thus they have not only the dental *n*, but also the palatal *ñ* and the lingual *ṇ*. The nominative masculine singular ends in *o*, not *e*. *L* is not substituted for *r*, and so on. Let us now see in what respects the dialects of the Uttarāpatha and the Dakshiṇāpatha differed from each other. The locative singular of both, no doubt, sometimes ended in *e*, in the case of the latter, often in *mhi* and of the former in *si* as of the Madhyadeśa. The former had the three sibilants *ś*, *sh* and *s*, but the latter had only *s* as in Madhyadeśa. *Vya* was generally retained in the latter, but was assimilated and became *vva* in the former. In the former, again, *y* and *i* were frequently interchanged, and the third letter changed to the first of its class. The

[1] The court draft may have been more faithfully copied in the Mānsherā than in the Shābhāzgaṛhī recension. That cannot, however, be taken to mean that morphologically the Mānsherā stands nearer to the Magadha language than the Shāhbāzgaṛhī dialect.

latter retained the diphthong *ai*, and had *sṭ* always for *shṭh* and sometimes for *st*.

Another point about Indian philology on which light is thrown by the Aśokan inscriptions is worth noting. Some philologists talk rather vaguely about phonetic decay when they speak of Pāli and Prākṛit, and maintain that it is an indication of a later age.[1] This phonetic decay, they contend, is represented by assimilation, hiatus, a fondness for cerebrals and aspirates, and so on. But must the language or dialect where these characteristics are perceptible be necessarily later than that where they are not? May they not rather denote a mode of pronunciation which is peculiar to one class, people or country, and not to another? Let us see at what solution the Aśokan records enable us to arrive. If we compare the Girnār version, for instance, with that of Kālsī, we cannot fail to notice that the language of the latter exhibits greater phonetic decay than that of the former. We have already seen that the original *r* of the conjunct consonants is as a rule retained by the former but invariably dropped by the latter. Thus in the former we may find *sarvatra*, but always *savata* (*savvatta*) in the latter. Again while Girnār has *hasti*, Kālsī gives *hathi* (*hatthi*). These are only a few out of the many instances of assimilation to be found in the language of the Kālsī version as compared with that of Girnār. Take, again, the fondness for cerebrals. For the Sanskrit

[1] R. G. Bhandarkar's *Wilson Philological Lectures*, pp. 8 and f.; pp. 34 and ff.

kṛita and *bhṛita*, Girnār gives *kata* and *bhata*, but Kālsī invariably *kaṭa* and *bhaṭa*. Similarly, for *dbādasa* or *edisa* of Girnār we find *duvāḍasa* and *heḍisa* in Kālsī. The latter word *heḍisa* again, along with *heta*, *hida* and so on shows also the fondness for aspirate in the case of the Kālsī dialect. It will thus be seen that according to the ordinary laws of Pāli and Prākṛits the Kālsī dialect shows greater phonetic degeneracy than the Girnār. Will any philologist, however, dare to conclude that the former is posterior in time to the latter? Most certainly he cannot, because the Girnār and Kālsī dialects were existing side by side in Aśoka's reign, and one cannot therefore be possibly said to be of later age than the other. Nevertheless, according to the canons of these philologists the Kālsī dialect evinces greater phonetic decay than the Girnār and must therefore be regarded as posterior to it.[1] The truth of the matter is that what are called the laws of the Pāli and Prākṛit speech do not at all indicate phonetic degeneracy and therefore a later age as contended by them, but rather a mode of pronunciation peculiar to a class, people or country, which was prevalent at all ages.

In this connection is worth remembering what Bharata has said in the seventeenth chapter of his *Nāṭya-śāstra*.[2] He clearly tells us that Sanskrit and Prākṛit are not two languages, but two modes

[1] See in this connection the thoughtful views of Prof. Michelson (JAOS., XXXIII, 145-9).

[2] V. 25 and ff. Even supposing that the work is of post-Christian age, all we have to infer is that the tradition, that there were two forms of speech—polished and vulgar, was current till a late period.

of speech, that is, of pronunciation and diction (*pāṭhya*). He recognises four languages only, namely, *abhibhāshā*, that of the gods, *ārya-bhāshā*, that of the kings, *jāti-bhāshā*, languages of the (human) species, and *jātyantarī*, those of other species, such as birds and beasts. The first two are *saṃskṛita-pāṭhya* or polished speeches, but the third comprises both, that is, the *saṃskṛita* or polished, and the *prākṛita* or popular mode, of speech. Much confusion has thus been caused by the loose use of these terms, and, above all, by thinking that the phonetic changes exhibited by Pāli, for instance, are phonetic degeneracy and therefore a criterion of later age. If we carefully divest our minds of the confusion and prejudices created and spread by some philologists, we shall find that the language in which the edicts of the Mauryan emperor, Aśoka, have been couched is just that language, whose grammar Pāṇini, Kātyāyana and Patañjali composed, but that while the former represent *prākṛita*, the works of the latter are concerned with the *saṃskṛita* form of that language. We will select here a specimen passage from Rock Edict IX of the Girnār recension :

Devānaṃ-piyo Priyadasi rājā evaṃ āha (:) asti jano uchāvachaṃ maṃgalaṃ karote ābādhesu vā āvāha-vivāhesu vā putralābhesu vā pravāsaṃmhi vā. Etamhi cha añamhi cha jano uchāvachaṃ maṃgalaṃ karote.

Now, if we make allowance for certain phonetic peculiarities, it is difficult to say that the language of this edict is not the *bhāshā* for which Pāṇini and Patañjali wrote. If we take a learned Pandit and a boor speaking any vernacular of India, we will find greater divergence of speech than here. An impartial scholar like Prof. F. W. Thomas has already remarked that "it is not too much to say that in modern English, both spoken and written, we find greater deviations from the norm than these Edicts display."[1] Of course, in Aśoka's time the phonetic peculiarities were of three different types, according as the three provinces, Madhyadeśa, Uttarāpatha and Dakshināpatha were concerned, and these no doubt constituted the three main dialects of the period. But if we once admit that these dialectic differences represented but so many different modes of pronunciation and diction, it is impossible to avoid the conclusion that the norm of these edicts must be just that language which is treated by the grammarians. This reminds us of the remark of Patañjali that the language for which Pāṇini wrote was the language of those *śishṭa* or disciplined Brāhmaṇas who spoke it naturally and without any study of grammar.[2] What is worthy of note is that the *śishṭas* referred to by Patañjali are precisely those who did not study the *Ashṭādhyāyī* and yet spoke the language as taught in that work.[3] This shows that up till *circa* 150 B.C., the time of Patañjali, the language for which *Ashṭādhyāyī* was the grammar continued to be the actual speech of the disciplined Brāhmaṇas of Āryāvarta which was no doubt the *Saṃskṛita* or polished form of the vernacular.

1 JRAS., 1904, p. 462.

2 R. G. Bhandarkar's *Wilson Philological Lectures*, pp. 295-6.

3 JRAS., 1904, pp. 479-80.

It may be admitted that the dialects of the Aśoka period represented but the modes of speech which were current mostly among classes of men who were not highly cultured. But it may be asked why no inscription has been found which is in the language of the *śishṭa* Brāhmaṇas? For has not the late Dr. Fleet, a renowned epigraphist, told us most emphatically that before A.D. 150, the time of Rudradāman of the Western Kshatrapa dynasty, there is not a single inscription in Sanskrit, clearly showing that up till then Sanskrit was not understood by the people at large and that it could not have been spoken by them?[1] It is not quite correct, however, to say that not a single inscription has been discovered of this period which is in this language. For the inscription of the Ghosuṇḍī step well found in the Udaipur State, Rājputānā, is in what is called Sanskrit, especially as we have here the dual form twice used.[2] It records a benefaction to Saṃkarshaṇa and Vāsudeva by Gājāyana Sarvatāta, who had performed a horse sacrifice. This record has been assigned by Bühler to the period between B.C. 350 and 250. The inscription cannot therefore be of any time later than that of Aśoka. Another epigraph in Sanskrit of an early period has been found in Ayodhyā [3] pertaining to Dhanadeva, son of Phalgudeva, a ruler of Kosala, who, just because he was a Śuṅga, was a Brāhmaṇ by extraction. It is not at all unreasonable to say that more of such Sanskrit records must have been

1 JRAS., 1904, p. 483.

2 MASI., No. 4, pp. 119-20. ASI-AR., 1926-27, p. 205.

3 JBORS., 1924, p. 203; E.I., Vol. XX, p. 57.

originally engraved but they have been lost. Such inscriptions could only be associated with Brahmanical monuments, which, just because they were in and near villages and towns, and not in solitary localities far removed from human habitation, as was mostly the case with the Buddhist and Jaina monuments, have now perhaps been irretrievably lost.

Dr. Fleet and Prof. Rhys Davids maintain that the inscriptions ranging between 300 B. C. and 100 A. D. are all in a sort of Pāli closely allied to, and based upon, the vernacular. This in their opinion conclusively proves that the language current up to 100 A. D. was practically Pāli and that Sanskrit or the *bhāshā* for which Pāṇini and Patañjali wrote could not have been a vernacular at all during that time. It is not possible to accept this view. In the first place, we have just seen that there are at least two epigraphs of the earlier part of the period which are in clear and unmistakable Sanskrit. Secondly, these scholars do not seem to have given any thought to what the French savant, E. Senart, has said in regard to the language of these inscriptions, or the Monumental Prākṛit as he calls it. We have, in the first place, to bear in mind the wide area over which they are dispersed, namely, from Gujarat and the caves of the Western Coast to Amarābatī at the mouth of the Kistna and the caves of Khaṇḍagiri in Orissa on the Eastern coast, and from Sāñchī and Barhaut in Central India to Banavāsī,[1] the southern extremity of the Bombay Presidency and Kāñchi or modern

[1] IA., 1892, p. 260.

Conjeeveram in the Madras Presidency. Secondly, these records extend over at least six centuries, from about 150 B.C. to 450 A.D., and do not disclose any appreciable variation between the most ancient and the most modern of them. Dr. Otto Franke [1] has, no doubt, shown some dialectical peculiarities noticeable among them, but they are so few, especially as compared to those we detect in the inscriptions of Aśoka, that they are of no consequence for our present purpose. Now the question arises : how is it possible for a vernacular, spread over such a wide area, to live seven centuries in the mouth of the common people without decay or transformation? This is certainly impossible, and this conclusion is more than amply confirmed by the fact that the earliest literary specimens which we possess of the Prākṛits, the stanzas of Hāla and the Prākṛits of the most ancient dramas, are of about the end of this period or shortly removed from it, and yet they reveal a phonetic alteration which was much farther advanced. The dialect of these inscriptions could not possibly have been the living popular language spoken over such an extensive area and over such a wide period as six centuries, but may, in all likelihood, have formed the *lingua franca* or the Hindustānī of Ancient India from *circa* 150 B.C. to 450 A.D. Even in the Hindustānī of the present day, provincial peculiarities are by no means absent. Certainly the Hindustānī of Mahārāshṭra is as much tinged with Marāṭhī phraseology and construction as that of Bengal is with Bengali, and the Hindustānī of both

[1] *Pāli und Sanskrit*, pp. 110 and ff.

Mahārāshṭra and Bengal is different from the Hindustānī that is spoken, for instance, at Benares. Nevertheless, nobody can dispute the proposition that Hindustānī is the *lingua franca* of Modern India. Such was the case with the Monumental Prākṛit, which, though some provincial differences were here and there perceptible in it as was first noticed by Dr. Franke, was nevertheless the Hindustānī of Bhāratavarsha from about 150 B.C. to at least 150 A.D. The question that we have now to answer is when and why it became the *lingua franca*. Through the unflagging missionary zeal of Aśoka there must have been an unprecedented activity all over India. All barriers which detached one province from another must have been broken and an interprovincial communication sprung up which was at once very brisk and frequent with the result that soon after Aśoka's death the necessity for a common language for the whole of India must have continued to be most keenly felt. But this time the province which was then the centre of this activity and where the parent of the Prākṛit called Mahārāshṭrī was spoken supplied its local dialect to meet the new demand. And what was once a provincial dialect began to rise to the eminence of the universal language in which not only the scriptures of the Buddhists were written in order that they may be understood all over India but which came everywhere to be recognised as the official or political language, and was adopted by people of other religions also. Thus the Vaishṇava inscription on the celebrated pillar of Besnagar, the Nānāghāṭ cave epigraph of Sātakarni enumerating his various Brahmanical sacrifices, and the royal charters issued by Gautamīputra Sātakarṇi and Vāsishṭhīputra Puḷumāvi of the Śātavāhana dynasty are all in the Monumental Prākṛit which was practically the same as the Pāli of the southern Buddhist scriptures.[1]

A few words may now be said in regard to the art that prevailed in Aśoka's time. Here too we shall confine ourselves entirely to the monuments, actually raised by him and not associated with his name. This is perhaps the only aspect of culture on which light is thrown by his monuments. They are, we know, the rocks and columns which bear his edicts of Dhaṃma and the caves he dedicated to the Ājīvikas. As pieces of sculpture and architecture they have been so well described that nothing need be said here. We have here to

[1] All these remarks about Pāli and Monumental Prākṛit have been extracted from the two lectures I delivered in 1919 before the Calcutta University. In the same lectures I have propounded the view that what is called the Gāthā dialect is practically the mixed Sanskrit of the Inscriptions of the Kushana period, and represents the spoken language, if not the vernacular, of the *śishṭa* people from the first century B.C. to the third century A.D., when, owing to the increasing supremacy of Brahmanism, Sanskrit was being largely studied even by non-Brahmanical sects but Pāli as a literary vehicle was not yet extinct. This is just the reason why we find some Buddhist scriptures written in this language. It is natural that the Buddhist sects that arose in the Kushana period should have their scriptures in a language that was spoken by the *śishṭas*. Things remained in the transitional stage till about the third century A.D. when Sanskrit was universally adopted for current use and thus took complete possession of the field as a literary vehicle which was destined never to escape it. Those Buddhist sects which sprang up at this time had their scriptures cast wholly in Sanskrit. This is the reason why we find the Dhammapada, for instance, in three versions, that is, composed not only in Pāli and mixed Sanskrit but also pure Sanskrit.

consider them only from the engineer's and the artist's point of view. It is not at all improbable, as was first pointed out by Senart, that the decrees of the Achæmenian monarch, Darius, suggested to the Mauryan emperor the idea of issuing religious edicts engraved on the rocks. And further Smith seems to be right in thinking that what, above all, served as the model here for Aśoka was the inscription of the former at Naksh-i-Rustam "which is supposed to be 'perceptive not historical' and to contain 'the last solemn admonition of Darius to his countrymen with respect to their future conduct in policy, morals and religion.'"[1] Aśoka, however, carried the idea one step further by bringing the columns also into requisition. If big rocks have been polished and inscribed, Aśoka's workmen probably did not show any superiority over their Persian brother-craftsmen. The case, however, was entirely different in so far as the pillars were concerned. Pillars were doubtless not unknown to the Persian structures. But the erection of pillars independent and not forming part of any edifices seems to have originated in India alone and is not found in Western Asia or Europe before the time of the Roman emperors. Again, the Aśokan columns are monoliths of singularly massive proportions from 40 to 50 feet in length and with an average diameter of 2′ 7″. Quarrying blocks nearly four feet square and fifty feet long is an occupation most taxing even to the powers of the twentieth century when we so much boast of our

[1] Smith's *Aśoka*, p. 141.

modern scientific knowledge, training and appliances. How the workmen of the Mauryan period achieved this gigantic task two thousand years ago cannot but fill our minds with wonder. But to cut true, dress, and proportion blocks of such stupendous dimensions into beautiful round columns and burnish it like mirror at which even a modern mason stands aghast was a still more arduous and delicate task. Of this even they acquitted themselves with eminent success. But this is not all. The pillars of Aśoka are one and all composed of sandstone from a quarry near Chunār in the Mirzāpur District, U.P. They are believed to have been chiselled there and transported to the different places. The carriage of such unwieldy masses to great distances (and some of the pillars were sent hundreds of miles away from the hill-sides where they had been quarried) and setting them up at diverse and remote places, demanded an amount of mechanical appliances and ingenuity which would have been most trying, if not impossible, to the modern age. Sixteen centuries later we find three of Aśoka's pillars removed to Delhi by Sultan Firoz Shah; and fortunately for us a graphic description of the extreme difficulty of conveyance and erection experienced by his engineers has been preserved in the case of one of these monuments, namely, that brought from Toprā in the Umbāllā District, Punjab. Shams-i-Sirāj, a contemporary historian, says :—

" After Sultan Firoz returned from his expedition against Thatta, he often made excursions in the neighbourhood of Delhi. In this part of the country there were two stone columns. One was in the village of Topra in the District of Salaura and Khizrabad, in the hills, the other in the vicinity of the town of Mirath. . . . . When Firoz Shah first beheld these columns, he was filled with admiration, and resolved to remove them with great care as trophies to Delhi.

"Khizrabad is ninety *kos* from Delhi, in the vicinity of the hills. When the Sultan visited that district, and saw the column in the village of Topra, he resolved to remove it to Delhi, and there erect it as a memorial to future generations. After thinking over the best means of lowering the column, orders were issued commanding the attendance of all the people dwelling in the neighbourhood, within and without the Doāb, all soldiers, both horse and foot. They were ordered to bring all implements and materials suitable for the work. Directions were issued for bringing parcels of the cotton of the sembal (silk-cotton tree). Quantities of this silk cotton were placed round the column, and when the earth at its base was removed, it fell gently over on the bed prepared for it. The cotton was then removed by degrees, and after some days the pillar lay safe upon the ground. When the foundations of the pillar were examined, a large square stone was found as a base, which also was taken out.

"The pillar was then encased from top to bottom in reeds and raw skins, so that no damage might accrue to it. A carriage, with forty-two wheels, was constructed, and ropes were attached to each wheel. Thousands of men hauled at every rope, and after great labour and difficulty the pillar was raised on to the carriage. A strong rope was fastened to each wheel, and 200 men (42 × 200 = 8,400) pulled at each of these ropes. By the simultaneous exertions of so many thousand men the carriage was moved, and was brought to the banks of the Jumna. Here the Sultan came to meet it. A number of large boats had been collected, some of which could carry 5,000 and 7,000 maunds of grain, and the least of them 2,000 maunds. The column was very ingeniously transferred to these boats, and was then conducted to Firozabad, where it was landed and conveyed into the Kushk with infinite labour and skill.

"At this time the author of this book was twelve years of age and a pupil of the respected Mir Khan. When the pillar was brought to the palace, a building was commenced for its reception near the Jāmi Masjid (mosque), and the most skilful architects and workmen were employed. It was constructed of stone and chunam (fine mortar), and consisted of several stages or steps. When a step was finished the column was raised on to it, another step was then built and the pillar was again raised, and so on in succession until it reached the intended height. On arriving at this stage, other contrivances had to be devised to place it in an erect position. Ropes of great thickness were obtained and windlasses were placed on each of the six stages of the base. The ends of the ropes were fastened to the top of the pillar, and the other ends passed over the windlasses, which were firmly secured with many fastenings. The wheels were then turned, and the column was raised about half a *gaz* (yard). Logs of wood and bags of cotton were then placed under it to prevent it sinking again. In this way, by degrees, and in course of several days, the column was raised to the perpendicular. Large beams were then placed round it as supports until quite a cage of scaffolding was formed. It was thus secured in an upright position straight as an arrow, without the smallest deviation from the perpendicular. The square stone, before spoken of, was placed under the pillar."[1]

Firoz Shah removed only three of Aśoka's pillars, which again were not the biggest and were transported to not more than 150 miles from the original places. On the other hand, Aśoka had not three, but nearly thirty, such columns erected and carried in many cases to much larger distances.

[1] Elliot, *Hist. India*, III. 350.

Thus not only the quarrying, and chiselling but also the conveyance of these monuments offers a most eloquent testimony to the highly specialised skill of labour and the extreme resourcefulness of Aśoka's engineers.

It is worthy of note that there was hardly any stone building prior to the time of Aśoka, and that India is indebted to this Buddhist emperor for the use of stone for architectural purposes. In his edicts Aśoka has told us in many places that one of the two objects which impelled him to engrave them on rocks and pillars is that they may endure permanently. This was the reason why Aśoka deemed it advisable to expend the skilled labour and resources of his state on these columns and have his Dhaṃma-lipis incised in stone. In the architecture of India before the time of Aśoka, wood seems to have been chiefly, if not solely, employed as it is in Burma, China and Japan almost to this day. Certainly, it is a better building material than stone except, of course, in point of durability. Megasthenes tells us that Pāṭliputra was "surrounded by a wooden wall pierced with loopholes for the discharge of arrows." If the very capital of Chandragupta was defended by such palisading, the inference is natural that the architecture of the period was almost solely wooden. Even in the Jātakas we find copious references to wooden buildings,[1] a few to brick structures,[2] but none at all to stone architecture. This should not, however, be taken to mean that the art and industry of the stone-cutter

[1] Jāt., II. 18. 7-13; VI. 332. 21 and ff.

[2] *Ibid.*, VI. 429. 17.8.

was unknown, as references to it in the Jātakas are by no means wanting.[1] Again, of about Aśoka's time there is at least one stone image, that found at Parkham,[2] for the sculpturing of which the royal masons were not responsible. Again, at Nagarī in Rājputānā we have the remains of a cyclopean enclosure wall of a shrine dedicated to Vāsudeva-saṁkarshaṇa, which has to be ascribed to a time slightly earlier than Aśoka.[3] Another stone structure, which according to Fergusson [4] was certainly anterior to Aśoka, is the one at Rājgīr, known as *Jarāsandh-ki baiṭhak.* If any further proof of the development of the stone art and industry prior to this king is required, it is furnished by the massive stone coffer exhumed from the Piprāwā Stūpa.[5] It is a huge monolith in grey sandstone measuring 4′ 4″ × 2′ 8¼″ × 2′ 2¼″, and bespeaks the highest quality of craftsmanship. When the idea of imparting a durable character to his Dhaṃma-lipis seized his mind, Aśoka seems to have availed himself of the stone-cutter's art which was already in a highly developed and flourishing condition.

So much for the monuments of Aśoka from the engineer's point of view. But what degree of development do they evince as works of art? Here too the columns are the most important of the three

1 See *e.g.*, Jat. I. 478. 5 and 12.

2 *Cat. Arch. Museum, Mathurā,* p. 83 and pl. XII.

3 MASI., No. 4, pp. 128 and ff.

4 HIEA., Vol. I, p. 75. For another view, see Dr. Kramrisch's *Die Indische Kunst,* Vol. VI (Springer, *Handbuch der Kunstgeschichte*), pp. 232 and 235.

5 SAMSJA., Vol. III, pt. I, p. 425.

classes into which they have been divided. Each column consists of three parts, the shaft with what is called the bell-shaped capital, the abacus, and the crowning sculpture in the round. The capital, abacus, and crowning sculpture together form the most important and artistic feature of the column. By far the best specimen of this is that found at Sārnāth, which is known as the Sārnāth capital. In regard to it Sir John Marshall says: " The Sarnath capital, on the other hand, though by no means a masterpiece, is the product of the most developed art of which the world was cognisant in the third century B.C.—the handiwork of one who had generations of artistic effort and experience behind him. In the masterful strength of the crowning lions, with their swelling veins and tense muscular development, and in the spirited realism of the reliefs below, there is no trace whatever of the limitations of primitive art. So far as naturalism was his aim, the sculptor has modelled his figures direct from nature and has delineated their forms with bold, faithful touch; but he has done more than this: he has consciously and of set purpose infused a tectonic conventional spirit into the four lions, so as to bring them into harmony with the architectural character of the monument, and in the case of the horse on the abacus he has availed himself of a type well known and approved in western art. Equally mature is the technique of his relief work. In early Indian, as in early Greek sculpture, it was the practice, as we shall presently see, to compress the relief between two fixed planes, the original front plane of the slab and the plane of the background. In the reliefs of the Sārnāth capital there is no trace whatever of this process; each and every part of the animal is modelled according to its actual depth without reference to any ideal front plane, with the result that it presents the appearance almost of a figure in the round which has been cut in half and then applied to the background of the abacus." [1]

The archæologists, however, are of opinion that the Aśokan architecture is an exotic. One view is that most of the features exhibited by the upper half of the column, especially the bell-shaped capital were borrowed from Assyria through Persia from where Aśoka "obtained those hints which in India led to the conversion of wooden architecture into stone." [2] The second, which is the latest, view is that the Aśokan column is entirely a Perso-Hellenic affair. The architectural features were Persian but the modelling of the living forms was entirely Hellenistic. For about this time the Hellenistic spirit was vigorous in Bactria and "was mastering and vitalising the dull, expressionless forms of Iran." [3] And so this Perso-Hellenic art was transmitted from Bactria to India. Now, if this Perso-Hellenic art is really represented by the Aśokan column and developed itself in Bactria, how is it that no specimens of it have been found in Bactria itself or its neighbouring region, *e.g.*, the north-west part of India? Unless such specimens are found, the Perso-Hellenic influnce is scarcely

1 CHI., I. 620-1.
2 HIEA., Vol. I, pp. 58-9.
3 CHI., I. 622.

more than a gratuitous assumption. The idea, again, of erecting pillars by themselves and not as forming integral part of any building, is as stated above, neither Persian nor Hellenistic, but Indian. Similarly, if the Bactrian Greeks took such a prominent part in the modelling and chiselling connected with the Aśokan column, it is rather strange that they have introduced no forms or features into this architecture which are typically Hellenic, such as those of the Ionic or Corinthian order. These last we find in the architecture of the Indo-Parthian and Kushana period, but not at all in the time of Aśoka. It is true that the honeysuckle, the cable and the bead and reel ornaments which are familiar to the student of the Hellenic art are found in the Aśokan column. But these ornaments are not typically Hellenic, because the Greeks themselves are known to have borrowed them from Assyria. And it is more natural to say that the other features of the column, such as the bell-shaped capital, smooth unfluted shafts, and lustrous polish are all adopted from the Assyrians, but directly, and not through the Persians. It is safer to say, as Rajendra Lala Mitra contended many years ago, that the Indians copied from the Assyrians, certainly at a time far removed from that of Aśoka.[1] This conclusion is quite in keeping with the fact that the structure, *Jarāsandh-ki Baiṭhak*, which is taken by all archæologists as of the pre-Mauryan period, is supposed by Ferguson to have an Assyrian origin and copied from the Birs

[1] *Indo-Aryans*, Vol. I, pp. 14 and ff.

Nimrud.[1] But when and where did the Indians and the Assyrians come in contact? These Assyrians are undoubtedly the Asuras, mentioned in the Vedic literature, as a people in India itself, with whom the Vedic Aryans were constantly warring. They seem to be already in possession of the greater portion of India before the Aryans came. The Asuras appear to have been great builders. For even in the Ṛig-Veda many references are found to their 'seven-walled' or 'iron-walled' cities or to their 'hundred cities of stone.' This must refer to the fortified ramparts of the period, some of which thus seem to have been of stone. Royal residences in the Ṛig-Veda, again, are said to be 'thousand-doored' and possess 'halls built with a thousand columns,' exactly as we find in the case of the hall built for Yudhishṭhira by Maya the Asura, as the Mahābhārata informs us. These most probably were of wooden construction. The special characteristic of the Asura architecture was the cyclopean style of the buildings. They raised structures on a colossal scale. The Indian civilisation in Aśoka's time had almost as much of the Assyrian as of the Aryan element; and, so far as architecture was concerned, India was greatly indebted to the Assyrians or Asuras, but certainly to those Assyrians who were settled in India and had made it their home. The Aśokan architecture thus, though dominantly Assyrian, was yet Indian.

---

1 *Cave-Temples of India*, pp. 34-5.

APPENDIX

It is a great pity that no scholar[1] has yet properly studied the Asura problem. Some scholars[2] have no doubt recently suggested that the Asuras referred to in the Vedic literature as a people were most probably the Assyrians and that these references are reminiscences of the times when the Aryans were in contact with the Assyrians somewhere in Mesopotamia or Central Asia but certainly outside India. But it has apparently been forgotten that the same conclusions were expressed long before them by H. H. Wilson and K. M. Banerjea. The former has told us that the Asuras were "the anti-Vaidik people of India" whose cities are said to have been destroyed by Indra.[3] The latter went one step further and identified these Asuras with Assyrians. He also pointed out that the three different senses in which the term *assur* is used in Cuneiform Inscriptions are also the senses in which the word *Asura* is employed in Vedic texts.[4] He, however, thought that the Aryans met the Assyrians in Central Asia, and not in India itself as Wilson maintained. Wilson's view, however, seems to be more correct. Prof. V. K. Rajwade has recently written an elaborate paper on the term *Asura*, in which he rightly says: "There is an overwhelming majority of instances in which the word Asura is used in a good sense, the bad instances being in a minority of about 15, *i.e.*, about 1/7th of the whole (105). This shows that the cleavage between the Rig-vedic religion and Zoroastrianism happened towards the end

[1] After the first edition of this book, the matter has received some attention from Dr. A. Banerji, Sastri (JBORS., 1926). Better work is still desirable.

[2] JRAS., 1916, pp. 363-64; JBBRAS., Vol. XXV, pp. 76 and ff.

[3] Wilson's *Rig Veda*, Vol. III, p. xiv.

[4] *Arian Witness*, pp. 49 and ff.

of Rigvedic period. *The enmity became bitter and bitterer in post-Ṛigvedic times.*"[1] The last sentence is very important, because it clearly shows that the bitter hostilities of the Aryans with the Asuras took place in India, as in the post-Rigvedic times the Aryans were certainly settled in this country. There is again one passage in the Śatapatha-Brāhmaṇa, where we are told that one Asura race was the Prāchyas, which we know was another name for Magadha.[2] Quite in keeping with this is the fact that the Asuras are still found as a non-Aryan tribe in Chhota-Nagpur in Behār.[3] This also agrees with the fact that in Rājgīr in Behār we have that *Jarāsandh-ki Baiṭhak*, which, as we have seen already, is, according to Fergusson, of the pre-Mauryan period, and is copied from the Birs Nimrud in Assyria. This also explains why a Babylonian seal should have been found in India.[4] The seal is at present deposited in the museum at Nagpur, and dates from 2000 B. C. The exact find-spot is not known, but in 1918 the Curator informed me that it was found somewhere in the Central Provinces.

In the time of the Śatapatha-Brāhmaṇa, the Prāchyas represented but one of the Asura tribes. But there must have been other Asura settlements in other parts of India. A critical and detailed study of the Vedic literature and of the epics may enable us to deduce a history of their migrations and kingdoms. One such settlement probably was in the western part of the United Provinces, the region including Khāṇḍava-vana from whose conflagration Arjuna saved the celebrated Mayāsura. The Asuras were known as a (fighting) people even as late as the time of Pāṇini, and are mentioned by him immediately after the

1 PTFOC., pp. 18-9.

2 XIII, 8. 1, 5; SBE., Vol. XLIV, pp. 423-4. For the Asura colonies and kingdoms in East India see my article in ABORI., Vol. XII, p. 108 & pp. 114 ff.

3 ERE., Vol. 2, pp. 157-9.

4 JASB., 1914, p. 462.

Parśus (the ancient Persians) who form his Parśu *gaṇa*. They spoke a Mlechchha language.[1]

If the Assyrians were thus already in India when the Aryans penetrated the country, it may naturally be asked: what traces of Assyrian civilisation do we find in India? The first and foremost Assyrian influence has of course been traced in the ancient architecture of India. And the late Mr. B. G. Tilak has also shown that some of the spirits or demons in the Atharvaveda were clearly Chaldean.[2] As the Atharvaveda is later in age than the Ṛigveda, this absorption of part of the Chaldean pantheon must have taken place in India. In fact, the civilisation of India prior to the rise of the Mauryan power was principally composed of the Aryan and Asura elements.

---

1 JBBRAS., XXV, 78; ZDMG., LXVIII, 719

2 *Bhandarkar Commem. Vol.*, pp. 29 and ff.

CHAPTER VII

Aśoka's Place in History

We have by this time obtained a sufficiently clear idea of the manifold and unflagging activity of Aśoka. We will now try to frame an accurate estimate of his work with a view to determine his real place in history. But this is not possible unless we try to ascertain what ideal guided him and what motive impelled him. Does Aśoka anywhere unbosom himself of the inner spring of action that prompted him to this activity? So many times has the Buddhist monarch given us glimpses into the inner recesses of his mind [1] that it is inconceivable that in this particular case alone which is of the greatest importance he has not thought fit to take us into his confidence. In Rock Edict VI he says: "There is no higher duty than the welfare of the *whole world*. And what little effort I make is in order that I may be free from debt to the *creatures*, that I may render them happy *here* and they may gain heaven in the *next world*." The words put in Italics here show exactly what ideal was before him. In the first place he feels that he is concerned with the whole world, the creatures in fact, not simply with men but with the whole animate world. And secondly, he feels that his supreme duty is to secure them not only temporal but also spiritual

[1] Prof. Charpentier, however, thinks that in his inscriptions Aśoka has rather concealed than laid open to us the greater part of his own personality (see Appendix to this Chapter).

weal. Let us proceed a little deeper and see whether the different parts of this statement are borne out by what his other records have to tell us. The most important feature of his Dhaṃma mission is the realisation of not only the temporal but also the spiritual good. The words he uses in this edict (RE. VI) are *idha* and *paratra*. And a student of Aśoka inscriptions need not be told how many times he has used words of this import in his various records, such as *hida-lokika* and *pala-lökika* (RE. XIII), *hida-palate* (PE. I), *hidatikāye* and *pala-tikāye* (PE. III), *hidataṃ* and *palataṃ* (PEs. IV and VII), *hidalogaṃ* and *pala-logaṃ* (J.-SRE. II), and so on and so on. Sometimes for *palata* he uses the word *svaga*. We thus see that what Aśoka thought himself bound to look after was not only the temporal but also the spiritual good. The next important feature of his mission to ascertain is how wide was the scope of his activity. In RE. VI he admits, as we have just seen, that it was co-extensive with the whole world and included all creatures. And it may be asked here whether there is anything in his other records which supports this inference. The animate world may be divided into three parts: (1) men, (2) animals, and (3) other creatures. Let us first confine our attention to the temporal welfare of the world which he sought to promote. In PE. VII he says: "On the roads have I planted the banyan trees. They will offer shade to man and beast. I have grown mango-orchards. I have caused wells to be dug at every eight *koses;* and I have had rest-houses. I have made many watering sheds at different places for the enjoyment of man and beast." It will thus be seen that some of the means he adopted for the promotion of Dhaṃma were connected with the material comforts of not only the man but also the beast. It may be argued that these measures of physical enjoyment were restricted to his own dominions and did not entitle him to claim that he promoted the temporal welfare of the world which was certainly more extensive than his empire. To remove this doubt, we have only to turn to RE. II where he not only specifies the philanthropic works just adverted to but mentions also the fact that he established medical treatment for men and for animals. What is most noteworthy about this edict is that he says he did all these things not simply in his kingdom, but also in the dominions of the independent kings known to him, such as the Choḍas, Pāṇḍyas, Sātiyaputra, Keralaputra and Tāmraparṇī which were in India, and also, outside this country, in those of the Yavana or Greek king called Aṃtiyaka (Antiochus) and four other Greek potentates who were his neighbours. Who these were we have already seen. But suffice it to say here, that his measures for the augmentation of the physical happiness of man and beast were not confined to his own empire but were spread over practically the whole world then known to him. Again, it may be contended that all this is very nice, but that this only shows that his philanthropic activity did not go beyond man and beast. There are other creatures besides these in this world. Did he show any concern for them? Two of the ethical practices constituting Dhaṃma in its narrow sense were *prāṇānaṃ anārambho*, 'non-destruction of life,' and *avihīsā bhūtānaṃ*, 'non-injury to creatures.' And quite in keeping with this, he admits in PE. II that he conferred various benefits "on the bipeds and quadrupeds, on birds and aquatic animals, even upto the boon of life." No reasonable doubt can possibly be entertained as to Aśoka's programme being so comprehensive as to have included the whole creature world and the whole earth accessible to him. His confession of his ideal in RE. VI is thus confirmed by his other records which set forth the programme of his Dhaṃma activity.

From the above consideration it follows as a corollary that so far as man was concerned, he thought that his duty lay in regard to the whole of mankind, not simply his subjects. He is quite explicit on this point. In both the Separate Kaliṅga Edicts he tells us that just as for his offspring he desires welfare and happiness, pertaining not only to this world but also the next, he desires it precisely for all mankind (*sava-munisa*); and in the second of these edicts, he goes further to instruct his officers to create in the mind of the alien subjects the belief: "the king (Aśoka) is unto us even as a father; he loves us even as he loves himself; we are to the king even as his children." This unmistakably shows that Aśoka's attitude as of a father to his children is by no means restricted to his own subjects but extended also to those of the foreign kingdoms, so as to embrace the whole mankind as he understood it. We thus obtain some insight into the ideal which Aśoka had placed before his mind and which stimulated him to this stupendous activity. His ideal was to promote the material and spiritual welfare of the whole world consisting not only of men but also of beasts and other creatures, not only again in his own kingdom but also over the world known or accessible to him. The question that now arises is : to what source was he indebted for this grand and noble ideal? Those who are conversant with Pāli literature and especially the Dīgha-Nikāya will perceive that Aśoka was evidently aspiring to be a Chakravartī Dharmarāja. The thirtieth Sutta of this Nikāya is entitled the *Lakkhaṇa-Suttanta,* and sets forth the thirty-two marks of the Superman. The *Sutta* itself begins by saying that to a Superman possessed of these marks, two careers alone are open. If he forsakes the worldly life, he becomes an Arahant, a Buddha Supreme. But if he chooses to live in the world and become a householder, he becomes *Rājā... chakkavattī dhammiko dhammarāja chāturanto vijitāvī...So imaṃ pathaviṃ sāgara-pariyantaṃ adaṇḍena asatthena dhammena abhivijīya ajjhāvasati,* "a King, Turner of the wheel, the Righteous One, Ruler of Righteousness, Lord of the four quarters, Conqueror...Having conquered this earth to its ocean bounds, not by the chastising rod, not by the sword, but by righteousness (*dhaṃma*), he lives supreme over it." The only question that now and here arises is : whether such a Chakravartī Dhārmika Dharmarāja has been described anywhere in the Pāli literature. Here also the Dīgha-Nikāya comes to our help, whose twenty-sixth *Sutta* called *Chakkavattī-Sīhanāda-Sutta* gives a reply to this question. Here we are told that in the days of yore there ruled a number of these Chakravartī Dharmrājas who occupied this exalted position, because they were abiding by the Aryan duty of a Chakravartī. In course of time kings arose who did not stick to this rule of conduct, and the result was that all kinds of immorality sprang up, shortening more and more the span of human life. The worst has not yet come, and the degradation and miseries that will confront men during this state of things have been graphically described. When the worst is once reached, things will take a better turn and continue improving till another Chakravartī Dharmarāja will come into existence. The first of these Chakravartīs in the age long past was Daḷhanemi. He reigned many thousand years, till the Celestial Wheel shone over his palace. When, however, it slipped down from its place, he retired to a forest, placing his eldest son on the throne. But on the seventh day after the royal hermit left, the Wheel completely disappeared. Thereupon the son hastened to the father and informed him of what had happened. The royal hermit exhorted him to act up to the noble ideal of duty set by the Chakravartins, which was thereupon expounded. The son returned to the palace, and things were soon alright as before. Let us now see what this Aryan duty of a Chakravartī is. "This, dear son," says Daḷhanemi, "namely, that thou...shouldst provide watch and ward and protection according to Dhaṃma, for thine own folk (*ante-jana*)...for town and country dwellers (*negama-janapadesu*), for the Brāhmaṇ and Śramaṇa ascetics, and *for beasts and birds*...And when, dear son, the Śramaṇa and

Brāhmaṇ ascetics shall come to thee from time to time and question (*paripuchchheyāsi*) thee concerning what is good and what is bad...what is to be done and what left undone, thou shouldst hear what they have to say, and thou shouldst deter them from evil, and bid them take up what is good." Whoever reads this passage from the *Sutta* cannot but be struck by the extreme similarity it bears to the life and action of Aśoka. It is scarcely necessary to dilate on these various points of similarity. To resume, however, the thread of our story, the son of Daḷhanemi followed his father's advice, and the Celestial Wheel which makes a king Chakravartī revealed itself. He followed the progress of the Wheel, which first went to the east, then to the south, west and north,[1] and the conquered enemy kings in each of these regions said: "Teach us, O mighty king." And what does this Chakravartī do? He does not receive any political homage from them, and he preaches to them, saying: "Ye shall slay no living thing. Ye shall not take that which has not been given," and so on, and so on. Anybody who reads this story carefully will be convinced that we have here a case not of

[1] There can be no doubt that the Chakravartī Dhārmika Dharmarāja whose account appears in these Suttas is modelled after the terrestrial Chakravartī described in the *Ait Br.*, VIII. 14 & 15 as being *samudra-paryanta* and carrying on expeditions of conquest in the east, south, west and north respectively (MCNL., pp. 91-3). The domain of the Chakravartī of the Brāhmaṇa period was confined to India, whereas in Aśoka's time the people of India had definite knowledge of land beyond this country and also of its rulers. Hence Aśoka's spiritual conquest is not restricted merely to India as is the case with the Suttas but extended over the whole world then known to him. This shows that these Buddhist Suttas were in existence before his time.

terrestrial, but of spiritual, conquest, and that the Chakravartī is a supreme ruler of the earth, not by physical might but by moral and spiritual power; and this is just what is meant by the *Lakkhaṇa-Suttanta* referred to above, when it says that the Superman 'lives supreme over the earth, conquering it, not by the chastising rod or the sword, but by Dhaṃma.' Evidently he becomes a Chakravartī, not by *vijaya*, but by *dhaṃma-vijaya*. There can hardly be any doubt that Aśoka took his cue for *dhaṃma-vijaya* from some such Buddhist Suttas.[1] This alone can explain why his charities were not confined merely to the human beings but extended to the beast, nay even to the bird, in fact, to the whole creature world, as we have just seen. This further explains why those activities were similarly not restricted to his own subjects only, but extended also to those of the independent kingdoms, in fact, to the whole human race; and those, again, not merely for their material comfort but also spiritual elevation. These last kingdoms were conquered by him, not by war or brute force, but by

[1] My attention to these Suttas was first drawn by Mr. Nanigopal Majumdar soon after the first edition of this book was out. The second of these has been incidentally referred to by Dr. Raychaudhuri in his *Political History of Ancient India* (2nd ed.), p. 205, n. 1. Recently Rai Bahadur Ramaprasad Chanda has brought the same Suttas to the notice of the scholars in No. 30 of the *Memoirs of the Archaeol. Sur. of India*, but in his opinion they "are probably post-Aśokan in date" (p. 16). Besides, he stoutly maintains that "Aśoka's Dharmavijaya . . . . is not a missionary movement, but a definite imperial policy" (p. 17). Whereas the view propounded in this book is that the ideal of the Chakravartī Dhārmika Dharmarāja is placed by the Buddhist scriptures before a pious king, that Aśoka left no stone unturned to realise this ideal and that consequently his Dharmavijaya was a missionary movement aiming at the moral and spiritual good of the world.

Dhaṃma or soul force. In other words, Aśoka aspired to become a Chakravartī Dhārmika Dharmarāja. From Rock Edict XIII it appears that Aśoka believed that he had attained to this lofty position through *dhaṃma-vijaya*. That he did not perhaps over-rate himself may be seen from the fact that the Divyāvadāna actually styles him *Chaturbhāga-chakravartī Dhārmiko Dharmarājo.*

We have thus seen what ideal was constantly before Aśoka's mind, and what motive power impelled him to all-embracing and unceasing activity. We are now in a position to determine what place he occupies in history. He has been compared to various fellow monarchs of the ancient world. But he does not in the least suffer by this comparison. Thus he has been compared to the Roman emperor, Constantine the Great, from two different points of view. Rhys Davids holds that Aśoka was like Constantine, because just as the religious benefactions of the latter were the cause of the spiritual decay of the Christian Church, Aśoka's conversion to Buddhism, and his munificent endowments to the Saṃgha were " the first step on the downward path of Buddhism, the first step to its expulsion from India." [1] In the first place, it is not quite correct to say that Buddhism has been expelled from India. For it still lingers in some parts of Bengal. But there can be no doubt that at present it is in a decrepit condition, and it was reduced to these straits soon after the twelfth century, that is nearly a millennium and a half

[1] *Buddhism*, p. 222.

years after Aśoka. How therefore he can be held responsible for the extinction of Buddhism which took place at such a remote period after him is more than we can understand. Where is the proof, again, of his misdirected endowments to the Buddhist Church? Rhys Davids would, of course, have us place implicit trust in the Buddhist accounts, but the greater portion of them, at any rate so far as Aśoka is concerned, is anything but reliable. And even supposing for the moment that the Sinhalese and other monks have preserved the tradition correctly, where is the evidence of the spiritual impoverishment of the Buddhist clergy in the centuries immediately following Aśoka? No traces of the decadence of the Buddhist religion are perceptible till after the beginning of the Gupta period, that is, *circa* 350 A.D. Some scholars again liken Aśoka to Constantine, because both were the royal patrons of their respective religions and materially aided their dissemination.[1] But they forget that the circumstances under which Aśoka strove for the propagation of his faith were entirely different from those under which Constantine worked.[2] "Constantine espoused a winning cause," whereas Aśoka put himself at the head of a religion which had made little headway. Constantine was "calculating, shrewd, superstitious, often cruel, cynical—whose one great instance of consummate foresight entitles him to be called 'Great'."[3]

1 Hardy, *Asoka: Ein-charakter-Bild.*, *etc.*, p. 30; Rhys Davids, *Buddhist India*, pp. 297-8; Rapson, *Ancient India*, p. 104.

2 *Times Literary Supplement*, August 7, 1914.

3 ERE., IV. 77.

Aśoka, on the other hand, was possessed of lofty ideals, and employed his shrewdness and calculating powers to raise Buddhism from a narrow provincial sect that it was to the position of a world-wide religion. "Constantine leaned to toleration for political purposes." Aśoka's toleration was a genuine commodity, because it had no political end in view. In the last years of life, Constantine displayed a reaction towards paganism and at its best his religion was a 'strange jumble.' Aśoka never evinced such moral degeneration, and from beginning to end he held fast to the same Dhaṃma.

A second ruler whose name is coupled with that of Aśoka is Marcus Aurelius Antoninus,[1] another Roman emperor who flourished from 121 to 180 A.D. In respect of private high noble life there can be no doubt that he was Aśoka's equal, and, in point of mental culture, was even his superior. But, in regard to the sublimity of ideal and the display of unflagging and well-directed zeal, the Indian monarch surpasses the Roman emperor. Some admirers of Marcus Aurelius have no doubt said that his was a life subordinated to a love of mankind which was allied to religion. But it is forgotten that he was "Roman in civil nobility and pride, Roman in tenacity of imperial aim," and that "the profession of Christianity remained under the imperial ban, and the Christians as such were judicially liable to death,"[2] just because "the prevalence of Christianity was incompatible with

[1] Macphail, *Aśoka*, p. 80; CHI., I, 509.
[2] ERE., VIII. 411.

his ideal of Roman prosperity." [1] The life and administration of the Buddhist monarch was not vitiated by any such narrow and sordid ideal or sullied by any such inhuman hostility to any section of human race. On the contrary, he exerted himself strenuously and systematically for the good not only of the whole mankind but also the whole creature world, and no racial, national or family pride or bias marred his life of self-effacement. It is not to be expected that Aśoka was free from the internal troubles of his kingdom. If we study Rock Edict XIII, it seems that Āṭavikas or Forest Principalities were causing him no small anxiety. He however gives them to understand that he is possessed of all terrestrial power to crush them, but that he would first strain every nerve to conciliate them and exhort them to follow Dhaṃma, to prevent bloodshed. This was the state policy of the Indian monarch. And can it be doubted that it was of a high spiritual order?

Aśoka has been compared by one writer to a good many other princes, such as King Alfred.

[1] EB., XVII. 695. On p. 807 of JRAS., 1925, Prof. Charpentier asks "what Aśoka would have done had he had to deal with a party steadily growing and violently preaching and conspiring against the existing government." But "if Aśoka were in the same position," replies N. C. Ganguly (IHQ., Vol. I, p. 785), "he would perhaps have given up the throne before acting like the Emperor, which marks out all the spiritual difference." What is noteworthy is that when the principles of Marcus were put to the test, he was found to be the Roman imperialist first and foremost, the Stoic teacher afterwards and in a leisurely fashion. In fact, he was in no mood to endanger the Roman sovereignty for the sake of the religious truth.

Charlemagne, Omar Khaliff I, and so forth.[1] There were many kings who were great warriors or great administrators like Aśoka. What however, entitles Aśoka to world-wide and everlasting fame, is the temporal and spiritual good of the people that he accomplished. And no prince is worthy of being compared to Aśoka unless he has shared and exhibited in some appreciable measure this special characteristic of the Buddhist monarch. The only other ruler, therefore, whose name is worth mentioning along with his is Akbar, the Mogul emperor.[2] There can be no doubt that Akbar strove very hard for the welfare and happiness of his subjects, but the particular and important point in which he resembles Aśoka is the religious toleration he granted and the noble example he set to them in his sympathetic endeavour to ascertain the truth in every religion. We know what delight he took in listening to and presiding over the debates of the ṣufī, the Sunnite, the Shī'ite, the Brāhmaṇ, the (Jaina) Jati, the Buḍdhist, the Christian, the Jew, the Sabaean, the Zoroastrian, and others. We also know why he had held these discussions. "He is truly a man," he often said, "who makes Justice his leader in the path of inquiry, and who culls from every sect whatever Reason approves of. Perchance in this way that lock whose key has been lost may be opened."[3] The result of this eclecticism was the inauguration of a religion called "Divine Faith" which was a monotheism.

1 Macphail, *Aśoka*, pp. 80 and ff.
2 ERE., II, 127.
3 *Ibid.*, I., 269 and ff.

"combined with a worship of light and fire, especially as represented by the sun, which is not to be distinguished from the religion of the Parsis." In the case of Aśoka, we have seen that the result of his religious quest was the espousal of Buddhism slightly tinged with Jainism. But it is to be remembered that Akbar was "before all things a politician and a man of the world, and was in no mood to endanger his sovereignty for the cause of religious truth." Thus whenever he found that his innovations in religion were provoking rebellions among the Muhammadans, he stopped all religious discussion. He was not disposed, for instance, to listen to Christian missionaries when his heresies were exciting a revolt in Bengal. Again, he was not tolerant all round. When a sect calling themselves *Ilāhis* sprang up, Akbar had its adherents arrested and deported to Sind and Afghānistān, where they were bartered for horses. Akbar's pursuit of religious enquiry was more or less of an academic nature, and when he proclaimed his "Divine Faith," there was also the motive of self-glorification behind it. He had absolutely no fire and enthusiasm for that religion, and, consequently though he was a mighty monarch, the Divine Faith did not spread beyond the royal court and died with its founder.

In the estimation of European historians, Alexander the Great, Cæsar and Napoleon are the world's greatest monarchs. They were probabiy greater warriors and greater administrators than Aśoka even. But because they were great warriors and great administrators, does it follow that they were great men? Mr. H. G. Wells,[1] author of *The Outline of History,* had recently to consider this question. Just because this history is a history of life and mankind, all the characters that figure in it had to be considered from a different point of view and appraised according to a different standard, that is, the standard whether they have rendered the world any way happier and better. In regard to Alexander, Cæsar and Napoleon, Mr. Wells therefore most pertinently asks : " what were their permanent contribution to humanity—these three who have appropriated to themselves so many of the pages of our history?"[2] What did Alexander create? Did he hellenize the east? No, hellenization had begun long before his time. For a time the whole world from the Adriatic to the Indus was under his rule. Hellenism, no doubt, spread in the wake of his world conquests. But he is not known to have devised and carried out any systematic plan of his own for the dissemination of that culture and civilisation. It spread only as the result of the Greek and Macedonian cities planted by him for military purposes. This is what the great historian, George Grote, says about Alexander : " To describe him as a son of Hellas, imbued with the political maxims of Aristotle, and

[1] Prof. Charpentier says that Mr. H. G. Wells, " . . . admirable as may be his achievements in other fields of action, is most certainly no historian " (JRAS., 1925, p. 808). And yet the most recent edition of the EB. (Vol. 23, p. 503) speaks of Mr. Wells as " English novelist, sociologist, historian and utopian " and remarks : " Obviously, the most important post-war work by Mr. Wells is *The Outline of History* (1920)."

[2] *The Strand Magazine*, September, 1922, pp. 216 and ff.

bent upon the systematic diffusion of Hellenic culture for the improvement of mankind—is, in my judgement, an estimate of his character contrary to the evidence. . . . Instead of hellenizing Asia, he was tending to asiatize Macedonia and Hellas.''[1] "As his power increased," remarks Mr. Wells, "his arrogance and violence grew with it. He drank hard and murdered ruthlessly. After a protracted drinking bout in Babylon a sudden fever came on him, and he died at the age of thirty-three. Almost immediately his empire began to break up. One custom remained to remind men of him. Previously most men had worn beards. But so great was Alexander's personal vanity that he would not let his face be covered. He shaved and so set a fashion in Greece and Italy which lasted many centuries. A good fashion perhaps, but not a very significant contribution to the race."

As with Alexander, so with Cæsar. Historians say that he had something of the vision in him, and refer to his marvellous world policies. But what do we find him to be? Nothing but a dissolute and extravagant man. Just when he was at the height of his power and might have done much good to the world, if he was really endowed with the lofty vision with which he was credited, we find him feasting and frolicking in Egypt with that Siren, Cleopatra, for nearly a year, who afterwards lived openly with him in Rome as his mistress. This happened not

[1] *A History of Greece* (John Murray, 1869 ed.), Vol. XII, pp. 87-8. And yet Prof. Charpentier gives credit to Alexander for hellenization of the east making headway in his time ! !

when he was young, but when he was fifty-four. Again, the historians have to admit that he treated with scant respect the historical institutions of Rome which were the organs of true political life and began the process by which the Roman emperors undermined the self-respect of their subjects and turned them into a nation of slaves.[1] That brands him as a gross elderly sensualist, and not the master ruler of men. As regards Napoleon this is what Mr. Wells says of him: "The old order of things was dead or dying; strange new forces drove through the world seeking form and direction; the promise of a world republic and enduring world peace whispered in a mulitude of startled minds. Had this man any profundity of vision, and power of creative imagination, had he been accessible to any disinterested ambition, he might have done work for mankind that would have made him the very sun of history. . . . . . There lacked nothing to the occasion but a noble imagination. And failing that, Napoleon could do no more than strut upon the crest of this great mountain of opportunity like a cockerel on a dunghill."[2] Napoleon may have done immense good to his country, but so far as his obligations to the human race are concerned, they are practically nil. And Mr. Well's estimate of him cannot be considered far from right.

As regards Aśoka we know what vision had taken possession of his mind. It was the vision of

[1] EB. (ed. XIV), Vol. IV, p. 525. And yet Prof. Charpentier wants me "to re-read carefully the history of the Roman Empire" before expressing my opinion about Cæsar ! !

[2] *The Outline of History*, p. 490.

the Chakravartī Dhārmika Dharmarāja. It was the brotherhood, not simply of the human, but of the living being. To put the same thing in other words, he was overpowered with the vision of promoting the physical happiness and moral elevation of the whole world. And he displayed his creative imagination in suiting the means to his end, in a fashion which was at once novel and unique. The Mauryan empire was in the heyday of its glory when with a rare imagination Aśoka seized the opportunity of dedicating all his energies and all the state resources to the realisation of his noble end. Well might Mr. Wells therefore say of the Buddhist emperor that "amidst the tens and thousands of names of monarchs that crowd the columns of history, their majesties and graciousnesses and serenities and royal highnesses and the like, the name of Aśoka shines and shines almost alone a star. From the Volga to Japan his name is still honoured. China, Tibet, and even India, though it has left his doctrine, preserve the tradition of his greatness. More living men cherish his memory to-day than have ever heard the names of Constantine or Charlemagne."[1] If however, Aśoka is at all to be likened to any monarch, it is not with one, but at least three, with whom he ought to be compared at one and the same time. And it is with Rev. Dr. Copleston[2] that we ought to say that "he was not merely the Constantine of Buddhism, he was Alexander with Buddhism for Hellas; an unselfish Napoleon, with 'mettam' in the place of 'glorie.'"

[1] *Ibid, l.c.*, 212.

[2] *Buddhism, Primitive and Present, l.c.*, 166.

In the history of Buddhism Aśoka's importance is second only to that of the founder of that religion.[1] Saint Paul is therefore the only historical character that can rightly be compared to Aśoka as has been correctly pointed out by Rev. Dr. J. M. Macphail.[2] It is true that the message preached by Jesus was for all mankind, but its universal character was not fully appreciated and emphasized by his immediate followers; and Christianity was thus deteriorating into but another, though perhaps more enlightened and liberal, sect of Judaism. It was Paul who broke the barriers of race and Law which were hemming it in. Some of his fellow preachers were no doubt for widening the door of the Christian Church so as to admit the gentiles. But Paul declared : " No, there must be, there is, no door, for there is no wall. Every partition has been broken down; every restriction and distinction, and division among men in the sight of God has been abolished. The love of God is as all-embracing as the sky above us ; His grace is as free as the air we breathe. In Christ Jesus there is neither Jew nor Greek, bond nor free, male nor female." Similarly, in Aśoka's time Buddhism had almost degenerated into a local provincial sect. He destroyed the barriers which detached one sect from another, by teaching them tolerance and respect for one another's principles and tenets, and thus promoted the essence of religion which they all shared in common. And there can be no doubt that in this matter the royal teacher rose to a higher level than the Buddhist

1 ERE., II, 127.
2 *Aśoka*, *l.c.*, 85.

Piṭakas attained. This, in fact, was the message of Buddha to all lay people, and it was this universal character of Buddhism that Aśoka clearly perceived and emphasized. Like Paul, again, Aśoka was supremely concerned with the dynamic of conduct, and left no stone unturned in restoring his faith to its proper rank, to wit, that of a world religion. Aśoka was thus not a mere patron, but a veritable apostle of Buddhism. Being, however, at the head of a big empire and consequently master of inexhaustible resources, he was able to accomplish far quicker and more tangible results.

We cannot conclude our estimate of Aśoka's work without also inquiring and determining how it has affected India, that is, what gain or loss it has conferred or inflicted on that country. It cannot be denied that indirectly India has gained considerably. We have seen how the missionary activity of Aśoka was a source of two boons. In his time, the whole of the country had become Aryanised. But the different provinces had their different dialects. Owing, however, to the stupendous efforts put forth by him for the diffusion of his faith, the communication between one province and another became more frequent and brisk, and the universal desire of having a common language was felt—a language which would be studied and understood in all provinces and become the medium of thought not only in secular but also religious matters. This led to the acceptance of Pāli or monumental Prākṛit as the *lingua franca* of India.[1]

[1] Above, pp. 209 and ff.

Originally Pāli must have been some local dialect, not an artificial concocted speech, as supposed by some. Probably it was the parent of the Prākṛit which was afterwards known as Mahārāshṭrī. And when this was raised to the rank of a universal language for all India, not only secular and religious documents but religious scriptures came to be written in Pāli. Originally the Buddhist scriptures must have been preserved in the Māgadhī dialect, but when this new Esperanto arose, they were all translated into Pāli in order that they might be understood from one extremity of India to another. The official documents and the records of religious benefactions also came to be couched in that language. This was no doubt a great boon to India caused indirectly by the almost superhuman activity displayed by Aśoka for the spread of Buddhism. Another result of this activity was the immense stimulus it imparted to Indian art.[1] The architecture up to his time was mostly wooden, and it was he who made it lithic. The stone-cutter's art and industry had been flourishing since a remote past, and, when the idea of giving a permanent character to his *Dhaṃma-lipis* first dawned upon his mind, he at once jumped to the requisition of that art to serve his end. The effect of it was the construction of huge monolithic pillars, the inscribing of big rocks, and, above all, the excavation of rock-cut temples which gradually developed into higher and higher dimensions but also more and more artistic forms, and has studded India with such a number

[1] *Ibid*, pp. 210 and ff.

of beautiful and sublime specimens that they have rightly been regarded as one of the wonders of the world.

We have seen that Aśoka's contribution to humanity was the goal of cosmopolitanism that he placed before them, the brotherhood not merely of the human but of the living being. We have also seen how his missionary efforts were a source of two boons to this country. And it may now be reasonably asked whether Aśoka's activity affected India directly in any way and cast her genius in a different mould. This is the question before us now for our consideration. If we make a critical survey of the India of this period, we find that Hindu civilisation had attained a perfectly equipoised condition between the forces making for material progress and those conducing to spiritual culture. But this equipoise was disturbed by the over-exuberant zeal displayed by Aśoka for the realisation of his vision, and the result was that the material element of the Hindu civilisation was so completely subordinated to the spiritual that it became unprogressive and decadent though never extinct.

The above view may perhaps sound strange and appear to be a little exaggerated. But what does the literature developed up till the time of Aśoka show? We learn from Kauṭilya that up till his time no less than four schools of the science of polity were known, and no less than seven individual authors of great eminence flourished, who were in no way connected with any schools. Again, what were the *vidyās* or sciences prevalent in his time? They were *Ānvīkshakī*, Philosophy, *Trayī*, Theology, *Vārtā*, Economics, and *Daṇḍaniti*, Polity. It is clear from this that the science of polity was separated from philosophy and theology and constituted an independent branch of study. Nay, one school, namely, the Bārhaspatyas, went so far as to declare *Trayī* or Theology as a pious fraud, and another school to the extremity of reducing all other sciences to Polity and laying down that Polity alone was the one science properly so called. This clearly shows that before the advent of the Mauryan power the Indians cultivated the science of politics with as much boldness and alacrity as they did theology and philosophy and that if in much later times religion and metaphysics encroached upon the political science, there was also a time when not only was Theology openly sneered at but Polity considered to be the only science that deserved to be called science. This is not the place to discuss what contribution the Hindus of the pre-Kauṭilyan period made to the political science, but those who have studied Kauṭilya's Arthaśāstra need not be told that the Indians had developed a definite conception of the State together with a fairly advanced idea of the International law. Side by side with Polity the Hindus developed another branch of learning called the *Vārtā* or Economics which concerned itself with 'agriculture, cattle-rearing and trade,' and which was freely drawn upon by Polity for the furtherance of its object.

Though the Hindus had reached the conception of a special science called Polity and developed many and manifold concepts and principles which were even added to by Kauṭilya, it seems to have come to a dead stop soon after he wrote. This is clear from the fact that hardly any work on Polity is known after Kauṭilya which contains any new idea or any kind of advance on the subject. In fact, Kauṭilya's Arthaśāstra, though it was more or less a compendium, seems to have superseded all the treatises on the Science of Polity that were known up to his time and to have been looked upon as the standard authority on the subject. But even this treatise was suspected to be unwieldily long, and, Kāmandaka, we know, set himself to the task of making it simpler and more concise. Surely Kāmandaka would not have undertaken this task if Kauṭilya's Arthaśāstra had not been the only work on Polity that was generally studied. There was no work on the subject composed after him which added to our knowledge of the Hindu Political Science. Evidently this science does not seem to have made any progress after Kauṭilya, and was practically dead just at a time when it was expected to make great strides and materially advance our political speculation and practice. We are all aware how the tiny State of Magadha in Behāṛ in the time of Bimbisāra had developed into the mighty Magadha empire in the reign of Chandragupta,[1] extending from the Hindukush to the frontiers of the Tāmil country. Aśoka himself had for a time aided this centripetal force that had originated with Bimbisāra, by conquering and annexing the

[1] CL., 1918, p. 84.

province of Kaliṅga.[1] And if the vision of the Chakravartī Dhārmika Dharmarāja had not haunted his mind and thus completely metamorphosed him, the irresistible martial spirit and the marvellous statecraft of Magadha would have found a further vent by invading and subjugating Tāmil States and Tāmraparṇi towards the southern extremity of India, and would probably not have remained satisfied except by going beyond the confines of Bhāratavarsha and establishing an empire like that of Rome. The Aryanisation of India had been completed long before Aśoka. This Aryanisation was to the different races of that country what Hellenism was to the non-Greek peoples. The Aryan speech and mode of life had already been assimilated almost all over India, and, even the *lingua franca*, corresponding to the Pāli language, was adopted. Here were present the solvents that were required for the fusion of the diverse Indian races into one nationality or rather imperialism. All that was now necessary to reach this consummation was political stability, that is, common political union. And if Aśoka had but continued the policy of his predecessors and helped the centripetal forces ushered in by Bimbisāra, his strong arm and administrative genius could have effectually consolidated the Magadha empire and ensured this political stability. As it was, he formulated a different foreign policy soon after the Kaliṅga war, that is, just after that event which would have stimulated

[1] *Political History of Ancient India* (2nd ed.) by Dr. H. C. Raychaudhuri, pp. 191 ff.; p. 205; pp. 218-9.

other kings of his opportunity and resources to establish a world-dominion. The very idea of war Aśoka thereafter abhorred. We have seen how, in describing the horrors of the Kaliṅga war, he says that if one-hundredth, nay, one-thousandth, of that misery were to befall men again, that would be a cause of extreme regret to him. And it is with a sense of relief and joy, as it were, that in another place he tells us that the sound of the drum has now become with him the sound of Dhaṃma, and not of war. But the incident of the Kaliṅga war he has mentioned with a purpose. There he naively confesses that he has abandoned all idea of *vijaya* or terrestrial conquest and adopted that of *Dhaṃma-vijaya* or conquest through Dhaṃma. This latter, says he, can with love and goodwill be achieved in all bordering regions, and has been so achieved by him, as he informs us. But he is not content with merely enunciating this new policy, but goes to the length of exhorting his sons, grandsons, and all his descendants to abandon all greed for terrestrial conquest, and follow in his foot-steps by continuing and completing the conquest through Dhaṃma inaugurated by him. The effects of this change of policy, of the replacement of *vijaya* by *Dhamma-vijaya*, were politically disastrous though spiritually glorious. Love of peace and hankering after spiritual progress were no doubt engendered, and have now been ingrained in the Indian character. The Hindu mind, which was already spiritual, became infinitely more spiritual. But that must have created some apathy to militarism, political greatness, and material well-being. This must be the reason why after Kauṭilya we find the progress of the political theory and practice suddenly impeded and stunted, especially at a time when the Magadha State was expected to create the feeling of nationality and raise India to a higher political plane. Aśoka's new angle of vision, however, sounded a death-knell to the Indian aspiration of a centralised national state and world-wide empire. The effects of his policy were manifest soon after his death. Dark clouds began to gather in the north-western horizon, and hardly a quarter of a century had elapsed since his demise when the Bactrian Greeks crossed the Hindukush which formed the north-western boundary of the Mauryan dominions, and began to cause the decay of what was once a mighty empire. We know how very afraid the Greeks were of the Magadha army, even when they were led by Alexander. Three battles were enough for them to dismantle and destroy the fabric of the wide Achaemenian empire; but when they entered India, they had to fight every inch of their ground, and their very leader, Alexander, was once almost mortally wounded. Of course, the Greeks were a band of mighty and brave warriors, and succeeded, though with difficulty, in conquering many Indian tribes and even king Poros of the Punjab. But, as Plutarch tells us, the battle with Poros so much depressed the spirits of the Macedonians and made them so very unwilling to advance farther into India that they most resolutely opposed Alexander when he insisted that they should cross the

Ganges and encounter the Magadha forces.[1] The Macedonian monarch was much vexed and enraged, but had to retreat. Such was the dread which the Magadha army struck in the mind of the Macedonians. But it looks that owing to the new foreign policy inaugurated by Aśoka for the promotion of Dhaṃma, everything had suddenly changed and the very Greeks who were in funks about the Magadha forces even when they were led by Alexander had little difficulty now in carrying their victorious arms into the heart of Northern India and disintegrating and dismembering the Magadha empire.

What is worse is that the Greek inroads, soon after the demise of Aśoka, for which his change of foreign policy appears to be responsible, opened a passage into India to the various wild hordes, such as the Śakas, Palhavas, Kushanas, Hūṇas, Gurjaras and so forth, whom we now find pouring unceasingly into the country till the sixth century A.D. and eclipsing the sovereignty of the indigenous rulers with such few exceptions only as the Śuṅgas and Guptas. It is true that these foreign tribes were all Hinduised soon after they were settled in India, but the fact can scarcely be contested that the political power of the country was practically monopolised by these foreigners up till the advent of the Muhammadans. The old Hindu genius for political originality and evolution thus remained dormant and died a natural death; and the world

1 *Ancient India: Its Invasion by Alexander the Great* by MacCrindle, p. 310. See also H. C. Ray's article: *Why did not Alexander cross the Beas* (JPASB., Vol. XIX, pp. 365 ff.).

dominion to which India at one time seemed to aspire resolved itself into a mere chimera.

Though, on account of the missionary activity of Aśoka, India, it appears, has been lost to nationalism and political greatness, she has doubtless gained in cosmopolitanism and humanitarianism which are the basic principles of Hindu society. It is true that as a consequence of this the progress of the Political Science was suddenly arrested, and that religion and philosophy began more and more to absorb the Hindu mind. It must not, however, be thought that the Hindu mind became completely averse or indifferent to the amenities of the worldly life or that India lost her importance commercially or industrially. Whether, on the whole, this is a gain or loss to India, different people will decide according to their different temperaments. This much, however, is certain that the world has considerably gained by the missionary activity of this Indian monarch and that while to the Farther East Buddhism has given not only her religion and philosophy but also other important features of the Hindu civilisation, it has exercised great influence not only on the Jewish sects of the Therapeutæ and Essenes but also on Christianity of the early period as well as of the Middle Ages.

APPENDIX

To no less a scholar than Prof. Charpentier the Aśokan records appear historically to be of a shadowy and doubtful character. "Different scholars," says he, "will look at the inscriptions of Aśoka from different points of view. To some of them their importance lies wholly in the information they are supposed to convey to us concerning Aśoka's personality and the history of his reign. But to the present writer it appears that the historical facts put on record here are extremely scanty and vague; and it is exceedingly questionable whether Aśoka has laid open to us or has concealed the greater part of his own personality."[1] It is not clear whether the Professor would have us believe that Aśoka was the great French diplomat Tallyrand, in one of his previous births,—Tallyrand who maintained that language was intended not to express, but to conceal, one's thought. But if the Buddhist monarch had seriously thought of throwing dust into the eyes of posterity, he would have shown himself to be a perfect master of words, as every successful diplomat is. But was Aśoka so really? "His sentences," says Senart, "are often short, even abrupt, and are always wanting in variety. His language is a 'prentice sailor, afraid to venture far from shore. When in an unlucky moment, he ventures on a period, he only makes his exit with great

[1] JRAS., 1926, p. 138.

difficulty."[1] And it is this "prentice sailor" of a monarch who is supposed to be such an expert in "doctored compositions" as to have concealed his thoughts and personality and completely hoodwinked the whole world! Again, it is possible to dupe mankind by promulgating two or three edicts by a cunning manipulation of words. But the inscriptions of Aśoka have been found in legion, and deal with many and manifold subjects connected with his Dhaṃma propaganda. Surely even a Tallyrand or Bismarck, if he had attempted to publish such numerous and multifarious records, would have contradicted and betrayed himself hopelessly in more than one place, in spite of his colossal cunning and superb power of fabrication. But has Aśoka done so? On the contrary, Senart has freely testified to "the unity of tone which reigns throughout all his edicts" and "their perfect agreement and the natural way in which they complete each other."[2] "It cannot, I think," says further the French savant, "be denied without injustice, that he exhibits, in his edicts, a spirit of moderation, a moral elevation, a care for the public good, which merit every praise." "By the various efforts with which he was inspired in his religious zeal, by his relations with nations not subject to his empire, nay, with peoples the most distant from the Peninsula, and finally, by the monuments, epigraphic or otherwise, of which he was the creator, Piyadasi certainly rendered services to the

[1] *I.A.*, 1891, p. 266.
[2] *Ibid.*, p. 229.

general civilisation of India, and the credit of these merits we are in justice bound to render to him." [1] If this is not *real* insight into Aśoka's personality, one wonders how any ruler can reveal his personality at all. Fortunately the above view of Senart has been countenanced by all scholars of repute. To say therefore that Aśoka in his records has not laid bare but rather concealed the greater part of his personality is as amusing as the opinion of Latham [2] that Piyadasi was none but the Egyptian Phrahate or of P. C. Mukharji [3] who identified the Sandracottus of the Greek writers with the Mauryan monarch, Aśoka.

---

1 *I.A.*, 1891, p. 266.
2 *JARS.*, Vol. XVII, pp. 273 ff.
3 *I.A.*, 1902, p. 233.

CHAPTER VIII

Aśoka Inscriptions

A.—THEIR PROVINCES, ETC.

Rock Inscriptions

(a) The Fourteen Rock Edicts

Inscriptions of Aśoka have been engraved either on rocks, stone pillars or in caves. We shall first take up those called the Fourteen Rock Inscriptions or Edicts. These together form a set of fourteen different inscriptions following a serial order and have been found incised in seven different localities with a few slight variants and dialectical peculiarities. Commencing from the north-west, the first recension or group of these inscriptions is found at Shāhbāzgaṛhī in the Yūsufzai subdivision of the Peshāwar District in the North-West Frontier Province, about 40 miles N. E. of Peshāwar. It was first made known by General Court who described it as being situated quite close to Kapurdagaṛhī after which it was formerly known as the Kapurdagaṛhī recension. Kapurdagaṛhī, however, is two miles distant, and the rock is actually within the boundary of the very much larger village of Shāhbāzgarhī, from which it is less than half a mile distant. The larger portion of the record, containing all the inscriptions except the twelfth, is engraved on both the eastern and western faces of a mass of trap rock, 24 feet long, 10 feet high and 10 feet thick, and lying about 80 feet up the slope of the hill with its western face looking down towards the village of Shāhbāzgaṛhī. Edict XII of this recension was however discovered as late as 1889 by the late Sir Harold Deane, and is engraved on a separate piece of rock about 50 yards distant from the main record. Shāhbāzgaṛhī is a modern name, but the present village is the site of a very old and extensive city, and, according to Cunningham, represents the ancient city of Po-lu-sha (Yuan Chwang) or Fo. sha-fu (Sungyun)[1] —a famous Buddhist Tīrtha, the scene of the Vessantara Jātaka. It was probably the capital of the Yavana province comprised in Aśokan dominions.

The next recension in order is that at Mānsehrā in the Hazara District of the North-West Frontier Province, about 15 miles north of Abbottabad. Here the edicts have been incised on three boulders. There are no vestiges of any old habitation in the neighbourhood, but as pointed out by Sir A. Stein, the record seems to have been engraved on a rock lying by an ancient road leading to a place of pilgrimage now called Brerī, which is the Kashmīrī equivalent of Bhaṭṭārikā = Devi or Durgā.[2] We have seen that Edict XII of the Shāhbāzgaṛhī copy is engraved on a separate rock, whereas the same inscription in the Mānsehrā version is incised on one whole side of a rock. At both these places,

1 C. ASR., V. 8-23; C. CII., I. 8-12.

2 PR.—ASNWFP., 1904-5, p. 17.

again, the characters are larger, and the engraving more accurate, than those of any other edict. There can be no doubt, as was first pointed out by Senart,[1] that special prominence seems to have been attached, on this side of India, at any rate, to Edict XII, which insists upon toleration being shown by one religious sect to another. It appears as if, in the eyes of king Aśoka counsels of religious peace were specially necessary in this extreme region of the north-west of his empire, which, being the main route of the invasions into India, must always have been the meeting place of diverse races, divided by religious ideas.

The third copy of the Fourteen Rock Edicts is engraved on a huge boulder of quartz on the western bank of the Jumna just above her junction with the Tons river and about fifteen miles to the west of Mussoorie (Mansurī). The rock is situated about a mile and a half of Kālsī in the Dehra Dun District, U.P., which is the nearest village to it and after which the inscription is called Kālsī Recension. The boulder is 10 ft. long, 10 ft. high, and about 8 ft. thick at the bottom. The south-eastern face has been smoothed, but rather unevenly, as it follows the undulations of the original surface.[2] It was originally discovered by Mr. Forrest in 1860. The letters of the inscription were then hardly visible, the whole surface being encrusted with the dark moss of ages. At first sight, the inscription looks as if it was

[1] I.A., 1890, p. 43.
[2] C. ASR., I. 244; C. CII., I 12-13.

imperfect in many places, but this is owing to the engraver having purposely left all the cracked and rougher portions uninscribed. Towards the bottom, beginning with the 10th edict, the letters increase in size until they become about thrice as large as those of the upper part. Owing either to this enlargement of the letters or perhaps, to the latter part of the inscription being of the later date, the prepared surface was too small for the whole record which was therefore completed on the left-hand side of the rock. On the right-hand side is traced in outline one elephant labelled *Gajatama* = 'the superlative elephant,' referring, of course, to Buddha.[1]

There are many sculptured stones lying about close to the rock indicating the former existence of structures in the neighbourhood, and the place itself was certainly situated near the ancient and prosperous city of Śrughna.

The fourth copy is the famous Girnār version, first described by Colonel Tod in 1822. It is inscribed on the north-eastern face of the large rock on the road to the Girnār hill, half a mile to the east of the city of Junāgaḍh in Kāṭhiāwāṛ. Girnār is the same as Girinagara, which was for long the capital of Surāshṭra. The *Prabhāsa-khaṇḍa* describes Girnār as a Śaiva *tīrtha*. It is also one of the places highly venerated by the Jainas. The record remained buried in a dense forest and might never have come to light, had not a local notable made a causeway through the

[1] See pp. 148-49 above.

jungle for the benefit of pilgrims.[1] The inscription consists of two main divisions which are separated by a line drawn from the top of the rock downwards. To the left are engraved the first five edicts, and to the right next seven edicts from 6-12. The 13th edict is placed below, and on its right is the 14th edict. The preservation is good, except where a portion of the stone, containing the 5th and 13th edicts, has been destroyed, it is said, during the blasting operations carried out to furnish material for the causeway referred to above. By turning up the soil close by, Captain Postans before 1877 recovered numerous fragments of the rock among which were two pieces bearing Aśokan letters, no doubt pertaining to Edict XIII, described and deciphered later on in JRAS, 1900, pp. 335 and ff. The edicts are separated from one another by horizontal lines drawn right across. Below Edict XIII, separated by an indentation, was engraved ......*va sveto hasti savaloka-sukhāharo nāma* (= 'the white elephant whose name is the bringer of happiness to the whole world'), where Prof. Kern was the first to recognise an unmistakable reference to Buddha.[2] It is possible there was here originally some stone representation of elephant similar to those found at Dhauli and Kālsī.

On the same rock are also inscribed the record of Rudradāman (A. D. 150) and that of Skandagupta (A. D. 457), informing us that in its vicinity was constructed under the orders of Chandragupta

1 ASWI., II. 95; PR.—ASWI., 1898-9, p. 15.

2 See p. 155 above.

Maurya, a lake named Sudarśana which was equipped with watercourses and sluices by the local representatives of the Mauryan dynasty and which was twice repaired, once in the reign of Rudradāman and once again in the reign of Skandagupta.

The discovery of a fragment containing a few words from Edict VIII is enough to prove that a copy of this set of documents once existed at Sopārā in the Ṭhāṇā District to the north of Bombay.[1] Sopārā, still a prosperous town, was an important port and mart under the name of Śūrpāraka (Mahābhārata), Suppara (Periplus), or Soupara (Ptolemy). The Mahābhārata seems to state that it was founded by Paraśurāma, and mention is made there of Rāma-tīrtha.[2] It was a very holy place and for long the capital of Aparānta. The stone is now preserved in the Prince of Wales Museum, Bombay.

Two copies [3] exist on the eastern side of India, near the coast of the Bay of Bengal, within the limits of the kingdom of Kaliṅga conquered by Aśoka 'when he had been consecrated eight years.' The northern copy (discovered by Mr. Kittoe in 1837) is inscribed on a rock called Aswastama, situated close to the village of Dhauli (the town of Tosali mentioned in the edicts as the seat of a Kumāra viceroyalty) about seven miles to the south of Bhubaneśvara, in the Purī District, Orissa. The Aśoka inscriptions are arranged in three

1 JBBRAS., XV., 282 and ff.; PR.—ASWI., 1897-8, pp. 7 and ff.

2 IA., 1882, p. 236.

3 C. ASR., XIII. 95 and 112; C. CII., I. 15 and ff.

parallel vertical columns, of which the Fourteen Rock Edicts (minus Edicts XII and XIII) occupy the whole of the middle column and one-half of the right column. Afterwards two local edicts were added, one completing the right-hand column, and the other filling the whole of the left-hand column. The latter is, therefore, the second of the two separate Edicts here. Immediately above the inscription is a terrace, on the right side of which is the fore-part of an elephant, 4 feet high, of superior workmanship; the whole is hewn out of the solid rock. From the grooves traceable here, the elephant seems originally to have been protected by a wooden canopy. The southern version (first copied by Sir Walter Elliot in 1850) is engraved on the face of a 'picturesque' rock in a large old fort called Jaugadā (Lac-fort), near the bank of Ṛishikulyā river, about eighteen miles to the west-north-west of the town of Ganjām. The Jaugaḍā inscriptions are engraved on three different tables on the vertical face of the rock. The first contains the first five edicts, but about one-half has been utterly lost by the peeling away of the rock. The second tablet comprises the next five edicts and Edict XIV. About one-third of this tablet has been mutilated. The third tablet contains the two separate Edicts which are found at Dhauli. These are less carefully engraved than those on the other two tablets.

Another copy of the Fourteen Rock Edicts was discovered in 1929 near Yerraguḍi, about 8 miles north by west from Gooty in the Karnul District, Madras Presidency. It is said that the Government Epigraphist is engaged upon deciphering and publishing them.

Separate Kalihga Edicts

Two separate edicts, the Borderers' Edict and the Provincials' Edict, take the place of Edicts XII-XIII of the ordinary series, at Dhauli and Jaugaḍā.

(b) *The Minor Rock Edicts*

At first, only three copies of these Edicts were known, what may be called the three northern versions.[1] Of these one is engraved on a rock in an artificial cave near the summit of the Channanpīr hill to the east of Sahasrām (Shāhābād District, Bihār), now surmounted by a shrine of the Muhammadan Pir (saint) after whom it is named.[2] Smith says that in Aśoka's time the place must have been visited by the Hindu pilgrims. But this is a mere conjecture. Another copy is inscribed on the Rūpnāth rock (Jabalpur District, Central Provinces), lying at the foot of the Kaimur range of hills. The spot is no doubt visited at present by pilgrims who worship the local deity, Rūpnāth (Śiva), and bathe in the three sacred pools named after Rāma, Lakshmaṇa and Sītā. The third northern version, discovered by Carlleyle in 1872-73, is engraved on a huge isolated block standing at the

[1] CASR., VI., 98; VII. 58; IX. 38; and XI. 133; C. CII., I. 20-4; PR.—ASWI., 1903-4, pp. 35-6; AR.—ASEC., 1907-8, p. 19.

[2] EC., XI. 1-5 (Intro.)

foot of a hill called the Hinsagir hill near the ancient city of Bairāṭ (Jaipur State, Rājputānā), where the Pāṇḍavas are said to have lived during the concluding portion of their exile. The surface of the rock is rough, and has suffered much from weathering. Of the southern version three were discovered in 1892 by Mr. B. Lewis Rice [1] incised in three localities, all close to one another, in the Chitaldrug District of Mysore, namely, Śiddāpur, Jaṭinga-Rāmeśwar and Brahmagiri, not far from the site of an ancient locality (probably Isila of the Edict). The Mysore versions alone contain each a short supplementary edict giving a summary of Aśoka's Dhaṃma. The discovery of these inscriptions for the first time clearly showed that Aśoka's empire had spread as far south as Mysore. The fourth southern version is the Maski Minor Rock Edict discovered in 1915.[1] It is in the District of Raichur, Nizam's Dominions. Though it is in a mutilated condition, it is a very important inscription as it is the only record that actually names Aśoka as its issuer, the other epigraphs ascribing themselves to Priyadarśin, another name of that king.

The fifth southern version came to light along with the Fourteen Rock Edicts found in 1929 near Yerragudi, in the Karnul District of the Madras Presidency. A facsimile, strange to say, has been printed topsyturvy in the September issue of the Telugu magazine *Bhāratī* of 1929. The sixth southern version was discovered in 1931 by

[1] HAS., No. 1, pp. 1-2.

Mr. Yazdani, incised on a bare rock on the highest point of the Palki Gunk hill near Kopbal in the extreme south-west corner of the Nizam's territory The text of neither of these has yet been published.

Pillar Inscriptions

(*a*) *The Seven Pillar Edicts*

The inscribed pillars of Aśoka have long been known to the Europeans owing to the favourite positions which they occupy in the very heart of the empire.[1] Of these the best known, and the earliest to be noticed by Europeans is the Delhi (Sivālik, or Toprā) Pillar, commonly known as Firozshah's *lāt*. According to Shamsi-i-Siraj, a contemporary of Sultan Firoz Tughlak, this pillar was brought (A. D. 1356) by the Sultan, from a place called Topra (v.l. Tohera, Tamerá, Nahera, etc.) on the bank of the Jumna, which was at the foot of the mountains, ninety *kos* from Delhi, and was erected on the summit of Kothila in Firozabad. It contains *seven* "pillar-edicts" whereas the other pillars contain six only. The first eleven lines of the seventh Edict have been incised on the eastern face of the column and the remaining round the whole of the shaft. This inscription is a later addition, as is clearly shown by the fact that it has been engraved in thinner and less carefully formed letters, many of which, again, have a sloping or cursive form.

[1] C. ASR., I. 76, 73, 161, 298; V. 143; XIV. 78; XVI. 110; XXII. 51. C. CII., I. 34 & ff.

The second of Aśoka's Delhi pillars, according to Shams-i-Siraj, was brought from Mirath (Meerat) by the same Sultan and was set up near the "Hunting Palace," which, we know, was situated on the Ridge to the north-west of the modern city. According to the popular belief, the pillar was thrown down by an accidental explosion of a powder magazine in the reign of Farokhsir (1713-19 A.D.). The inscribed portion of this fallen shaft was once in the Museum of the Asiatic Society of Bengal. But this piece was afterwards returned to Delhi, and the pillar again set up (1867 A.D.) in its old position. The inscriptions on this pillar are very imperfect, partly owing to its mutilation, and partly to the worn surface of the existing pieces.

The Allāhābād pillar now stands near Ellenborough Barrack in the Fort. It is inscribed also with two minor edicts of Aśoka, and as one of these is addressed to the officials at Kauśāmbī, the pillar appears to have been originally set up in that ancient city identified with Kosam on the Jumna, about 30 miles south of west from Allāhābād. This pillar contains Samudragupta's *Praśasti* also. Jahangir ruthlessly destroyed, by his vainglorious inscription, the third and fourth edicts of Aśoka. Shortly before his time, however, the pillar had been removed to Prayāga, and it is surmised that it was brought there by Firoz Tughlak who, we know, was responsible for the removal of at least two Aśoka columns to Delhi.

In the Champāran District of North Behār, there are three pillars inscribed with edicts of this series. The Lauriyā Ararāj (or Rādhiah) pillar is situated close to the small hamlet of Lauriyā, at a distance of one mile to the south-west of the much frequented Hindu temple of Ararāj-Mahādev, two miles and a half to the east-south-east of the village of Rādhiā and twenty miles to the north-west of the Kesāriā *Stūpa*, on the way to Bettiā. Proceeding from this spot and going N. W. towards Nepāl, one will see the graceful Lauriyā Nandangarh or Māthiah pillar which is the only one of Aśoka's columns which still retains its original capital. It stands near the large village of Lauriyā, 3 miles north of Māthiah and very close to the ancient site of Nandangarh, the remarkable ruins of which date, according to Dr. Bloch,[1] from pre-Mauryan period and where has been located the sacred site of the 'Charcoal Stūpa' of Pippalavana. A Persian inscription, dated 1071 (A.D. 1660-1) recording the name of *Mahiuddīn Muhammad Aurangazib Pādshāh Alamgīr Ghāzi* was probably inscribed by some zealous Moslem in Jumla's army, which was then on its return from Bengal whose attempt to demolish the Kafer monument is still visible in the form of the round mark of a cannon shot just below the capital. Some twenty miles N. N. E. of it and more than a mile N. E. of Piparīā village is the Rāmapurwā hamlet.[2] The Champāraṇ pillars were supposed by the late Dr. Smith[3] to have marked the course of the royal road from the

1 ASI.—AR., 1906-7, pp. 119 & ff.
2 *Ibid.*, 1907-8, pp. 181 and ff.
3 Aśoka, p. 120.

northern bank of the Ganges opposite the capital to the Nepāl valley.

(b) *The Minor Pillar Edicts*

The Allāhābād pillar contains two minor edicts—the Queen's Edict and the Edict specifying the penalty of schism in the Church. Of the Queen's Edict we have no other version. But besides the mutilated version of Allāhābād and Sāñchi [1] (inscribed on a fallen and broken pillar at the southern entrance to the Great Stūpa of Sāñchi in Bhopāl State, Central India), the Edict on the penalty of schism in the Church is also preserved in the nearly complete and fuller version engraved on the Sārnāth Pillar [2] discovered by Mr. Oertel in 1905, at Sārnāth about 3½ miles N. of Benares.

The most important of the minor pillars of Aśoka is the Rummindeî pillar standing at the shrine of Rummindeî about one mile north of Paderia and 2 miles north of Bhagwānpur in the Nepalese Tashil of that name situated to the north of the British District of Basti.[3] The commemorative record inscribed on it states that Lord Buddha, the Śākya sage, was born there. It thus locates the famous Lumbinī grove, the birthplace of Buddha. A similar commemorative pillar is that discovered on the western bank of Niglīva

1 *A Guide to Sāñchi*, pp. 90 and ff.

2 ASI.—AR., 1904-5, pp. 68 and ff.

3 Führer's *An. Prog. Rep.*, 1894-95, para. 3: JRAS., 1897, pp. 429 and ff.; pp. 365 and ff.

Sagar, near the village of Niglīva in the Nepalese Tarāi to the north of the Basti District. The inscription on this pillar, now situated at a distance of about 13 miles to the north-west of the last-mentioned pillar, records that it was erected to mark the site of the *stūpa* of Konāgamana.

An inscribed stone-slab was procured in March, 1928, by Mr. Birendranath Roy for his museum at Puri from a farmer of the village of Kapilesvar, situated nearly a mile to the south of the famous Lingaraj Temple at Bhubanesvar (*Pravasi*, Sravan, 1335 B. S.). It was found to be a copy of the Rummindeî Pillar Inscription and was first brought to public notice by Mr. H. C. Chakladar of the Calcutta University.

Cave Inscriptions

The famous caves of Barābar and Nāgārjunī are situated sixteen miles due north of Gayā, or nineteen miles by the road, in two separate groups of hills on the left or west bank of the Phalgu river.[1] There are four caves in the Barābar hill. Three of them have their walls inscribed with Aśoka characters, informing us that these caves were dedicated by king Piyadasi to the Ajīvikas.

Chronology of Inscriptions

So much for the *provenance* of the various inscriptions of Aśoka. We have now to consider other questions connected with them. First, what are the forms of stone on which they were

[1] C. ASR., I. 44 and ff.: C. CII., I. 30-1.

engraved ? How are they spoken of by Aśoka ? At the end of PE. VII, he refers to *śilā-stambha* and *śilā-phalaka*. The first obviously represent the stone pillars, and we know that many of his records were inscribed on them. *Śilā-phalaka* signify ' the stone slabs,' but except perhaps the Bhābrū Edict,[1] no inscription of Aśoka has yet been found incised on a stone slab. About the end of the Sahasarām and Rūpnāth Edicts we meet with the words *śilā-stambha* and *parvata*. The last of these must refer to such rocks as have been inscribed with not only his Minor Rock Edicts but also Fourteen Rock Edicts. And, as a matter of fact, the Dhauli and Jaugada versions of the last series speak of their having been engraved on a *parvata*. The name of the *parvata* was in each case specified, but that in the Jaugaḍā copy is alone preserved, and that is Khapiṁgala. It will thus be seen that Aśoka caused his records to be incised on a three-fold material, namely, rock, stone pillar and stone slab.

The second question that we have now to consider is : how does Aśoka speak of his inscriptions ? By what names does he refer to them ? Those who have studied the Fourteen Rock and the Seven Pillar Edicts know full well that they have been designated Dhaṃma-lipis by him. What does this phrase mean ? We have seen above that Aśoka is very fond of instituting a comparison between his Dhaṃma and the ordinary practices of life. Thus he compares *vijaya* with Dhaṃma-vijaya, *maṅgala* with Dhaṃma-mangala,

[1] C. ASR., II. 247; C. CII., I. 24; PR.—ASWI., 1909-10, p. 45.

dāna with Dhaṃma-dāna, and so forth. We also know that he distinguishes between ordinary Mahāmātras and Dhaṃma-Mahāmātras. The same must have been the case with Dhaṃma-lipis, which he must have used in contrast with ordinary *lipis*. Now, *lipi* is a word which signifies a 'writ' or 'record,' and is found employed in this sense not only in the Separate Kaliṅga Edicts but also Sārnāth Pillar Edict. The use of this word, especially in the last inscription, is of special importance. This Edict, it is worthy of note, calls itself a *śāsana* or Order, and yet we are told that two *lipis* of it were to be deposited—one for the guidance of the officials and the other for the Buddhist laity. *Lipi* cannot but mean 'a document' here. As king, Aśoka must have issued a great many decrees relating to secular matters. And the writings conveying those decrees are obviously *lipis*. And further as he was also a preacher, he must have issued similar decrees for the advancement of Dhaṃma. These can therefore most appropriately be called *Dhaṃma-lipi*. It is true that the Fourteen Rock and the Seven Pillar Edicts alone have been styled *Dhaṃma-lipi*; but it does not follow that the other inscriptions of Aśoka, except perhaps those engraved in the caves, were not so. All these epigraphs were records relating to the promotion and propagation of Dhaṃma and can with perfect propriety be designated *Dhamma-lipi*.

The third question that we have to discuss is: the time when the different records were engraved. It is not, however, an easy question to answer.

Because the word *likh* which means ' to engrave ' also means ' to write,' and sometimes it is very difficult to understand which sense is intended. Thus RE. IV has *idaṃ lekhāpitaṃ* twice, *e.g.*, in Girnar (J) and (K). Here it no doubt seems tempting to take *likh* in the sense of ' to engrave.' But if we do so, we shall be compelled to suppose that while this edict was inscribed in the 12th, the next was in the 13th year, because, as a matter of fact, RE. IV is dated in the 12th and RE. V in the 13th year of Aśoka's reign. And Senart has adduced some solid grounds to prove that this series of Rock Edicts forms one *ensemble* and was not engraved in successive additions. Similarly, there is nothing to show that the term *likh* is necessarily used in the sense of ' to engrave ' in the case of *iyaṃ dhaṃmalipi likhitā* which occurs about the end of RE. XIII. It seems safer and better to take *likh* in the sense of ' to write ' in all cases except where there are definite indications pointing to the other sense, such *e.g.*, as where the words *chira-thitikā hotu* occur as they do in REs. V and VI and PEs. II and VII. In one instasce even the engraver, we find, confounded these two senses of the word. Thus in RE. I, the Dh. and Jaug. versions have *pavatasi* before *lekhāpita* in the very first line, and one is therefore inclined to translate the latter by ' caused to be engraved ' instead of merely ' caused to be written.' It seems, however, that this reference to *parvata* was not in the original draft of Aśoka and was inserted locally when it was incised at Dh. and Jaug. For in the same edict further on are repeated the words *iyam dhammalipi......lekhitā*, just where Aśoka says that two peacocks and one deer alone shall be killed for the royal table. He could not have said this, if *lekhitā* had meant ' engraved,' for this series, *viz.*. the Fourteen Rock Edicts, must have been inscribed at different times as their find-spots are situated at different distances from Pātaliputra. They could not have been engraved at one and the same time. that is, at any particular time when Aśoka could make that reference to his royal table. This is possible only if by *lekhitā* is meant ' the writing ' and issuing of that edict, because it is only when the edict was drawn up in his palace that he could say that only two pea-fowls and one deer were being slaughtered that day in the royal kitchen. This shows that the reference to *parvata* at the beginning of RE. I in Dh. and Jaug. was inserted by local officers at the capital town of Kaliṅga without understanding what the following word *likhāpitā* really meant there.

It will thus be seen that the question when the different edicts were inscribed is not easy to answer. Nevertheless, we are on pretty safe grounds in regard to the first six of the Seven Pillar Edicts. There can be no doubt that together they form one *ensemble*. For in the first place, PE. VII is found engraved only on one column, *viz.*, on Delhi-Toprā. Secondly, that it is a subsequent addition may be seen also from the fact that the letters of this epigraph are in an entirely different hand from that of the preceding six, as we have already observed in our notice of this Pillar. Now, it is worthy of note that PEs. I and IV begin and PE.

VI ends by informing us that they were *likhāpitā* in the twenty-sixth year of Aśoka's reign. Of course, it is natural to say that here *likhāpitā* means 'written, drawn up.' But about the close of PE. II we have *etāye me aṭhāye iyaṃ dhaṃma-lipi likhāpitā* (I) *hevaṃ anupatipajaṃtu chilaṭhitīkā cha hotu ti.* As we have here the words *chilaṭhītīkā hotu, likhāpitā* in this connection cannot but mean 'inscribed.' Putting all these facts together, it seems that every one of the first six of these Edicts was drawn up and promulgated in the twenty-sixth year of Aśoka's reign and that the six afterwards arranged in their present order into one *ensemble* and also engraved on the pillar in precisely the same year. There can thus be no doubt as to the first six of the Seven Pillar Edicts being inscribed in the twenty-sixth year of Aśoka's reign. As to PE. VII we know it was *likhāpāpitā* or written in the twenty-seventh year. But there is nothing to show in what year it was incised on the Delhi-Ṭopra Pillar. All that we can say about it is that it could not have been inscribed before the twenty-seventh year of his reign.

Though there is thus a perfect certainty about the date of the first six of these Pillar Edicts, the same thing cannot unfortunately be said in regard to the other records, not even in regard to the Fourteen Rock Edicts. It is true that no less than four different dates are found mentioned in this series (RE. IV, V, VIII and XIII), but it is nowhere stated that this whole set of Dhaṃma-lipis or any component thereof was *inscribed* in any particular year They are dates of the different events alluded to in the different parts of this series, and not of the actual engraving. The latest of these is the thirteenth year of Aśoka's reign, and this has been proposed by Senart as the date when the Fourteen Rock Edicts were incised. The French savant, it is true, has been followed by other scholars, both Indian and European. But this date cannot reasonably be taken as the actual date of the inscribing. All that we can logically conclude is, not that the whole set was engraved in the thirteenth regnal year, but only that it could not have been engraved before that year. We have, therefore, to fix the date for this series on independent grounds. If it cannot be fixed with any certainty, we shall do so at least approximately. The line of argument we have to adopt in this connection has already been indicated above.[1] Pillar Edict VII has been looked upon by all scholars as giving a resumé of the measures that Aśoka devised and followed for the promotion of Dhaṃma up to the twenty-seventh year of his reign, which, we have just seen, is the date of that edict. But we find absolutely no reference made in it to the works of charity he executed in and outside India and which have been described in Rock Edict II or to the successes which crowned his missionary efforts, as we learn from Rock Edict XIII, not only in his empire but also in the dominions of his neighbouring sovereigns, Greek and Indian. Both these matters are of such paramount importance in Aśoka's estimation that he would never have failed to make

[1] Above, p. 45, n. 1.

mention of them in Pillar Edict VII, if he had known about them before the twenty-seventh year, the date of that edict. We are, therefore, compelled to infer that Rock Edicts II and XIII, in fact the whole set of the Fourteen Rock Edicts, came to be engraved after the Seven Pillar Edicts were promulgated. Another consideration also points to the same conclusion.

After giving the date of its promulgation, P.E. VII ends thus : *etaṃ devānaṃ-piye āhā* (:) *iyaṃ dhaṃmalipi ata athi silāthaṃbhāni vā silāphalakāni vā tata kaṭavîyā ena esa chilaṭhitike siyā.* "This the Beloved of the gods saith : this *Dhaṃmalipi* should be inscribed where there are stone pillars or stone tablets so that it may long endure." This clearly shows that whatever records he had already engraved were engraved on stone pillars and stone slabs only.

There is, indeed, no reference here to the inscribing of Dhaṃma-lipis on *parvatas* or rocks. The idea does not seem to have occurred to him till after the twenty-seventh year of his reign, the date of Pillar Edict VII. This shows that all his Rock Edicts, whether they are the Fourteen Rock Edicts or the Minor Rock Edicts, must have been engraved when the work of inscribing the Seven Pillar Edicts came to an end.

As regards the question : which were first inscribed—the Fourteen Rock Edicts or the Minor Rock Edicts, it deserves to be noticed, as we have seen, that in the Sahasarām and Rūpnāth epigraphs Aśoka orders that edict to be inscribed on a *parvata*, and on a stone pillar wherever it exists. The phrase 'on a stone pillar wherever it exists' shows that these edicts were engraved after he had set up his pillars. This also shows that the idea of inscribing *parvata* or rocks was new to him at that time. It seems therefore that soon after the pillars were engraved Aśoka took up the work of incising Minor Rock Edicts, which must have been followed by that of the Fourteen Rock Edicts. When the latter series was being inscribed, the idea of engraving rocks as well as pillars had become so familiar that Aśoka makes absolutely no reference to either and that if he makes any reference at all to such material, he makes the general remark that those (Fourteen) Rock Edicts were engraved on stone in order that they might endure permanently.

Aśoka does not seem to have been able to carry out his whole programme of inscribing his edicts. He orders PE. VII to be engraved on stone pillars and stone slabs. But so far as we can see, it was incised only on one pillar, *viz.*, the Delhi-Ṭoprā Pillar. As to stone slabs, none has been found with this edict inscribed on it. Probably none was engraved. Similarly, he intended inscribing Minor Rock Edicts on stone columns, but this too does not seem to have been done. It does appear after all that Aśoka commenced this work rather late in his life and was not thus able to carry through his whole programme of inscribing his Dhamma-lipis.

After a hard strenuous missionary career of at least fourteen years, the idea first occurred to Aśoka of inscribing on imperishable stone his manifold thoughts about Dhamma and the various measures he adopted for its propagation. We have seen already why this idea commended itself to his mind. His object evidently was that if he gave in a lithic form a succinct account of the activities of his career as a missionary, it would be preserved for his remote descendants to see, read and reflect upon, and would stimulate them to push forward, over the whole world, the *Dhaṃma-vijaya* or conquest through Dhaṃma, which was inaugurated by him with such *eclát*. The different parts of his Dhaṃma-lipis, whether we take the Fourteen Rock Edicts or the Seven Pillar Edicts, are by no means bound together by any natural order. Aśoka perhaps was in such a hurry to preserve an account of his missionary life in a durable form that he put together the different components of his series of epigraphs without any connected sequence. Nevertheless, we are exceedingly obliged to the Buddhist monarch that he at all conceived and forthwith executed the idea of transmitting to posterity in an enduring form the thoughts, feelings and motives that agitated, animated and guided his soul and, above all, galvanised him into an all-round and unflagging activity to promote not only the temporal but also the spiritual weal of mankind.

B.—TRANSLATION, NOTES, ETC.

Introductory Note

Many are the scholars who have dealt with the Aśoka inscriptions since the second quarter of the 19th century. The labours of Prinsep, Wilson and

Burnouf, the pioneers of Indian epigraphy, were brought together in 1877 by Sir Alexander Cunningham in the handy form of *Corpus Inscriptionum Indicarum*, Vol. I. But they have now become more or less obsolete on account of the faultiness of their texts. Some new inscriptions have been discovered and also many of the old known records have been differently read and interpreted since this volume was published. An exhaustive list of references to all publications brought out up till 1902, is contained in R. Otto Franke's *Pali und Sanskrit* (Strassburg, 1902, pp. 1-5). Aśoka inscriptions are a literature by themselves, and very few indeed are the scholars who have edited and annotated his whole set of epigraphs. The following are the only works that will generally be useful to a student of these inscriptions.

Senart, Emile—*Les Inscriptiones de Piyadasi* (Paris, in two vols.). Though this edition has suffered from faulty texts and later discoveries and researches, it is still considered to be an important work which no student can afford to ignore. The English translation of Vol. II, by G. A. Grierson has been published in *Ind. Ant.*, Vols. XVII-XXI.

Bühler, George—*Beitrage zur Erklärung der Aśoka-Inscriften* (Leipzig, 1909), off-print from ZDMG., 1883-1894. This gives many improved readings and emended translations, together with useful notes. This work is indispensable. Part of it in English garb was published in EI., Vol. I, pp. 16-20, and Vol. II, pp. 245-274 and 447-72; ASSI., Vol I, pp. 114-125.

Smith, V. A.—*Aśoka, the Buddhist Emperor of India* (3rd Ed., 1920), Chapters IV-V. This, however, contains only translations and comments, and gives no text of the records. This is a carefully prepared compilation, and serves as a useful handbook.

Hultzsch, E.—*Inscriptions of Aśoka.* The new revised edition of *Corpus Inscriptionum Indicarum*, Vol. I, which was begun in 1912 but was delayed on account of the war, was out after the first edition of my book, and is now accessible to scholars. It settles many controverted points about the text, and is thus a most meritorious production. But it does not go very much beyond a judicious selection from among the interpretations of Senart, Bühler, Thomas, Lüders and the author of this book. Not much originality is displayed in the matter of interpretation or the historical portion of the tome, though his construction of a passage from MREI., is invaluable to the chronology of Aśokan Inscriptions.

Woolner, A. C.—*Aśoka Text and Glossary*, Parts I-II, published by the Lahore University. It is impossible to overrate the importance of Part II., which deals with Aśokan glossary. Every word is explained in every philological detail; and the different interpretations proposed of the different terms by the different scholars have all been given lucidly, interspersed here and there with the author's own interpretation. Part II is useful not only to a student or a lecturer but also to a researcher.

Mookerji, R. K.—*Aśoka : Gaekwad Lectures.* Its main design is to serve as a " convenient textbook " for University students reading for the M.A. Examination. It is thus an excellent epitome of Hultzsch's work. But it seems to have been somewhat hastily published. See, *e.g.*, into what inaccuracies he has fallen in note 2 on p. 151 of his book which have been pointed out in note 2 to my translation of RE. VIII. The book, however, is not a mere compilation, but contains here and there some thought-provoking suggestions.

Different articles by different scholars have been published from time to time, either annotating single words or passages from the Aśoka Inscriptions or dealing with special questions connected with them. They are too numerous to mention here, and will be referred to in the following pages as occasion arises. There are however, some invaluable papers of T. Michelson published in *Indo-Germ. Forschungen*, 1908, 1910, 1911; *Amer. Jour. Philology*, 1909, 1910; and JAOS., 1909, 1911 and 1916. They are concerned more with textual criticism and questions of phonetics than with interpretation.

But the scholar who has recently done yeoman's service to the interpretation of these epigraphic records is H. Lüders, whose papers is SPAW., 1913 and 1914, have proved exceedingly valuable to E. Hultzsch and A. C. Woolner. Unfortunately they have all been written in German which is still unknown to a good many Indian scholars. An English translation of the same is a keenly felt desideratum. We cannot close this note without drawing the attention of scholars to an interesting and informing paper of B. M. Barua entitled

Inscriptional Excursions in respect of Aśoka Edicts and published in the IHQ., 1926, p. 87ff. The same was reprinted in an amplified form under the title *Aśoka Edicts in New Light.* "Here my immediate purpose," says he, "is to show how the vehicle of Aśokan study has gone off the track and how this can be put back on it. This, I believe, can be best achieved by ascertaining the chronology of the edicts and the exact significance and historical bearings of certain technical terms and expressions in the edicts." In regard to Hultzsch's edition, he remarks: "As one turns over its pages, reading written records of the Buddhist emperor of India, depending on Dr. Hultzsch's amended texts, interpretation, notes and introduction, the suspicion begins to grow that the position of his readers is no better than that of the caravan merchants in the Buddhist parable in which they are said to have at the end of their journey returned almost to the same spot whence they had started. For example, his rendering of the Bhābrū Edict or Second Bairāṭ Rock inscription goes to show that he has overlooked the note of the present writer in the *JRAS.*, 1915, used in the third edition of Smith's *Aśoka.*" It is however unfortunate that Barua has himself completely overlooked Hultzsch's interpretation of *ekaṃ chu kho savachharaṃ*, etc., in MRE. I., which is so valuable for 'the chronology of the edicts' (see below my n. 2 to the translation of that Edict). Besides, he has taken the technical terms *lipi* and *lekhita* invariably in the sense of 'inscription' and 'inscribed.' In these circumstances how far his dissertation' which occupies three-fourths of his publication has helped the vehicle of Aśokan study being put back on the track from which it has gone off is not yet clear. His 'excursus,' however, contains valuable quotations from Pāli and other Buddhist literature of which he is a real master and help much towards the proper interpretation of some knotty Aśokan words and passages. No serious student of Aśoka Inscriptions can afford to ignore it.

(a) THE FOURTEEN ROCK EDICTS.

I.

Translation.

This *Dhaṃma-lipi*[1] has been caused to be written[2] by king Priyadarśin, Beloved of the gods.[3] No life should here[4] be immolated and offered as a sacrifice ; nor should any *samāja*[5] be held ; for king Priyadarśin, Beloved of the gods, sees much evil in a *samāja*. There are, however, certain *samājas*, which are considered excellent by Priyadarśin, Beloved of the gods.

Formerly in the kitchen of king Priyadarśin, Beloved of the gods, many hundreds of thousands of animals were every day slaughtered for curry.[6] But now when this *Dhaṃma-lipi* is written, only three lives have been killed[7] for curry, namely, two peacocks and one deer ; but even that deer not regularly. Even these three animals shall not be afterwards killed.

Notes

[1] The phrase *dhaṃma-lipi*, which occurs in this as well as in many other Aśoka inscriptions, has been translated 'righteousness-edict' by Kern, simply 'edict' by Senart, and 'religious edict' by Bühler. For the meaning of *Dhaṃma-lipi*, see *Above*, p. 282f.

[2] *Likh* means both 'to write' and 'to engrave.' For what meaning the word signifies in Aśoka inscriptions and when, see *Above*, p. 283ff.

[3] For the meaning and significance of *devānaṃ-priya*, see *Above*, pp. 6-8: also my note in JBBRAS., XXI. 393 and Kielhorn's remarks in JRAS., 1908, pp. 504-5.

[4] The word *iha* has been taken by some to mean "here, that is, on this earth," and by others "here, that is, in Pāṭaliputra." But it had rather be taken to denote his "palace or royal establishment," because all the other items mentioned in this edict are connected with either Aśoka personally or his royal household. He may therefore be supposed to have prohibited the performance of sacrifice not universally in his empire but only so far as he and his family were concerned.

[5] The real sense of *samāja* was unknown to scholars till it was first pointed out by me in 1902 in JBBRAS., XXI. 395ff. A more detailed note by me on the same subject will be found in IA., 1913, p. 255 & ff. Some additions to our knowledge of the exact nature of a *samāja* has recently been made by F. W. Thomas in JRAS., 1914, pp. 392-4 and 752. See also N. G. Majumdar, IA., 1918, pp. 221-3. The word was interpreted by Senart as denoting 'a convivial assembly' (I.A., IX. 286), by Pischel 'a battue (*Gott. Gel. Anz.*, 1881, p. 1324), and by Bühler 'a festive assembly' (EI., II. 466). None of these scholars was, however, able to substantiate his meaning by any literary evidence or to show why some *samājas* were condemned and some extolled by Aśoka in an inscription directed against the slaughter of animals. This point has been clearly set forth by me, *Above*, pp. 20-21 and p. 137.

[6] The question arises: why did this daily slaughter of hundreds of thousand animals take place in the royal kitchen of Aśoka before the inscription was engraved?

Attention may in this connection be invited to IA., 1913, pp. 255 & ff., and also *Above*, pp. 21-2.

[7] *Ārabhisu* or *ālabhiyisu* stands for the third pl. Aor. pass.; *ārabhare*, 3rd pl. Pre. pass.; and *ārabhisare* or *ālabhiyisaṃti*, 3rd pl. Fut. pass. Note that *ā + rabh* is used here in the sense of 'ordinary killing,' not 'killing for any sacrificial purposes.'

II

Translation

Everywhere in the dominions of king Priyadarśin, Beloved of the gods, as well as of those of his frontier sovereigns,[1] such as the Choḍas, Pāṇḍyas, Sātiyaputra, Keralaputra, as far as the Tāmraparṇī, the Yona (Greek) king called Aṃtiyaka (Antiochus) and also those who are the neighbours[2] of Aṃtiyaka (Antiochus)—everywhere has king Priyadarśin, Beloved of the gods, established medical treatment[3] of two kinds, medical treatment for men and medical treatment for animals. Wherever medicinal herbs, wholesome for men and wholesome for animals, are not found, they have everywhere been caused to be imported and planted. Roots and fruits, wherever they are not found, have been caused to be imported and planted. On the roads wells have been caused to be dug, and trees caused to be planted for the enjoyment of man and beast.

Notes

[1] *Vijita*='conquered country, realm, dominions.' *Aṃta* or *pachaṃta* (*pratyanta*)='bordering dominions,' or 'rulers or people of bordering dominions.' For Choḍa, etc. see *Above*, pp. 40 & ff. For Paṃḍiya (Pāṇḍya), see also CL., 1918, pp. 10-11. In regard to Sātiyaputra, R. G. Bhandarkar draws attention to the fact that along the westernmost portion of the Deccan tableland we have Marāṭhā, Kāyastha, and Brāhmaṇ families, bearing the surname Sātpute, which seems to be derived from the Sātiyaputta of this inscription. The independent state of Sātiyaputra may, therefore, have been situated along the Western Ghuts and the Konkan Coast below (*Ind. Review*, 1909, pp. 401 & ff.). Bühler, however, identifies Sātiyas with Sātvats mentioned in the *Aitareya-Brāhmaṇa*, VIII, 14. and included in the *Parśvādi-gaṇa* referred to in Pāṇini, V. 3. 117 (*Beiträge zur Erklärung der Aśoka-Inscriften*, pp. 13 & ff.). V. A. Smith holds that Sātiyaputra may be either the Tuluva country or the region round about Satyamangalam (EHI., 171, 194 n., 464; *Aśoka*, p. 161). Mr. S. V. Venkateswara takes it to be "the name of the country or people having Kānchipuram for its capital" (JRAS., 1918, pp. 541-2; IA., 1919, p. 24). According to S. Krishnaswami Aiyangar, Sātiyaputra refers to the region north of Cochin, where the Matriarchate or Aḷiyasantānam Law prevails (*Beginnings of South Indian History*, p. 73; JRAS., 1919, pp. 581 & ff.). For my view, see *Above*, pp. 45-6.

Ā-Taṃbapaṃṇi should be taken as one word forming an *Avyayībhāva* compound like *ā-bālaṃ*, *ā-gopālaṃ* and so forth.

[2] Bühler renders *sāmaṃta* by 'vassal-kings.' This is the reading of all the versions except that of Girnār which has *sāmīpaṃ*. This indicates that *sāmanta* must

here signify 'neighbouring or bordering' which is exactly the sense that Childers' *Pāli Dictionary* gives for the word.

[3] Senart takes *chikīchhā* to signify 'remedies,' and Bühler 'a hospital.' It is safer to render it by 'medical treatment.' For the proper understanding of the passage, see *Above*, pp. 192-4.

III

Translation

Thus saith king Priyadarśin, Beloved of the gods:—This was ordered by me (when I had been) consecrated twelve years:—Everywhere in my dominions the Yuktas,[1] the Rājūkas[2] and the Prādeśika[3] shall proceed on circuit[4] every five years as well for this purpose (for the instruction of Dhaṃma) as for other business, to wit,—"meritorious is hearkening to mother and father, meritorious is liberality to friends, acquaintances and relatives, to Brāhmaṇs and Sramaṇas;[5] meritorious is abstention from the slaughter of animals; meritorious is small expense and small accumulation."[6] The council (of ministers) shall order the Yuktas in regard to the reckoning (of accounts)[7] both according to the specification and according to the object.

Notes

[1] Yuta has been separated by Senart from Rājūka and Prādeśika and taken in the sense of 'the faithful.'

Bühler, however, takes it as an adjective of Rājūka and translates it by 'loyal.' As was first pointed out by Senart (IA., 1891, 246, n. 50), the insertion of the word *cha* thrice in the Girnār text makes Bühler's rendering of Yuta untenable. That word clearly must be taken as a substantive, and, like Rājūkas and Prādeśikas, Yutas must be taken to be officers. For the correct sense of Yuta (=Yukta), see *Above*, pp. 57-8. See also *Jāt.*, Vol. V., p. 117, v. 20.

² For Rājūkas see *Above*, pp. 59-60. Jayaswal, however, derives *rājūka* from *rājan*, and takes Rājūkas to denote "the rulers or Ruler-ministers, the Committee of the Parisā vested with real executive powers over the empire" (JBORS., 1918, p. 42). Jayaswal has been criticised by Ghoshal (IHQ., VI. 426 ff.).

³ According to Kern, Prādeśika was a local governor, and Senart seems to agree with him. Bühler renders the word by ' vassals ' and understands by them the ancestors of the Thākurs, Raos, Rāwals, etc., of the present day. As Prādeśikas have been associated with Yuktas and Rājūkas, they must denote Aśoka's officers, and not his vassals. This agrees with the fact that they had to go on their circuit like the other officers, and during tours to do the work of preaching over and above their office duties. See also *Above*, pp. 58-9.

⁴ Kern, and after him Bühler, translate *anusaṃyānam* by 'on tour of inspection.' This seems to be correct, and Bühler has quoted authority in support of it from Brahmanical literature with the help of the St. Petersburg Dictionary. Authority of the Pāli texts for this sense is also not wanting. See *e. g. Aṅg.-Nikāya*, I. 59-60, a gloss on which is quoted in IHQ., II. 128. Senart, however, understands it in the sense of "assembly." But this seems to be improbable, first because there is no authority in

favour of this meaning. Secondly, the object of the verb *nish-kram* which occurs in most of the versions must always be something physical. We might thus speak of *anusaṃyānaṃ niyaṃtu*, but not *anusaṃyānaṃ nikhamaṃtu*. Of course, we speak of *sabhāṃ nishkrāntah*, but only in the sense of 'went to the assembly house' and not 'went to or joined the assembly.' Thirdly, the word *anusaṃyāna* occurs in the Separate Jaugada Edict, but not in its Dhauli version. If its meaning is 'assembly' as Senart takes it, the omission of such an important word in any version is inexplicable, but if it simply signifies 'a tour or a tour of inspection,' the same sense is brought out by the causal form of the root *nishkram*, the use of the word *anusaṃyāna* being not absolutely necessary. The same word has also been traced in a seal found at Basarh, whose legend I read as *Vesāla-anusaṃyāna-kaṭak-āre*, 'from the touring campof the Vesāli (officers)' (ASI.AR., 1913-14, pp. 111 and ff. and plate L). Jayaswal takes *anusaṃyāna* to mean "going out of office or on official transfer," and quotes an authority from the *Śukra-nīti*, not, however, in support of this meanings of the word, but of the desirability of transferring officers (JBORS., 1908, pp. 36-40).

[5] This is a Dvandva compound signifying "recluses and mendicants of the Brāhmaṇ and Śramaṇa sects." See *Above*, pp. 174-5.

[6] *Apavyayatā apabhāṃḍatā sādhu* has been rendered by Senart thus: "good to shun prodigality and violence of language." Bühler omits *apavyayatā*. *Apabhāṃḍatā sādhu*, according to him, means "meritorious is the abstention from reviling heterodox *men*." Both these scholars find, in *apa*, the first component of the two words, the privative use of the preposition *apa* and derive *bhāṃḍatā* from *bhaṃḍ*, 'to reprove, deride.' I agree with Thomas in taking it as equivalent to *alpa* for the reasons specified

by him (IA., 1908, p. 20). *Bhāṇḍa*, if we derive it from *bhaṇḍ*,' to reprove, deride,' can no doubt mean 'reviling' or 'violence of language,' as understood by Bühler and Senart; but as *apabhāṃḍatā* has been placed in juxtaposition with *apavyayatā bhāṇḍa* must be so interpreted as to show that *bhāṇḍatā* is one extreme and *vyayatā* is another. This is possible only by taking *bhāṇḍa* in the sense of "goods, property." *Apabhāṇḍatā* thus means 'little accumulation' corresponding to *apavyayatā*, 'little expense.' Compare the story of *Bahu-bhāṇḍika Bhikkhu* mentioned in the Dhammapada Aṭṭhakathā.

[7] This is one of the most knotty passages from Aśoka inscriptions. Let us try to arrive at the correct sense of it. In the first place, what is the meaning of the word Yuta here? Obviously it must denote the same thing which the word denotes above in this inscription. We have seen that as Yutas are mentioned in conjunction with Rājūkas and Prādeśikas who were officers, they must denote a class of officers; and we have also seen what class of officers they were. Secondly, what is the meaning of *parisā*? It is worthy of note that this word occurs also in Rock Edict VI., where, as we shall see further on, Jayaswal has conclusively shown us that it means 'the council of ministers.' This fits here excellently, because it is the council of ministers that can with propriety issue orders to the Yuktas. Now remains the word *gaṇanā* which signifies, 'reckoning, counting.' We have seen that Aśoka asks his officers to preach the development of the virtues of *alpa-vyayatā* and *alpa-bhāṇḍatā*. But how was it to be determined that his people were developing these homely virtues? It was, therefore, necessary that some of his officers should make a house-to-house inspection and count how much of expense and how much of goods each householder had incurred or accumulated. But it was impossible to lay down one inflexible rule for all house-

holds. So the Parishad was ordered to advise them as each difficulty arose, so as not to violate the text (*vyaṃjana*) or the object (*hetu*), of the king's orders (*Above*, p. 66).

This passage is susceptible of another interpretation. The third important word here is *gaṇanā*, which occurs in the form of *gaṇayati* and *gaṇīātha* in the Queen's Edict, where it obviously signifies 'to register (a grant).' This meaning also suits here excellently. Whosoever, being inspired by the king's *dhaṃmānusathi*, makes a grant shall have that grant registered by the Yuktas, both by recording the name (*vyañjana*) of the donor and his object (*hetu*). This is exactly in consonance with the import of the Queen's Edict.

For *vyañjana*, see ZDMG., LXVII. 345 f. Hultzsch, following Lüders, translates it by "the council (of *Mahāmātras*) also shall order the Yuktas to register (these rules) both with (the addition of) reasons and according to the letter." But when he wrote, he had not my views before him. Mookerji, however, adopts them in his *Aśoka*, p. 136, n. 1.

IV

Translation

For a long time past, for many hundreds of years, have ever increased the slaughter of animate beings, injury to creatures, unseemly behaviour to relatives, (and) unseemly behaviour to Brāhmaṇs and Śramaṇas only increased. But now, in consequence of the practice of Dhaṃma by king Priyadarśin, Beloved of the gods, the sound of drum has become the sound of Dhaṃma, after (his) having shown to people spectacles of aerial chariots, spectacles of elephants, masses of fire and other divine representations.[1] As has not happened for many hundred years before, have now increased, through king-Priyadarśin-Beloved-of-the-gods' instruction in Dhaṃma, non-slaughter of animate beings, non-injury to creatures, seemly behaviour to relatives, seemly behaviour to Brāhmaṇs and Sramaṇas, hearkening to father and mother, hearkening to the aged. The practice of Dhaṃma of this and other manifold kinds has grown, and king Priyadarśin, Beloved of the gods, will ever cause this practice of Dhaṃma to grow. And the sons, grandsons and great-grandsons of king Priyadarśin will cause the practice of Dhaṃma to grow until the æon of destruction,[2] (and), abiding in Dhaṃma and virtuous conduct will give instruction in Dhaṃma. For the highest work is instruction in Dhaṃma, and the practice of Dhaṃma is not for one devoid of virtuous conduct. Growth and non-diminution in this matter are therefore excellent. For this purpose, namely, that they (*i.e.*, my descendants) may enjoin the growth of this matter and that no diminution should be noticeable, has this (Dhaṃma-lipi) been caused to be written.[3] This was caused to be written by king Priyadarśin, Beloved of the gods, when he was consecrated twelve years.

Notes

[1] This passage has been variously interpreted, but these interpretations may be divided into two classes according as they are taken to refer to terrestrial objects or atmospheric phenomena. The first kind of interpretation has been favoured by Senart and Bühler, and the second by Kern and for some time by Hultzsch (JRAS., 1911, 785 & ff.). I confess the first interpretation commends itself to me as being more natural. But the actual sense I deduce from the passage differs from that of Senart and Bühler, and has been set forth in IA., 1913, 25 & ff., and it is a matter of extreme gratification that Hultzsch has accepted my view (*ibid*, 1913, 651 & ff.; CII., I. 6, ns. 5 & 6.

The passage in question was discussed by S. Krishnaswāmi Aiyangar after my interpretation was published (JRAS., 1915, p. 521; IA., 1915, p. 203). He renders it as follows: "But now, in consequence of the adoption of the Dharma (law of morality) by Devānāmpriya Priyadarśin, the sound of the drum is lo! but the sound of the Dharma; the spectacles represented to the people, processional cars, elephants, bonfires and others, the representations of the *Devas*." I am afraid, the translation is not quite admissible. Because the word *aññāni* clearly shows that the *vimānas, hastins* and *agniskandhas* which Aśoka showed to his people were *divyāni rūpāni*. They could not therefore be the processional cars, elephants and bonfires, which are earthly objects. F. W. Thomas also gives 'bon-fire' as the meaning of *aggikhaṃdha* (JRAS., 1914, 395), but has not shown how the display of bonfire could create and develop righteousness among the people.

For my elucidation of this passage, see *Above*, pp. 130-2 and 141-5. In my note referred to above (IA., 1913, p. 25 & ff.), the word *vimāna* alone has been satisfactorily explained. For this purpose attention was drawn to a Pāli work called *Vimāna-vatthu*. The same work also explains the words *hastin*, and *agi* or *joti-khandha*. From it we learn that of those who live pious lives, some obtain in the next world not only *vimānas* or heavenly palaces, but also *hastins* or all-white celestial elephants (p. 4, l. 1; p. 56, ll. 16 & 35) and *agi* or *joti-khandhas*, that is, a complexion resplendent like lightning (p. 1, l. 9), stars (p. 7, l. 28), or fire (p. 12, l. 33). *Aññāni cha divyāni rūpāni* include such vehicles as celestial horses, ships, and so forth mentioned in the same work, that is, the *Vimāna-vatthu* (p. 12, l. 28; p. 4, l. 26). Hultzsch had no time to adopt this my later interpretation in CII., but this has been done by Mookerji in his *Aśoka*, p. 136, n. 7.

[2] For *Saṃvaṭa-kapa* (= *Saṃvartakalpa*), see JRAS., 1911, p. 485, n. 1.

[3] See *above*, p. 246.

V

Translation

Thus saith king Priyadarśin, Beloved of the gods: Good is difficult to perform. He who initiates good does something difficult to perform. Hence by me much good had been done. If my sons, grandsons, and my descendants after them, until the æon of destruction, follow similarly, they will do what is meritorious, but in this respect he who abandons even a part (here), will do ill. Verily, sin is easy to commit.[1]

Now, for a long time past previously, there were no Dharma-Mahāmātras.[2] Dharma-Mahāmātras were created by me when I had been consecrated thirteen years. They are employed among all sects; and (also) for the establishment of Dhamma, promotion of Dhaṃma, and for the welfare and happiness of those devoted to Dhaṃma.[3] They are engaged among the Yavanas, Kaṃbojas and the Gandhāras,[4] and the hereditary Rāshṭrikas and others on the Western Coast (Aparānta); among the Brāhmaṇs and Gṛihapatis who have become hirelings,[5] and, among the helpless and the aged, for (their) welfare and happiness; and (also) for the unfettering[6] of those devoted to Dhaṃma. They concern themselves with (money) grant, the unfettering[7] or the release, of (any one) who is bound with fetters, according as he is encumbered with progeny, is subjected to oppression, or is aged.[8] They are everywhere employed in (my) closed female apartments, or among my brothers, sisters, and other relatives,[9] whether in Pāṭaliputra or outlying towns Everywhere in my dominions they are occupied with those devoted to Dhaṃma according as there is any one who is leaning on Dhaṃma, is an abode of Dhaṃma, or is given up to almsgiving.[10] For this purpose this document of Dhaṃma has been engraved, namely, that it may long endure and that my progeny may follow (me).

Notes

[1] It has been customary to separate the initial portion of the inscription from the part where mention is made of the creation of the Dharma-Mahāmātras, as if both these parts were disconnected. But such a procedure is unwarranted. Every inscription of Aśoka is permeated by a certain idea which connects its different parts. The initial portion must therefore be so translated as to show that it is connected with what follows. What he means by *kalyāṇa* he has explained in PE. II. Aśoka thus tells us that he has done much good of this nature, and exhorts his sons, grandsons, and descendants to follow in his path. He insists upon their performing this duty in full and not partially, because *pāpa* or sin comes naturally to a human being. Hence the latter, especially if he is a ruler, can never be too much on his guard, and ought to fulfil his whole duty to his subjects, without omitting any part thereof. In the Mānserā, Kālsī and Dhaulī copies we have *pāpe hi nāma supadālaye*, which, I think, means "indeed one ought well to weed out sin." Aśoka then informs us that contributory to his plan of doing *kalyāṇa* or good deeds was his appointment of the Dharma-Mahāmātras, who, as we shall soon see, were set to bring about both these kinds of weal to the people. For his contrast of *kalyāṇa* with *pāpa*, see Pillar Edict III.

[2] The term *Dharma-Mahāmātra* has been translated 'Overseer of the Sacred Law' by Buhler (EI., II. 167) and 'Censor of the Law of Piety' by Smith (*Aśoka*, p. 168). It had better be left untranslated, as any translation of it must be misleading. There were many Mahāmātras before Aśoka's time, but he was the first to create Dharma-Mahāmātras, that is, Mahāmātras for the promotion of Dhaṃma.

[3] The construction of this passage has rather become abstruse by the indiscriminate use of the conjunction *cha* in the various recensions, particularly after *dhaṃmayutasa* in the Girnār copy. Nevertheless, I think that what is here intended is that the Dharma-Mahāmātras were to concern themselves with all the Pāsaṁḍas and Dharmayuktas in Aśoka's dominions. For *Pāsaṃḍa*, see *above*, pp. 156-57. The word *Dhaṃma-yuta* occurs thrice in this inscription, and each time Bühler interprets it differently. Senart's criticism seems to be unanswerable (I.A , 1891, p. 239, n. 30), and he proposes to render it by 'the faithful of the (true) religion.' It, however, seems better to translate it by 'one devoted to Dhaṃma, the righteous.' Thomas takes it in the sense of "the officials of the *dharma* (or ecclesiastical) department" (JRAS., 1915, pp. 102-3), and Smith "Subordinates of the Law of Piety" (*Aśoka*, p. 170). They thus take the word to be Dharma-Yukta, and not *dharmayuta*. But this procedure is open to objection. In the first place, Aśoka nowhere tells us about the creation of the Dharma-Yuktas, which he certainly would have done, if he had created them as he no doubt does in the case of the Dharma-Mahāmātras. And we are not warranted in supposing that there already existed before the time of Aśoka any officials of that description. Secondly, it is inconceivable why the Dharma-Mahāmātras have to show solicitude for the welfare and happiness of and even preach to the Dharma-Yuktas, if the *dhaṃma-yutas* were the king's officials, and not his subjects. Thirdly, in PE., VII., Rājūkas are spoken of as preaching to the *Dhaṃma-yuta jana*, who can there stand only for those people who follow Aśoka's Dhaṃma.

The duties of a Dharma-Mahāmātra, it will be seen, were of a twofold nature, according as they pertained to the material or the spiritual welfare of the people. See *above*, pp. 63 and ff.; also pp. 132 and ff.

[4] Bühler proposes a punctuation after *Apalaṃtā* and connects *Yona-Kaṃboja-Gaṃdhālānaṃ* with what precedes. Hultzsch follows him. But I agree with Senart in taking the latter along with what follows. The reasons for this procedure have been ably set forth in I.A., 1891, p. 240, n. 30. For the identification of the Yonas, Kambojas, Gandhāras and so forth, see *above*, pp. 26 and ff.

On pp. 29-30 it has been suggested that *pettenika* corresponds in sense to *pettanika* of *Aṅg.-N.*, but philologically it must be derived from *Paitrayaṇika* as pointed out by Michelson (IF., XXIV. 52 ff.). Aparānta is taken by Hult. in the sense of 'Western borderers' (*apar-Ānta*), and Mookerji follows him. But if Yonas, Kambojas, etc., are really 'borderers' (*antas*), that is, obviously independent kingdoms, why are they included by RE., XIII in the *rāja-vishaya* or royal dominions of Aśoka?

[5] *Bramaṇibha* and its variants correspond exactly, as was pointed out by Bühler (VOJ., XII, 76), to the literary Pāli *brahmanibbha* (brāhmaṇ-ebhya) which occurs in no less than three verses in the Mahānāradakassapa-Jātaka. The term *ibbha* of this compound has been explained as *gahapati* in the commentary. Patañjali, however, equates *Ibhyā* with *Kshatriyā* in his gloss. on Pāṇini, IV. 1. 63. For the social group exactly denoted by it, see *above*, p. 165-66. The phrase *bhatamaya* (G.), *bhaṭamaya* (S. M. & K.), or *bhaṭimaya* (D.) has very much exercised the epigraphists, and has been variously explained; 'soldiers and warriors' =*bhaṭa-marya* (Senart); 'hired servants'=*bhṛita-maya* (Bühler); and 'servants and masters'=*bhata-m-ayesu* (Franke). I can agree with Bühler only. *Bhaṭa* cannot possibly stand here for 'warriors'. This is forbidden by the variant form *bhata* furnished by Girnār. *Maya*, again,

cannot be equivalent to *marya* as its *r* would have then been preserved in the Shāhbāzgarhi and Mānserā versions. It is therefore natural to equate the phrase with the Sanskrit *bhṛita-maya*. I, however, take this expression as qualifying *bramaṇibha*, and translate the whole by 'Brāhmaṇs and Gṛihapatis, consisting of hirelings.' Not all individuals of the Brāhmaṇ and Vaiśya classes are meant here, but rather those who were in the same condition as *anātha* and *vṛiddha*, 'the helpless and the old.' We need not doubt that some of the Brāhmaṇs and Vaiśyas were in this degraded condition. Rhys Davids says: "Brahmins are also frequently mentioned as engaged in agriculture, and as hiring themselves out as cowherds and even goatherds" (*Buddhist India*, p. 57). For Gṛihapatis reduced to such a condition, see Fick's *Social Organisation*, etc., Trans., pp. 255-6.

Mookerji explains (*loc. cit.*, p. 141, p. 1) "*bhaṭamayeṣu* = *bhṛita-m* (euphonic) = *āryesu*." He thus takes *bhaṭa* = *bhṛita* = servant; and yet in the same breath he adds "*bhaṭa* (= a soldier) is not the same word as *bhaṭaka* (= a servant)" and translates it by "among the soldiers and their chiefs." Besides, as pointed out above, it defies all phonetic laws, because *bhata* or *bhaṭi* (D.) must correspond to *bhata* (G.) = 'hirelings' and cannot possibly signify 'soldiers'; and, secondly, if it is really *āryeshu*, it would have been *aliyesu* and not *ayesu* in D. and G.

6 In Separate Kaliṅga Edict I., Aśoka warns a certain class of his officials against any *bandhana* or *parikleśa* (*e.g.*, Dhauli, J) befalling any one of his subjects. At the end of the same Edict, while repeating this warning, he uses the words *paribodha* and *parikleśa* (Dhauli, Y). *Paribodha* is thus practically the same as *bandhana*, and may be translated by 'bonds or shackles.' The same meaning suits the word very well in the passages quoted by Thomas

in JRAS., 1915, pp. 99-106. As regards the other reading, *parigodha*, presented by Girnār, he seems to be right in ascribing this confusion between the two words to the usage of the time.

[7] In regard to the interpretation of this passage I agree, on the whole, with Senart. Bühler takes *badha* in *bandhana-badhasa* to mean 'corporal punishment.' The word is *badha* in all recensions, and not *vadha*. And the rule *va-bayor=abhedaḥ* was certainly not applicable to the Aśokan records. The phrase is equivalent to the Sanskrit *bandhana-baddhasya*, and means "of one bound with fetters," that is. 'imprisoned.' *Paṭividhāna* has been used in Rock Edict VIII in the sense of 'distribution or grant (of money),' and suits here very well. *Kat-ābhikāra* is translated 'victim of a trick' (Senart), 'overwhelmed by misfortune' (Bühler) and 'bewitched (incurably ill?)' (Hultzsch). The word *abhikāra* has been traced by Bühler to the root *abhi+kṛī*, and he refers us to *Jāt.*, IV. 121, v. 72, where the word *abhikirati* means 'overpowers, oppresses.' For a different interpretation, see JBORS., 19 8, pp. 144-6.

[8] I have nowhere seen a translation of this passage where its parts are intelligently connected one with the other. For an elucidation of the exact kind of work which in this passage the Dharma-Mahāmātras are expected to do, see *above*, p. 63 f.

[9] Hultzsch translates the passage "in the harems of our brothers, of (our) sisters, etc." Mookerji follows him. One wonders what sort of harems Aśoka's sisters had! *Aṃnesu vā nātisu* of Dhauli clearly shows that the locative sense is intended even in the case of *bhātinaṃ me bhaginīnaṃ* which precedes it.

[10] See *above*, p. 133.

VI

Translation

Thus saith king Priyadarśin, Beloved of the gods:—For a long time past previously there was no dispatch of business and no reporting at all hours. This, therefore, I have done, namely, that at all hours and in all places,—whether I am eating or am in the closed (female) apartments, in the inner chamber, in the royal rancho,[1] on horseback [2] or in pleasure orchards, the Reporters may report people's business to me. People's business I do at all places. And when in respect of anything that I order by word of mouth, for being personally issued or proclaimed, or, again, (if) in respect of any emergent work that may superimpose itself on the Mahāmātras, there is any opposition or argumentation in the council,[3] I have so commanded that it shall be forthwith communicated to me at all places and at all hours. I am never satisfied with (my) exertions or with (my) dispatch of business. For the welfare of the whole world is an esteemed duty with me. And the root of that, again, is this, namely, exertion[4] and dispatch of business. There is no higher duty than the welfare of the whole world.[5] And what little effort I make,—what is it for?—(in order) that I may be free from debt to the creatures, that I may render some happy here and that they may gain heaven in the next world. For this purpose have I caused this document of Dhaṃma to be engraved: what for?—in order that it may endure for a long time and that my sons, grandsons and great grandsons may similarly follow me for the welfare of the whole world. This, however, is difficult to accomplish without the utmost exertion.

Notes

[1] The exact meaning of *vacha* is not settled. It is translated 'secret retreat' (Senart), 'latrine' (Bühler), 'closet' (Smith), and 'cow-pen' (Hultzsch). Bühler and Smith evidently take it as equivalent to *varchas* which, however, means 'excreta,' and not 'latrine.' Jayaswal (IA., 1918, pp. 53-55) rightly remarks that "no king in his senses would ask officers to announce the business of suitors in his latrine," and says that *vacha* stands for *vraja* and explains the philological difficulty, namely, the change of *j* to *ch*, by referring us to *vrachaṃti* in RE., XIII (Shāhbāzgarhi) which stands for *vrajanti*. He also shows that *vraja* is mentioned thrice in Kauṭilya's Arthaśāstra, where the word is used to denote 'herd of cattle, whether of horses, or camels, and so forth.' RE. XII mentions *vacha-bhūmikas*, or Officers connected with *Vrajas*. See *above*, p. 55, for my view. Jayaswal, however, takes it in a different sense. The only objection to the full acceptance of Jayaswal's proposal is that the philological difficulty is not wholly removed, because the change of *j* to *ch* in the present instance is a peculiarity of the Shābhāzgarhi and Mansherā edicts only, and hence *vacha* of the Girnār and other recensions cannot normally be taken to stand for *vraja*. Vidhushekhara Bhattacharya Sastri also takes

vacha as equivalent to *vraja*, but takes the latter to mean 'a road' (IA., 1920, p. 56). This, in his opinion, refers to the king when he is on the road for a short walk.

[2] Bühler takes *vinīta* as *vinītaka* 'a litter or palanquin,' Hultzsch follows him. Jayaswal (IA., 1918, p. 53) takes it as equivalent to Kauṭilya's *vinaya*, and interprets it to mean 'military exercise' and quotes in support of his position a passage from the Arthaśāstra. Reasons against Jayaswal's interpretation have been set forth by Radhagovinda Basak (IA., 1919, pp. 14-15). Basak further shows that the Amarakosha (II. 8. 45) has *vinītāḥ sādhu-vāhinaḥ*, that is, *vinītas* are easy-riding or well-trained horses. This is supported by the Medinī which gives *vinītaḥ suvah-āśve syāt*. From the same word has been derived *vainītaka* which Amarakosha explains as *paraṁparā-vāhana*. It signifies, I think, any conveyance that is borne by relays of *vinītas* or well-trained horses. In the Majjhima-Nikāya, as pointed out by Vidhushekhara Sastri (IA., 1920, p. 55), Pasenadi, king of Kośala, is referred to along with his seven *ratha-vinītas* when he has to go from Śrāvastī to Sāketa. These *ratha-vinītas* are placed at successive stages, so that the first is disposed off as soon as the next one is reached. What is this *ratha-vinīta*? He takes it to mean 'a *vinīta* in the form of a *ratha*.' Perhaps it is better to take it as denoting 'a horse trained for the chariot.' *Vinīta* can thus be brought to bear the same sense that has been assigned to it in the lexicons. Mookerji takes it as a place where Aśoka studied *vinaya*. *Vinaya*, however, was intended for a Buddhist monk, and not for a layman such as Aśoka was.

[3] The most important word here is *parisā* (=*parishat*), taken to signify "the Buddhist clergy" (Senart), and "the committee of any caste or sect" (Bühler). Jayaswal alone seems to be correct in taking it as equivalent to

the *mantri-parishat* mentioned in Kauṭilya's Arthaśāstra (IA., 1913, 282 and ff.). This is just what might be expected in an administrative edict, such as this Edict undoubtedly is. But for a different meaning of this word and also of this passage, see JASB., 1920, pp. 331 and ff.) The next important word is *nijhati*, which occurs also in PE. VII. The verbal root of this word occurs also in PE. IV. and Separate Kalinga Edict I. The word seems to have been used differently in different edicts as in Pāli literature. So far as the word in this edict is concerned, attention may be drawn to two of the multifarious passages quoted by Barua (IHQ., II. 125-7). The first is from *Aṅg.N.*, I. 76 and runs thus: *yassa parisāyaṃ bhikkhū adhikaraṇaṃ ādiyanti...na cheva aññamaññam saññāpenti na cha saññattiṃ upāgachhanti*, etc. The second passage is from the *Maj.-N.* commentary on the *Kosambika-sutta* and is, as follows: *atthaṃ cha kāraṇañ cha dassetvā aññamaññam jānāpanaṃ nijjhāpanaṃ*. In the first passage the words *saññatti* and *nijjhatti* occur in connection with a cause or dispute (*adhikarana*) in an assembly (*parisā*). There can be no doubt that it is this *nijjhatti* which is intended here also. The meaning of this word is made clear in the second passage, from which it appears that *nijjhatti* is 'making the matter intelligible to one another by placing facts and reasons.' It thus seems to signify 'argumentation.' For the full sense of this passage, see *above*, pp. 58 and ff.

[4] Bühler quotes verses from the *rājadharma* of the Sānti-parvan (Chap. 58, vs. 13-16) of the Mahābhārata, which are apparently from Bṛihaspati's Arthaśāstra, and where 'exertion' is ordained for all rulers. The same is prescribed in the *Kauṭilīya* also (p. 39).

[5] *Loka* had better be understood in the sense of 'the world' so as to bring it into accord with *bhūtānaṃ*.

VII

Translation

King Priyadarśin, Beloved of the gods, wishes that all sects may dwell at all places, because they all desire self-restraint and purification of heart. People, however, are of various likings and various attachments. They will perform either the whole or a part (of their duty). But even the lavish liberality and firm attachment (of a man to his sect) are quite worthless,[1] if he has no self-restraint, purity of heart or knowledge of what is right.

Notes

[1] The last clause of this edict is rather difficult to interpret. It depends upon correctly understanding the meaning and force of the word *nichā* or *niche*. Bühler translates it as follows: "But self-control, purity of mind, gratitude and firm attachment are laudable in a lowly man, to whom even great liberality is impossible." But this is untenable, because in the first place *nichā* does not mean 'a lowly,' but 'a low person.' Secondly, *nichā* of G cannot possibly stand for *nichāya*. Thirdly, *bāḍhaṁ* here is an adverb and not an adjective, and can never mean 'laudable.' Smith, following F. W. Thomas, translates: "Even for a person to whom lavish liberality is impossible, the virtues of mastery over the senses, purity of mind, gratitude, and steadfastness are altogether indispensable." Thomas thus takes *niche*=*nityaṃ*, that is, 'permanent,' 'indispensable,' in contradistinction to *naimittikaṃ*, 'occasional.' If *niche* here had really been equivalent to *nityaṃ*,

we should have had *nitiaṃ* at least in K, D and J. *Nichā* seems to have been used as an adjective and to be going with apparently the preceding word *diḍha-bhatitā*. The variant *nīche* corresponds to Skt. *nīchāiḥ*, as suggested by Hultzsch, which is often used adjectively. What Aśoka means is that *saṃyama, bhāvasudhi* and *kataṃñatā* are virtues of such paramount excellence that every individual ought to develop them in himself. They, again, are superior to *dāna* and *daḍhabhatitā* inculcated by every sect along with them. The latter will be practised by any member of a sect. But it is supremely imperative on him to cultivate the former virtues, the negation of which can never be compensated by any degree of development of the latter. This edict looks like a replica of RE., XII, where Aśoka distinctly says that he does not think of *dāna, pujā* and *bhati* so highly as of 'restraint of speech' *vachaguti*, and willingness to learn the tenets of other sects. In the present edict also Aśoka does not attach so much importance to *dāna*, etc., as to *saṃyama* which doubtless corresponds to *vacha-guti*. For further elucidation of this point, see *above*, p. 98 and ff. *Kataṃña*=*Kṛitajña*="Knowing what is right, correct in conduct, MBh. xii, 104,6"—Monier-William's Dictionary.

VIII

Translation

For a (long) time past, kings used to go out on tours of pleasure.[1] Here there were chase and other similar diversions. Now, king Priyadarśin, Beloved of the gods, repaired to Saṃbodhi (Bodhi Tree),[2] when he had been consecrated ten years. Hence this touring for Dhaṃma.

Here this happens, namely, visits and gifts to the Brāhmaṇ and Śramaṇa ascetics, visits and largesses of gold to the aged, and visits to, instructions in Dhamma to, and enquiries about Dhamma of, the provincials. The great delight that (springs) from it is the extraordinary luck of king Priyadarśin, Beloved of the gods.[3]

Notes

[1] A *vihāra-yātrā* has been described in the M. Bh., *above*, pp. 15 & ff.

[2] The most difficult expression to understand here is *ayāya Saṃbodhiṃ*. For the various renderings of the passage and also my interpretation, see IA., 1913, pp. 159 and ff. But the word *Saṃbodhi* in the sense of Mahābodhi or the Bodhi Tree actually occurs only in v. 81 of the *Kaliṅgābodhi-jātaka* (Jāt., IV, p. 236). See in this connection my paper in DMMV., pp. 445-6.

In this connection, again, Prof. Mookerji (p. 151, n. 2) says: "The term *Saṃbodhi* is used in the *Mahāvaṃsa* [v. 266] in the sense of Buddhism which was taught Aśoka by Upagupta..." In the first place, according to the *Mahāvaṃsa*, Buddhism was taught Aśoka not by Upagupta, but by Moggaliputta Tissa. Secondly, the word signifying 'Buddhism' is not *Saṃbodhi* as wrongly asserted by the Professor, but *Saṃbudha-samaya* (=the religion of the Sambuddha) which word again occurs not in v. 266 but v. 265.

[3] *Tadapayā* has been taken to stand for *tadauparayāt*, meaning 'since then.' Should we not have expected *tadopaliyā* in Dhauli and Jaugada copies at least? Possibly it stands for *tad-upayā*=*tad-upagā* as suggested by Franke.

Bhāge aṃne is taken by Bühler to mean "in exchange for past pleasure." But Hultzsch, following Lüders, rightly says: "this is impossible, because in the eastern dialect the two locatives would end in *asi*." I take it as equivalent to *bhāgoḥ anya*='unusual luck, extraordinary fortune.'

IX

Translation

Thus saith king Priyadarśin, Beloved of the gods: People perform various (lucky) rites in sicknesses, at marriages,[1] on the birth of offspring (sons—G.), and on journey. On these and other similar occasions people perform various rites. In this matter, however, womankind[2] performs much manifold, (but) trivial, useless rite. Rites should undoutedly be performed. But a rite of this kind bears little fruit. That rite, however, bears great fruit, which is Dhaṃma-maṃgala.[3] There seemly behaviour towards the servile and menial classes, reverence towards preceptors, self-control in regard to animals, (and) liberality to Brāhmans and Śramaṇas are meritorious. These and other similar (items) are indeed the Dhaṃma-maṃgala. Therefore, a father, a son, a brother, a master (K. S. & M.—a friend or acquaintance, nay, even a neighbour) ought to say: "this is meritorious, this rite ought to be performed till that object is attained; (S. & M.—and after it is performed, I shall do it again).''

(G. D. & J. Texts)

And it has been said : "gift is meritorious."[4] But there is no gift or favour comparable to the gift or favour of Dhaṃma. Therefore, a friend, a sympathiser, a relative, or a companion ought to exhort (one another) on this and that occasion, saying : "this is a duty, this is meritorious ; with this it is possible to attain heaven." And what thing is more worthy of achievement through this than the attainment of heaven?

(K. S. & M. Texts)

For (every) other rite is of a dubious nature. Perchance it may accomplish that object, and perchance it may not remain in this world. But this Dhaṃma-maṃgala is not conditioned by time. Even though it does not achieve that object here, it begets endless merit in the next world. But if it achieves that object, both are here gained, to wit, that object of his world and the begetting of endless merit in the next through that Dhaṃma-maṃgala.

Notes

[1] For the phrase *āvāha-vivāha*, see *Dīgha-N.*, I. 99. "*Āvāha* is a son's marriage as opposed to a daughter's (*vivāha*) in the 9th rock edict of Piyadaśi. So *Jātaka*, I. 452, 2 ; IV, 316, 8 and VI. 71, 32."—Cowell's Trans. of *Jāt.*, Vol. V, p. 145, n. 1.

[2] K. has *abaka-jani*[*yo*] and M. *abaka-janika* which

corresponds to *ambika-janyo*='Old venerable women and mothers.'

[3] For the explanation of the different parts of the edict, see *above*, pp. 104-5, 160-1 and 165.

[4] See *above*, p. 112.

X

Translation

King Priyadarśin, Beloved of the gods, does not deem glory or fame as conducing to any great thing except in that, whether at the present time or in future,[1] his people may show desire to hearken to Dhaṃma and practise the utterances of Dhaṃma. In this matter only does king Priyadarśin, Beloved of the gods, desire glory of fame. Whatever exertions king Priyadarśin, Beloved of the gods, puts forth are all with reference to the other world—why is it?—in order that every one may be free from *parisrava*.[2] But that is *parisrava* which is *apuṇya* (demerit).[3] This, however, is difficult to accomplish whether by the lower or the higher class (of officials),[4] except by the utmost exertion [5] and by renouncing every other duty. But it is most difficult for the higher (class).

Notes

[1] *Tadātva*=the time being, present time; *āyati*= future time, the future; *dighāya*=for a long time.

[2] Compare *apa-parisrava* with *ap-āsinava* of PE. II. See also *above*, pp. 117-8.

[3] *Apuṇya* may be either *pāpa* or *āsinava* of PE. III.

[4] *Esa* or *ese* must refer to the work of freeing people from *parisrava*. *Chhudaka* and *usaṭa* (=*uchchhita*) must therefore refer to the lower and higher classes of his officials who alone can help him in his mission. G. alone has *jona* here, the other recensions giving *vaga* instead. About the beginning of this edict, however, we have *jano* in all recensions. This clearly shows that the word *jano* in G. at the second place down below has a different sense, namely, that denoted by the other word, *vaga*, that is "a body of men," that is, I believe, "a class of officials." Compare the use of this word in separate Dhauli Edict I, l. 23. See also n. 4 on MRE. I.

[5] I have already said that the Arthaśāstra recommends *parākrama* or exertion to kings and officials. And it is worthy of note that Aśoka also speaks of the necessity of *parākrama* for himself or his sons and grandsons as in RE. VI, or for his officials as in the present edict. These two edicts may therefore be compared to MRE. I.

XI

Translation

Thus saith king Priyadarśin, Beloved of the gods : There is no such gift as the gift of Dhamma, (no such acquaintance as) acquaintance in Dhamma, (no such participation as) participation in Dhamma, and (no such kinship as) kinship in Dhamma. Therein this happens " seemly behaviour towards slaves and servants, meritorious hearkening to father and mother, meritorious gifts to friends, acquaintances, and relatives, and to Brāhmaṇs and Sramaṇas (and) meritorious non-slaughter of animals."

This ought to be said by a father, a son, a brother, a master, a friend or acquaintance, nay even a neighbour:[1] "This is meritorious; this ought to be done." Thus acting, he attains this world and begets endless spiritual merit through that gift of Dhaṃma.

Note

[1] This clause explains the *dhaṃma-saṃstava, dhaṃma-saṃvibhāga* and *dhaṃma-sambaṃdha* mentioned above. Fathers, sons and brothers are *saṃvibhāgīs* as well as *saṃbandhīs.* The others are connected with one another by *saṃstava.* But these are material ties which should be replaced by spiritual links. This is possible only by kinship, acquaintance and participation in Dhaṃma.

XII

Translation

King Priyadarśin, Beloved of the gods, honours (men of) all sects, ascetics and householders and honours (them) with gift and manifold honour.[1] But the Beloved of the gods does not think so much of gift and honour as—what?—as that there should be a growth of the essential among (men of) all sects. The growth of the essential, however, is of various kinds. But the root of it is restraint of speech,[2]—how? —namely, there should not be honour to one's own sect or condemnation of another's sect without any occasion; or it may be a little on this and that occasion. On the contrary, others' sects should be honoured on this and that occasion. By so doing one promotes one's own sect, and benefits another's sect. By doing otherwise one injures one's own sect and also harms another's sect. For one who honours one's own sect and condemns another's sect, all through attachment to one's own sect,—why?—in order that one may illuminate one's own sect in reality by so doing injures, more assuredly, one's own sect. Concourse[3] is therefore commendable,—why?—in order that they may hear and desire to hear (further) one another's Dhaṃma. For this is the desire of the Beloved of the gods,—What?—that all sects shall be well-informed and conducive of good.[4] And those who are favourably disposed towards this or that sect should be informed: "The Beloved of the gods does not so much think of gift or honour as—what?—as that there may be, a growth of the essential among all sects and also mutual appreciation." For this end are engaged the Dharma-Mahāmātras, Superintendents of women, the Vr ajabhūmikas[5] and other bodies (of officials). And this is its fruit—the exaltation of one's own sect and the illumination of Dhaṃma.

Notes

[1] For properly understanding this edict, see *above*, pp. 99 and ff. See also *Sīha-sutta* in the *Aṅg.-N.* (Pt. IV, p. 185 f.) where Buddha exhorts Sīha to give alms not only to the Buddhist but also to the Nirgrantha ascetics. Compare also *na cha nāma sadhaṃmokkaṃsanā bhavissati na paradhaṃmavambhanā* occurring in the *Majjhima-N.* (Pt. I, ll. 35-6).

[2] For *vachaguti* and *bhatiyā*, compare RE. VII.

[3] *Samavāya* is derived from the root *samav-e*, which means "to come together, assemble." What Aśoka means is that if the adherents of the different sects come in contact with one another, they would learn many good points of religions other than their own. Sh. has *sayumo* = 'restraint,' corresponding to *vachaguti* above.

[4] *Kalāṇa* has been explained by Aśoka in PE. II.

[5] For the elucidation of the function of these officials, see *above*, pp. 54 and ff. Vrajabhūmika of this edict may be compared to the official *hasty-aśva-go-mahish-āj-āvik-ādi-vyāpṛitaka* of the Sena copper-plate grants.

XIII

Translation

The country of Kaliṅga was conquered when king Priyadarśin, Beloved of the gods, had been anointed eight years. One hundred and fifty thousand were therefrom captured, one hundred thousand were there slain, and many times as many died. Thereafter, now,[1] when the country of Kaliṅga has been acquired, the Beloved of the gods has zealous compliance with Dhaṃma, love for Dhaṁma, and teaching of Dhaṃma. That is the remorse of the Beloved of the gods on having conquered Kaliṅga. Verily the slaughter, death and captivity of the people, that occurs when an unconquered (country) is being conquered, is looked upon as extremely painful and regrettable by the Beloved of the gods. But this is to be looked upon as more regrettable than that, because there dwell Brāhmaṇic Śramaṇic, and other sects and householders, among whom is established this, *viz.*, hearkening to the elders, hearkening to the parents, hearkening to the preceptors, seemly behaviour and steadfast devotion to friends, acquaintances, companions and relatives, and to slaves and servants. There (in the war) to such (pious) people befall personal violence, death, or banishment from the loved ones. Or there are those who are well-circumstanced[2] and possess undiminished affection, but their friends, acquaintances, companions and relatives meet with a misfortune; there that (misfortune) becomes a personal violence to those (former All this is the lot of (these) men, and is considered regrettable by the Beloved of the gods. And there is no country except that of the Yavanas[3] where there are not these orders, namely, the Brāhmaṇa, and the Śramaṇa ascetics; and there is no place in any (such) country where men have no faith in one sect or another. Even one-hundredth or one-thousandth part of those who were slain, died, or were captured in Kaliṅga, is to-day[4] considered regrettable by the Beloved of the gods. Nay if any one does (him) wrong, the Beloved of the gods must bear all that can be borne. And (the people of) the forests[5] which are in the dominions of the Beloved of the gods he conciliates and exhorts.[6] The might of the Beloved of the gods, though he is repentant, is told them—why?—in order that they may express sense of shame, and not be killed.[7] The Beloved of the gods desires for all beings non-injury, self-control, equable conduct and gentleness.

And this conquest is considered to be the chiefest by the Beloved of the gods, which is conquest through Dhaṃma. And that again has been achieved by the Beloved of the gods here and in the bordering dominions, even as far as six hundred *yojanas*, where (dwell) the Yavana king called Aṃtiyoka, and, beyond this Aṃtiyoka, the four kings called Turamāya, Aṃtekina, Maga and Alikasu(ṃ)dara,[8]—(likewise) down below, where are the Choḍas, the Pāṇḍyas, as far as the Tāmraparṇiyas,—likewise here in the king's dominions among the Yavanas and Kambojas, the Nābhakas and Nābhapaṃtis, the hereditary Bhoja rulers, Andhras and Pāriṃdas—everywhere they follow the teaching of the Beloved of the gods in respect of Dhaṃma. Even where the envoys of the Beloved of the gods do not go, they, hearing the utterances of Dhaṃma, the ordinances, and the instructions in Dhaṃma by the Beloved of the gods, practise Dhaṃma, and will so practise. And the conquest, which is thereby achieved, everywhere becomes a conquest flavoured with love. That love has been attained (by me) in the conquest through Dhaṃma. A petty thing, however, is that love. That which concerns the next world, the Beloved of the gods esteems, as alone bearing great fruit. And this edict of Dhaṃma has been engraved for this purpose,—why?—in order that whosoever may be, my sons and great-grandsons, may not think of a new conquest as worth achieving, that in regard to a conquest, possible only through (the use) of arrow,[9] they may prefer forbearance and lightness of punishment, and that they may regard that to be the (real) conquest which is a conquest through Dhaṃma. That is (good) for here and hereafter. May attachment to Dhaṃma develop into attachment to all kingdoms (*chakras*).[10] That is (good) for here and hereafter.

Notes

[1] *Adhunā* (now) and *aja* (to-day) referred to in note 4 below clearly show that Aśoka's zealous protection of Dhaṃma in Kaliṅga pertains to the time when the edict was promulgated. *Dhaṃmavāya* of G. & K. must correspond to *Dhaṃma-sīlana* of S. As proposed by Senart the former must be taken as equivalent to *Dhaṃmāvāya*, *avāya* signifying 'yielding to,' 'compliance with.'

[2] *Saṃvidhā* signifies 'mode of life,' 'means of leading lif'e (*Raghuvaṁśa*, I. 94). *Saṃvihita* may therefore be taken to denote 'those who are well-circumstanced, well-provided for.'

[3] The *Yona* denotes the Yavana people, and consequently the province inhabited by them must be distinguished from the dominions of the Yavana-rājas referred to further in this edict. The Yona province was included in Aśoka's empire, as may also be seen from RE. V. see *above*, p. 27 f.

[4] The word *aja* strengthens the conclusion in note 1.

[5] For the identification of this province, see *above*, pp. 41-2.

[6] See n. 9 on PE. VII., below.

[7] Previously scholars took *vuchati* to begin a new sentence. Hult. seems right in taking the words from *anutape* to *haṃñeyasu* as forming one sentence. This yields a better sense.

[8] For these and the following names, see *above*, pp. 26 and ff. For another interpretation of *a-shashu*, see IA., 1918, p. 297.

[9] G.—*Sarasake* (*Sara-śakye*) *eva*, *vijaye* 'when a conquest is possible only through an arrow.' K.—*Shaya-*

kashino (=śaly-ākarshiṇo) *vijayashi*, 'in a conquest by (a warrior) who draws an arrow.' What Aśoka probably means is that if the policy of expansion commends itself to any one of his successors, the latter should in such cases exercise as much forbearance and inflict as light punishment as possible, so as to make this terrestrial *vijaya* well-nigh bloodless.

Sh. has *spa[kaspi]yo vijaye* which yields no sense, and in fact, the reading seems doubtful. Hult. takes it as equivalent to *svake eva vijaye* which curiously he translates by 'if a conquest does please them,' instead of 'if it is their own conquest.' It is also not clear how *spakaspi=svakasmin*, because here one and the same letter *spa* stands once for *sva* and another time for *sma*. In the *K*. wording, he separates *no* from *Shayakashi* and arbitrarily takes it as standing for *ye*. As regards *shayaka* he derives it from Sk. *svayam* although the latter is an indeclinable. We should naturally expect some derivative from *svīyaka*, and not *svayam*, but the actual K. reading is *shayaka*, and not *shiyaka*. In respect of *sarasake* of G., Hult., "considers it as a Bahuvrīhi of *sva+rasa*." If it is any Bahuvrīhi, *sva* of the compound must refer to *vijaya* and not to the descendants of Aśoka, as Hult. takes it when he translates it by "if a conquest does please them." Besides, it can never be a Bahuvrīhi in this sense.

[10] According to Hult., K. should read *shavā-chakū-nilati hot[u] uyāma-lati*; S., *sava-chati-rati bhotu ya [dh]-ramma-rati*; and M., *sava-cha[ka]-nirati hotu ya dhrama-rati*. The most important word here *chaka=chakra=* kingdom,' a word technical to Hindu polity. *Chati* of S. seems to be a mistake for *chaka*. It is, however, strange how Hult. splits it up into two: *cha ka*, correcting the latter into *kam*. Mookerji, of course, follows him.

What Aśoka says is that attachment to Dhaṃma with his descendants should develop into attachment to all kingdoms on earth. *Uyāma* of K. should properly speaking stand for *udyāma* for which Monier Williams' *Dictionary* gives a sense of 'the act of erecting or stretching out' with one reference to the *Satapatha-Br*. This suits the text fairly well. What Aśoka means is that 'expansion' with his descendants should take place through 'strong attachment to all kingdoms,' that is, by carrying out the Dhaṃma propaganda in them. As in his case so in theirs, *Dhaṃma-vijaya* should enable them to conquer the dominions of the Antas.

XIV

Translation

This *Dhaṃma-lipi*[1] has been caused to be inscribed by king Priyadarśin, Beloved of the gods, either in abridged, medium or expanded form. The whole was not executed at every place. Vast, indeed, is (my) kingdom, and much has been written, and much will I cause to be written. And, owing to their sweetness, various things have been uttered over and over again. And why? In order that the people may act accordingly. But it may be that something has here been inscribed incomplete, considering either the locality or (a good) reason for deletion, or through the fault of the scribe.[2]

Notes

[1] *Ayaṃ dhaṃmalipi* can mean either '*this* edict,'

that is, R.E. XIV or '*this* series of edicts,' that is, the Fourteen Rock Edicts. It cannot denote *dhaṃma-lipis* in general, as supposed by Hultzsch and also by Mookerji who follows him. The same phrase occurs both in REs. I & XIV, where it has been differently translated by these scholars,—which does not seem to be the right procedure.

[2] The last sentence has been variously interpreted. "But it may be that something has been written here incompletely, be it on account of the space, be it on account of some reason to be *especially* determined, or through a mistake of the writer"—Bühler. "It may be that something may have been written incompletely, by reason of a mutilation of a passage, or of misunderstanding, or by a blunder of the writer"—Smith. "In some instances (some) of this may have been written incompletely, either on account of the locality, or because (my) motive was not liked, or by the fault of the writer"—Hultzsch.

I take *sa(ṃ)chhaya*, *shaṃkheya*, and *saṃkhaya* as standing for the Sk. *saṃkshaya* or *saṃksheya* and signifying 'deletion, omission'. *Ālochetpā* governs *desaṃ* and *sa(ṃ)chhāya-kāraṇaṃ*.

(*b*) PILLAR EDICTS

I

Translation

Thus saith king Priyadarśin, Beloved of the gods: " When I had been crowned twenty-six years, this *Dhaṃmalipi* was caused to be written. One may with difficulty promote [1] things of this and the next world, except through intense love of Dhamma, rigorous scrutiny,[2] extreme obedience, utmost fear, (and) extreme energy. But through my instructions, this regard for Dhamma and love of Dhaṃma have grown and will grow day by day [3] (among my people). And my Purushas, whether of high, low,[4] or middle rank, conform to and promote (them). And they are (quite) able to urge others (to do it).[5] So also the Mahāmātras for the Frontier Kingdoms. This is the precept [6]: namely, protection by Dhaṃma, administration by Dhaṃma, causing happiness by Dhaṃma, and guarding by Dhaṃma."

Notes

[1] The same word occurs in line 8 below, as *saṃpaṭīpādayaṃti*. *Du-saṃpaṭipādaye* = 'Difficult to gain' (Bühler), 'difficult to secure' (Smith). But this is philologically impossible, as remarked by Michelson. Better to take

Sampaṭipādaye=*sampratipādayet*. *Sampratipādayaṃti*= carry out (my orders), (Bühler), 'lead others in the way' (Smith). It is clear that both these scholars are taking the same word in two senses at two different places in one and the same edict. Besides, they take it once as referring to Aśoka's subjects in general and at another time as referring to his officials. The word should, however, be so interpreted as to have the same sense in both the places. The concluding portion of the inscription, again, clearly shows that Aśoka is here addressing himself not to the people in general but to his officers of all ranks. *Sampaṭipād* must, therefore be taken to mean "cause (people) to attain to," of course, things of this and the next world.

According to Senart, *du-sampatipādye*='difficult to provide', and *saṃpaṭipādayaṃti*='direct (the people) in the Good Way. He has no doubt taken the word in both places in the causal sense and as referring to officials, but not, however, in the same sense.

[2] *Palīkhā*='scrutiny,' that is, as to whether one's actions are lawful or not. *Susūsā* and *bhaya* are, of course, with reference to a king. As regards *usāha* compare RE. VI. & D.-J.S.I., I. Of course, all these qualities are to be exhibited by the king's officials.

[3] *Suve suve*='every day,' 'from day to day' (*cf.* Dhaṃmapada, v. 229)—Senart.

[4] *Gevayā* "is derived from the Sanskrit root *gep* or *glep* which the *Dhātupāṭha* explains by *dainye*. The corresponding Sanskrit word was no doubt, *gepya—glepya*, literally 'the poor' or 'wretched.'"—Bühler. Later, he derived it from *gevaka*. Both are phonologically untenable, as pointed out by Michelson. The meaning, however, is clear. For Purushas, see *above*, p. 57.

[5] *Chapala* is taken generally to mean 'the fickle-minded.' But S. N. Mitra separates *chapalaṃ* into *cha palaṃ* and refers us to *Ang*.-N., II. 253-6 (IHQ., VII. 193), His interpretation seems better. *Alaṃ* (Jaugada-L)=*patibalā* (Dhauli-K) in Separate Kaliṅga Edict II. *Samādapayitave* is the infinitive of *samādāpeti*, the causal form of *samā+dā*, which means "to take upon oneself, solemnly undertake, generally used of a religious undertaking or vow to fulfil some or all of the religious precepts, either for a time or permanently"—Childers. This suits here excellently. What Aśoka means is that his officials are able or fit enough to cause or induce the people to take upon themselves the performance of some or all the precepts of Dhaṃma prescribed by him.

[6] *Vidhi* means 'a sacred rule, precept'. Aśoka is here apparently quoting from some scripture. Compare *dhaṃmikaṃ rakkh-āvaraṇa-guttiṃ* which a *Chakkavatti* is enjoined to carry out in *Dīgha-N.*, III. 61. 2 (*above*, p. 204). Here *rakkhā* and *gutti* correspond to *pālanā* and *goti* of this edict.

II

Translation

Thus saith king Priyadarśin, Beloved of the gods: Dhaṃma is meritorious. But what does Dhaṃma consist of? (Of these things:) freedom from depravity,[1] much good, mercy, liberality, truthfulness, purity. The gift of sight[2] have I given in manifold ways: (and) various favours have been conferred by me on bipeds and quadrupeds, birds and aquatic animals, even up to the boon of life. And many other good deeds[3] have I done. For this purpose I have caused this *Dhaṃmalipi* to be engraved, that they may follow (me) and that it may long endure.[4] He who acts thus will do what is good.

Notes

[1] In the next edict *āsinava* is taken as allied to *pāpa*. This may be compared to *parisrave* of R. E. X. where it is taken to be identical with *apuṃne*. This makes Senart's derivation of *āsinava* from *ā+sru* more probable than that of Bühler from *ā+snu*. This derivation was suggested originally by Burnouf as pointed out by Michelson (I.F., XXIII, 268). For the correct meaning of the word, see *above*, pp. 111 and ff.

[2] Senart's "interpretation of *chakhudāne* by *cha khu dāne* cannot stand, because the enclitic words *cha* and *khu* cannot begin a sentence, and because the continuousness of the syllables in the text does not permit their being taken as parts of two sentences"—Bühler. *Chakhu*= 'spiritual insight,'—Bühler. But it had rather be taken in its physical sense, and probably refers to the remission of such punishment as that of "eye for eye, tooth for tooth." This agrees with *ā-pāna-dakhinā*, 'Even the boon of life'—Bühler, and not 'even to securing them water'—Senart.

[3] The preceding clauses explains what Aśoka understands by *kalyāṇa*. The same thing is doubtless intended where he uses the word, as *e.g.* REs. V & XII, and PE. IV. In PE. VII (EE.), he uses *sādhava* as an equivalent of *kalyāṇa*.

[4] Compare this with the concluding portion of REs. V and VI. See *above*, pp. 247-9.

III

Translation

Thus saith king Priyadarśin, Beloved of the gods: "(A person) seeth the good deed only, (saying unto himself:) 'This good deed has been done by me.'[1] In no wise[2] doth he see (his) sin, (saying unto himself:) 'this sin have I committed,' or 'this, indeed, is a depravity.' But this certainly is difficult[3] to scrutinise. Nevertheless, it should certainly be looked into thus: 'these (passions), indeed, lead to depravity, such as violence, cruelty, anger, conceit, envy and by reason thereof may I not cause my fall.'[4] This should certainly be seen to—'this is to my good for this world, and this again[5] to my good for the next world.'

Notes

[1] Compare this to the initial portion of RE. N.

[2] *No mina=no manāk*, 'not in the least, in no wise'—Bühler.

[3] *Paṭiveka*, as pointed out by Senart, is the same as the Pāli *pachchavekkhanam*, 'self-examination'. He refers to a passage from the *Visuddhimagga*, quoted by Childers *sub voce*. *above*, pp. 95 and ff.

[4] Senart takes *isyā* separately from *māne*, and joins it to *kālanena* which follows it. But this proposal, says Bühler rightly, is barred by the fact that all versions have breaks between the two words. The root in *palibhasa-*

yisaṃ is *paḷibhāsati*, 'to calumniate,' 'to defame'—Senart. Bühler takes it as equivalent to *paribhraṃśayishyāmi*, which is better.

[5] Michelson translates *mana* by 'also.' It is, however, better to take *idaṃmana* with Hult. as equivalent to *idam-anyat*. But I translate it differently.

IV

Translation

Thus saith king Priyadarśin, Beloved of the gods : This *Dhaṃmalipi* was caused to be written by me when I had been consecrated twenty-six years. The Rājūkas have been set[1] by me over people (consisting of) many hundred thousands of souls. Any reward or punishment by them has been placed by me under their sole control[2]—why?—in order that the Rājūkas may perform their duties with confidence and without fear, cause welfare and happiness to the people of the provinces and confer favours (upon them). They will make themselves acquainted with what gives happiness or pain, and exhort the people of the provinces as well as those devoted to Dhaṃma[3]—how?—so that they may gain the here and the hereafter. The Rājūkas are eager to obey me.[4] And just because the Rājūkas desire to obey me, Purushas also will obey my wishes and orders,[5] and will also exhort some (people). Certainly, just as (a person) feels confident after making over his offspring to a clever nurse, (saying unto himself) 'the clever nurse desire to bring up my offspring,' even so have I appointed the Rājūkaṣ for the welfare and happiness of the provincials. In order that they may perform their duties without fear, with confidence, and without perplexity,—for this (reason) any reward or punishment by the Rājūkas has been placed by me under their sole control. For this is desirable,—what?—uniformity of administration and uniformity of punishment. And even so far goes my order; to men who are bound with fetters, on whom sentence has been passed and who have been condemned to death, have I granted three days as something rightfully and exclusively their own.[6] (In that interval) (their) relatives will indeed propitiate some (of the Rājūkaṣ) in order to grant their life; and to propitiate Deatḥ; they (*i.e.*, the convicts) will give alms and observe fasts pertaining to the next world.[7] For my desire is that even when the time (for their living) has expired,[8] they may win the next world and that manifold pious practices, self-restraint and liberality may thus grow among the people.

Notes.

[1] The word *āyata* occurs also in PE. VII (N.) and SEI. (D). Senart seems right in recognising here an

instance of the popular confusion between *āyatta* and *āyutta*. 'Caring for, occupied with'—Lüders.

[2] *Atapatiye*=*ātmapatiya* (Lüders). *Abhihāra* means 'honour, honorarium' according to Bühler, who refers us to Jat., Vol. V, p. 58, v. 143 and p. 59. l. 28f., where the commentary explains the word by *pūjā*. Senart has no doubt shown that we have further on in this edict a direct parallelism between *abhihāla* and *daṃḍa* on the one side and *viyohāla-samatā* and *daṃḍa-samatā*, on the other. But *abhihāra* need not be here exactly equivalent to *vyavahāra*. It is enough if *vyavahāra* is more extensive than *abhihāra* and is thus understood in the sense of the general administration of a district committed to the charge of the Rājūkas. *Above*, pp. 53-54. *Asvatha* is from *āśvas*, for a note on which by F. W. Thomas, see JRAS., 1915, pp. 106 and ff.

[3] *Dhaṃmayutena cha viyovadisaṃti janaṃ jānapadaṃ* of this Edict may be compared to *hevaṃ cha hevaṃ cha paliyovadātha janam dhaṃmayutaṃ* of PE. VII (N). This shows that *dhaṃmayutena* of the former cannot be taken to mean "in accordance with the principles of the sacred law" (Bühler), but rather "at the same time as the faithful" (Senart). *Dhaṃmayuta* cannot here be "taken as the name of some officials," as proposed by Michelson (JAOS., 46, 261). See my n. 3 on p. 273.

[4] Senart corrects *laghaṃti* into *chaghaṃti*. This is inadmissible, because all the versions have *laghaṃti*. Bühler takes *laghaṃti* to be the representative of Sk. *raghaṃte*, 'they hasten, are eager.' Senart is, however, right in taking *paṭichalati* as *paricharati*, meaning 'to serve, obey.' Compare *paribhogāya* of Girnār with *paṭibhogāya* of other recensions at the end of RE. II.

[5] *Chhaṃdaṃnāni* Bühler takes as a Tatpurusha com-

pound going with *pulisāni* and signifying *chhaṃdaṃ jānāt=īti chhaṃdajñaḥ*, 'knowing the will.' Senart explains it as a Dvandva compound: *chhaṃdaś=cha ājñā cha*, and takes it as the accusative of *paṭichalisaṃti*. Bühler objects to this interpretation on the ground that there is no instance of any feminine *ā* being declined as a neuter *a*. But we know that in the language of our inscriptions there is a great confusion of genders. In the Rūpnāth MRE. we have *kāla* declined as if the word was *kālā*. This is a very clear instance, but it is only one instance, where masculine *a* is declined like feminine *ā*. Similarly, in many edicts we meet with the expression *etāye aṭhaye*. Why not suppose similarly that in PE. IV we have an instance, though it is only one instance, where feminine *ā* is declined like neuter *a*. Again, *chhaṃdaṃnāni* is separated from *pulisāni* in all recensions, but is joined to *paṭichalisaṃti* at least in one recension. This shows that *chhaṃdaṃnāni* goes rather with *paṭichalisaṃti* as its accusative than with *pulisāni* as its adjective. The meaning also is quite clear, if we accept Senart's procedure. If Rājūkas, who are functionaries of a very high order, obey Aśoka, the Purushas or minor officials must follow in their footsteps. Bühler, however, would lead us to suppose that the Purushas, though they are minor officials, are to be an example for the Rājūkas to imitate. This is also what Hultzsch apparently means, though his translation is anything but clear and intelligible. Mookerji follows Hultzsch in his translation, but explains in a note that Purushas of a rank higher than the Rājūkas are here intended and were to exhort the remiss among them to duty. If there is such a distrust in Aśoka's mind about the Rājūkas, one wonders what he means by saying that he feels confident by entrusting the provincials to the care of the Rājūkas just as a man feels confident by handing over his child to an expert nurse. But if he has such a high opinion of them as is quite unmistakable from his words, the passage must be interpreted in exactly the opposite manner so as to show that the Rājūkas were an example to the Purusha and not *vice versa*. Secondly, the Purushas are here referred to in a general manner; and if we take into consideration the fact that according to PE. VII, the Rājūkas ruled over a much larger population than the Purushas, the latter appear to be inferior in rank to the former. How therefore Mookerji gets hold of Purushas of a rank higher than that of the Rājūkas is far from clear.

Senart takes *chaghati* as standing for *chagghati* and as alteration of *jāgrati*, like *pati-jaggati*, 'to take care, watch.' Grierson derives it from a root *chagh* 'to rise, ascend,' found in the Chhattisgarhi dialect and traces it to the Sanskrit *chargh* 'to go' (JPTS., 1891-3, pp. 28 and ff.). Kern explains the verb *chagh* by the Hindi *chā-nā*, and Bühler agrees in this view and adds that *chāh* occurs in all Indian vernaculars and must therefore belong to the ancient stock of Aryan speech.

6 *Yote* Kern rightly connects with the Sanskrit *Yautaka*, and is taken by European scholars in the sense of 'respite.' But *Yautaka* does not mean 'respite' but 'something exclusively and rightfully belonging to a person. This sense is by no means inapplicable here. What Aśoka means is that such culprits as have been sentenced to death can claim three days of grace as a matter of right.

7 This is the most knotty passage in the edict. Senart:—*Nātikāvakāni* = *na* + *atika* + *avakāni*(= *avvakāni* = *alpakāni*) = "neither more nor less." Bühler:—*nātikā va kāni* = *jñātikā eva kāni*(*chit*) = "(their) relatives (will make) some of them." Bühler's reading out of these

letters is better and has now been accepted. As regards *nijhapayisaṃti*, Lüders has drawn our attention to the word occurring in a verse in the Ayoghara-Jātaka (*Jat.*, Vol. IV, p. 495, v. 334), which has the sense of 'to soften, propitiate.' This point has been lucidly expatiated upon by Barua (IHQ., 1926, p. 125), and it will be seen that this sense really comes out of that explained for the word on p. 280 above. Further it is worthy of note that in this Jātaka *nijjhapana* is predicated not only of the king but also of Mṛityu or death. This fits here also, with just a small difference. For, instead of the king, we have here the Rājūkas. Mṛityu may easily be recognised in the word *nāsaṃta*=*nāś-ānta*=' (One) whose nature or disposition (*anta*) is destruction (*nāśa*).' Anta in this sense is too well-known to require any explanation. There will thus be a two-fold propitiation according to Aśoka: (1) propitiation of the Rājūkas by the relatives of the convicts by adducing proofs of their innocence, and (2) the propitiation of Death by the convicts themselves. Lüders, however, takes *nāsamtam*= 'not being, there being none,' as the nom. sing. *absol.* of the pres. part. of *nāthi*. As regards *nijhapayitā* of some copies, Bühler has rightly equated it with *nijhapayitave* of others, and explained its formation by saying that *tā* is a short form of *tāya* (compare *esanā* with *esanāya*).

[8] *Niludhasi pi kālasi* is taken by Senart as 'during the time of their imprisonment'; Bühler 'even during their imprisonment': Lüders 'even in a limited time'; and Thomas 'though their hour of death is irrevocably fixed (there being no *nijhati*)' (JRAS., 1916, p. 123); Hultzsch 'even when the time (of respite) has expired.' *Niruddha* is taken by Hultzsch in the sense of 'expired,' and he refers us to Childers' Dictionary. This is alright, but the *kāla* does not seem to be 'the time (of respite).'

It had rather be taken in the sense of *Jīvana-kāla.* What Aśoka means is that even when the time for their living has expired,—they should seek the hereafter during the extension of this time by means of *yauta.*

V

Translation

Thus saith king Priyadarśin, Beloved of the gods: When I had been consecrated twenty-six years, the following species[1] were declared exempt from slaughter, namely, parrots, *mainas*, ruddy geese, [2] swans, *Nandimukhas*,[3] *Gelāṭas*, flying-foxes, queen-ants, female tortoises, boneless fish, *vedaveyakas*, *Gaṅgā-papuṭakas*, skates, tortoises and porcupines, hare-like squirrels, twelve-antler stags, bulls set free, household vermins, rhinoceros, gray doves, village pigeons, and all quadrupeds which are neither used nor eaten.[4] She-goats, ewes, and sows, which are with young or in milk, are unworthy of slaughter, and those of their young ones up to six months of age. Cocks shall not be caponed. Husks containing living things shall not be burnt. Forests shall not be set on fire for mischief or injury (to life). The living shall not be fed with the living. About the three Chāturmāsīs [5] and the Tishyā full-moon days fish may neither be killed nor sold during three days, namely, the fourteenth (and) fifteenth (of the fortnight) and the first (of the following fortnight), and invariably on fast days. On the same days these and other species of life also shall not be killed in the elephant forest and fishermen's preserve. On the eighth of (each) fortnight and on the fourteenth and fifteenth, on the Tishyā and Punarvasu days, on the full-moon days of the three seasons,—on (such) auspicious days, bulls shall not be castrated: he-goats, rams, boars and such others as are castrated shall not be castrated. On the Tishyā and Punarvasu days, on the Chāturmāsīs and during the fortnights connected with the Chāturmāsīs, the branding of horses and oxen shall not be done. Twenty-five jail deliveries have been effected by me, who am consecrated twenty-six years, just in this period.

Notes

[1] *Jāta* literally means 'a born being.' Here it stands for 'species,' or 'classes' of creatures.

[2] *Aluna* has been taken as a separate name. It had better be taken as an attribute of *chakavāke* so as to distinguish the ruddy geese from the *haṃsas* which are wild geese.

[3] In connection with the different species of life mentioned in this edict, Monomohan Chakravarti's monograph on *Animals in the Inscriptions of Piyadasi*, published as *Memoir* of the As. Soc. Bengal, Vol. I, No. 17, may be read with great profit. *Nandīmukha* occurs, as

pointed out by Barua, in the *Praśna-vyākaraṇa-sūtra*, I, 7, where it is explained by the commentator as *sārikā-viśeshaḥ*. What is worthy of note is that Aśoka lays an embargo on the slaughter of those animals only that are neither eaten nor used for any purpose. Hence *jatūkā* should be taken to stand for 'flying-foxes' (Bengali, *chāmchikā*) whose flesh is not taken, and not for bats (Bengali, *bāduḍ*) whose flesh is eaten at least by the lower classes. Bühler has rightly interpreted *ambā-kapīlikā* as mother-ant, *i.e.*, queen-ant, the Sanskrit *pipīlikā* having the Pali form *kipilika*. *Daḍi*=(Sk.) *duḍī*=particular type of female tortoise, *Anaṭhika*=*anasthika*=' boneless, the boneless fish being 'prawns' according to Senart and Bühler. *Saṃkuja-machhe* lit. means the fish that can contract or withdraw itself in, and has therefore been taken to stand for 'skate fish.' *Kaphaṭa*=*kamaṭha*=tortoise (Senart). *Seyaka*=(Sk.) *salyaka*=porcupine. *Paṃnasasa* lit. means a hare-like animal living in the leaves of trees, and has been taken by Bühler to denote the large white-bellied red-squirrel which is found in the forests of the Western Ghats and whose skinned body looks exactly like that of a hare. *Simale*=*Sṛimara*=*Bārashing* or twelve-antler stag. *Saṁḍake* corresponds to the vernacular *sāṇḍ*, 'a bull which has been set at liberty and cannot therefore be killed.' *Okapiṃḍa* Senart connects with the *ukapiṇḍa* of the Mahāvagga which are said to eat the provisions of the monks and are, according to Budhaghosha, 'cats, mice, iguanas and mungooses.' This fits excellently, because these animals are neither eaten nor utilised for any other purposes. Hence they should not be killed simply because they destroy household provisions. *Pālasate* =(Pāli) *palāsādo* or *parasato*=rhinoceros (Bühler). *Above*, pp. 161 and ff.

[4] *Paṭibhoga* is, of course, *paribhaga* 'enjoyment' as

contrasted with 'nourishment.' Aśoka here evidently "means to forbid the slaughter of all animals, whose skins, fur, feathers, etc., are not required, as well as of those which are not eaten." *Above*, pp. 135.

[5] *Chātuṃmāsi* (=Sk. *chāturmāsī*) is the particular full moon of each one of the three seasons: Summer, autumn and winter, each consisting of four months. It is the full moon of the initial month of each season. *Tisā puṃnamāsī* is the full-moon of Taisha or Pausha. Posatha stands midway between the Buddhist Pāli *uposatha* and the Jaina Prākrit *posaha*. It corresponds to the Brahmanical Parvan days, and denotes the 8th and 15th day of each fortnight. As shown by Bühler, Piyadasi thus forbade the sale of fish on 56 days: (1) six in each initial month of the three seasons and in the Taisha or Pausha month, *viz.*, the 8th, 14th and 15th of the bright fortnight and the 1st, 8th and 15th of the dark,—thus in all 24; (2) four in the remaining eight months, *viz.*, the 8th and 15th of each fortnight,—thus 32 in all. The whole total comes to 24 + 32 = 56 days, on which Aśoka prohibited the killing and sale of fish.

[6] Various are the occasions on which jail deliveries are made by kings. One such occasion is the birthday of a king when, the Arthaśāstra (p. 146) lays down, he shall set free such prisoners as are children or aged, diseased or helpless persons. This fits here admirably, first because this edict, which is intended for the prevention not of wholesale slaughter but of wanton and unnecessary butchery and injury, cannot be taken to refer to the wholesale or promiscuous liberation of prisoners but of such prisoners only, in whose case imprisonment would be a wanton and unnecessary cruelty. Secondly, as, during twenty-six years no less than twenty-five jail deliveries were effected, they most probably refer to the setting free of prisoners on

Aśoka's birthday and further show that the regnal years mentioned in his inscriptions must be, not elapsed, but current, years of his reign. (*Above*, p. 9.)

VI

Translation

Thus saith king Priyadarśin, Beloved of the gods: "Since I was consecrated twelve years, I have caused *Dhaṃma-lipis* to be written for the welfare and happiness of the people, so that without violation thereof,[1] they might attain to this and that growth of Dhaṃma. (Perceiving): 'thus (lies) the welfare and happiness of the people,' I scrutinise[2] whether, as among (my) relatives, so among those who are far and near, —what ?—whether I cause happiness to them; and I act accordingly. Thus do I scrutinise about all congregations. All sects I have honoured with various honours; but voluntary advances[3] (to a sect) are considered by me as the chief thing. This *Dhaṃma-lipi* has been caused to be written by me when crowned twenty-six years."

Notes

[1] *Apahaṭa* = *a* + *prahitvā* = (Sk. *a-prahṛitya*) = "not injuring, not violating"—Franke (VOJ., IX. 344, n. 2); *tam* refers, of course, to *hita-sukha* which precedes it. The *Dhaṃmalipis*, says Asoka, were promulgated in order that both the temporal and spiritual welfare of the people may

be promoted. For *pāpāva*, see H. K. De in JPASB., 1920, pp. 336-7. Michelson, however, dissents from this view (JAOS., 46, 262).

[2] The meaning of the root *paṭivekh* is determined by *paṭivekhā* which occurs in PE. III. What Aśoka says is that he always scrutinises whether he is causing happiness to the people who are far and near as he does to his own relatives.

[3] Hultzsch translates the passage thus: "But this is considered by me (my) principal (duty), *viz.*, visiting (the people) personally." But *pachupagamana*=*pratyupagamana*='advancing towards to meet or greet.' And if we compare this part with the gist of RE. XII, *pachupagamana* seems to correspond to *añamañasa dhramo śruṇeyu*, &c.

VII

Translation

Thus saith king Priyadarśin, Beloved of the gods: "Those who were kings in times past wished thus: 'how may men grow with the growth of Dhaṃma?' But men did not grow with a befitting growth of Dhaṃma. On this king Priyadarśin, Beloved of the gods, saith thus: 'This occurred to me: in times past kings had wished that men should grow with a befitting growth of Dhaṃma. But men did not grow with befitting growth of Dhaṃma. How then may men be moved to conform (to Dhaṃma)? How may men grow with a befitting growth of Dhaṃma? How may I uplift them with a growth of Dhaṃma?" On this king Priyadarśin, Beloved of the gods, saith thus: "This occurred to me: 'Proclamations of Dhaṃma will I proclaim. Instructions in Dhaṃma will I instruct. Men, hearkening thereto, will conform (to it), will be uplifted, and will grow with the growth of Dhaṃma.' For this purpose have I proclaimed proclamations of Dhaṃma and directed various instructions in Dhaṃma. My Purushas have been set over many people. These will preach and disseminate it. Rājūkas have been set over many hundred thousands of lives. They too have been ordered: 'Preach thus and thus to those devoted to Dhaṃma'."

Thus saith Priyadarśin, Beloved of the gods: "This same thing being considered, I have set up Pillars of Dhaṃma,[1] appointed Dharma-mahāmātras, (and) caused discourses on Dhaṃma to be heard."

Thus saith Priyadarśin, Beloved of the gods: "On the roads have I planted the banyan trees. They will offer shade to man and beast. I have grown mango-orchards. I have caused wells to be dug at every eight koses;[2] and I have had rest-houses. I have made many watering sheds at different places for the enjoyment of man and beast. This (provision of) enjoyment, however, is, indeed, a trifle, because mankind has been blessed with many such blessings by the previous kings as by me. But I have done this with this intent, namely, that (they) may practise (such) practices of Dhaṃma.[3] "

Thus saith Priyadarśin, Beloved of the gods: "Those Dharma-Mahāmātras of mine have been occupied [4] in various matters of grace, with the ascetics and with the householders. They are also occupied with all sects. I have arranged that they shall be occupied with the affairs of the Saṃgha. Likewise, I have arranged that they shall be occupied with the Brāhmanic Ājīvikas, the Nirgranthas, and the various sects.[5] The various Mahāmātras are for various (affairs) and for various specific (classes of men). But my Dharma-Mahāmātras are occupied only with these and all other sects." Thus saith king Priyadarśin, Beloved of the gods: "These and many other head officers[6] are employed in the distribution of charity both my own and those of the Queens, and in all my gynaeceum. Both here and in the provinces, they are making various abodes of the contented[7] in manifold ways. And I have arranged that they shall be occupied with the distribution of charity, both of my sons and of other Queens' sons."

[Thus saith king Priyadarśin, Beloved of the gods: "I have also caused discourses on Dhaṃma to be heard[8]] for the development of Dhaṃma and for conformity to Dhaṃma. And this development of Dhaṃma and conformity to Dhaṃma, which consist of mercy, liberality, truthfulness, purity, gentleness and good deeds will thus grow in the world (*loka*)." Thus saith king Priyadarśin, Beloved of the gods: "Whatever good deeds I have performed, these have been conformed to in the world; and these (they) will perform (in future). They have thereby grown and will grow in respect of hearkening to father and mother, hearkening to preceptors, following in the footsteps of the aged, and seemly behaviour towards Brāhmaṇs and Śramaṇas, towards the poor and the wretched, and even towards slaves and servants."

Thus saith king Priyadarśin, Beloved of the gods: "And men (*munisā*) have grown this growth of Dhaṃma in two ways, namely, through restriction of Dhaṃma and exhortation.[9] And in this matter restrictions of Dhaṃma are of small account, and much more has been done through exhortation. The restrictions of Dhaṃma, indeed, are such as have been adopted by me, namely, that 'such and such species (of creatures) shall be exempt from slaughter,' and numerous other restrictions of Dhaṃma effected by me. But through exhortation such as non-injury to (all) creatures and non-slaughter of (all) life, the growth of Dhaṃma has been fostered much more among men.

For this purpose has this been engraved, in order that my sons, great-grandsons, etc., may continue as long as the sun and the moon endure[10] and in this way follow (in my footsteps). By thus following, both this world and the next are attained. This *Dhaṃma-lipi* was caused to be engraved by me when I had been anointed twenty-seven years.

Concerning this the Beloved of the gods saith: this *Dhaṃma-lipi* should be inscribed where stone pillars and stone tablets are found, so that it may long endure.

Notes

[1] What Aśoka says is that in order that there may be a growth of Dhaṃma, he has resorted to the following means: (1) erection of Dharma-stambhas, (2) appointment of Dharma-Mahāmātras, and (3) preaching of Dhaṃma. In Section EE and ff., Aśoka explains what sort of Dhaṃma he proclaimed, that is, what qualities and what practices go to make up that Dhaṃma. In the para. preceding it, that is, in Section Y-DD, he tells us for what different purposes he has appointed the Dharma-Mahāmātras. In the sections preceding these last, that is, in Sections R-W, he gives an account of his charitable works, such as growing of mango-orchards and so forth. It is difficult to avoid the conclusion that it is these charities that are indicated by the word *dhaṃma-stambha*, which therefore here stands not for any material pillars, but rather spiritual columns. That these humanitarian works were considered to be of much spiritual efficiency is clear from the quotation given above (p. 131)

from the *Saṃ-N*. If this line of reasoning is not accepted, the enumeration of charities in this connection becomes unmeaning and irrelevant. Besides the mention of *dhamma-stambhas* alone remains unexplained, when the other two items are so fully explained. See also above, p. 131, n. 1.

[2] For *aḍhakosikyāni*, see Fleet's note in JRAS., 1906, p. 401 and ff. For the occasional change of *ṭh* to *ḍh*, compare *aṃbā-vāḍikyā* preceding it in this Edict. See also my n. 2 on Rummindēī inscription. For *niṃsiḍhiyā*, see Bühler EI., II. 274 and Fleet JRAS., 1906, pp. 404-5. Hultzsch, following Lüders, takes the word to mean 'a flight of steps,' but does not derive it like the latter from the Skt. *niśrayaṇī* but rather from *niślishṭakā*.

[3] The subject of *anupaṭipajaṃtu* is Aśoka's descendants understood. Compare the same word occurring in l. 31 (OO) below. Philologically *etadathā me*=*etad-yathā me* (Michelson). But this does not yield any sense, as the meanings of *iti*, *etad* and *yathā* cannot be brought out. It is best to take it as equivalent to *etad-arthāya*. It is one dot that changes *ṭha* into *tha*, and it seems that this dot has been inadvertently engraved.

[4] Note that *viyāpaṭāse* which occurs thrice in this inscription has the Vedic nominative plural termination -*āsaḥ*, as was pointed out by Franke (VOJ., IX. 349 f.).

[5] It is worthy of note that here we have three clauses, each giving the name of one sect. The expression *Bābhanesu Ājīvikesu* is in perfect agreement with this, because there is no *cha* which would certainly have been put in here if *Bābhanas* were really intended to be separate from Ājīvikas. There is thus no other help but to take this expression to mean 'Brāhmaṇic Ājīvikas.' That the Ājīvikas were not simply Śramaṇic, but also Brāhmaṇic, has been pointed out *above*, pp. 155-6. It seems that

Ājīvika was a general term and could be used to denote any sect, Brāhmaṇic or Śramaṇic. Thus the Nirgranthas have actually been called Ājīvakas in the Buddhist work, (*Divyāvadāna*, p. 247). Similarly, they were known as Buddhist Bhikshus to the Digambara Jainas (IA., XLI. 89). And Utpala, in his commentary on Varāhamihira's *Bṛihajjātaka*, takes Ājīvaka to mean by *upalakshaṇa* 'devotees of Nārāyaṇa' (*ibid.*, 1912, p. 287 f.). There were thus different sects of Ājīvikas, and by inserting *Bābhanesu* Aśoka tells us that it was the Brahmanical Ājīvikas whom he had in view.

B. M. Barua says "*babhanesu ājīvikesu* is grammatically the same expression as *bābhana-ājīvikesu*." I am afraid no grammarian can agree with him. *Bābhan-ājīvikesu* is a *dvandva* compound like *bhābana-samanesu* occurring in Section HH of this edict. But there is no *cha* between *bābhanesu* and *ājīvikesu*. We thus cannot but interpret the first expression to mean "among Brahmanical Ājīvikas" and not "among Brāhmaṇs and Ājīvikas" as he takes it.

6 *Mukha* is taken by Senart in the sense of 'intermediaries' and by Bühler 'chief officials.' F. W. Thomas draws our attention to the various places in which the terms *mukha* or *mukhya* occurs in Kauṭalya's Arthaśāstra (JRAS., 1915, pp. 97-9), and takes *bahukā mukhā* of this edict to denote either 'many departments' or 'many different officials.' In the first place, it is worthy of note that as pointed out by Michelson, *mukha* here does not stand for *mukhya*, *khya* being unassimilable in the dialect of the PEs.; see same word, *e.g.* in PE. VI. Secondly, Thomas's quototion (3) from the Arthaśāstra and also the one from the *Yājñavalkya-smṛiti* show clearly that *mukha* can also signify 'head official,' which suits here very well.

[7] Bühler takes *tuṭhāyatanāni*=*tushṭy-āyatanāni*= 'sources of contentment,' 'opportunities for charity.' Hultzsch takes *āyatana* in the sense of *pātra* and renders the expression by 'worthy recipients of charity.' *Tuṭhāyatanāni* ought really to mean 'the places or abodes (*āyatana*) of the contented (*tushṭa*).' By the distribution of charity by Dharma-Mahāmātras, many houses have become 'places of the contented.'

[8] *Dhaṃmāpadānaṭhāye* &c. has been tacked on to the preceding *hohaṃti-ti* by previous translators. This is the fourth time we have here this last phrase. In the previous three cases *hohaṃti-ti* ends a clause or sentence. And there is no reason why this *hohaṃti-ti* also should not be taken as ending a sentence. Obviously some words after it seem to have been inadvertently omitted. In the portion missing between *hohaṃti-ti* and *dhaṃmāpadānaṭhāye* &c., Aśoka is telling us what he means by *dhaṃmasāvaṇe kaṭe*, occurring in P. of Hultzsch's transcript. The lacuna may therefore be perhaps filled up as follows: [*Devānaṃ-piye Piyadasi hevaṃ-āhā* (:) *dhaṃmasāvaṇe-pi me kaṭe*] *dhaṃmāpadānaṭhāye* &c. &c. The filling up of the lacuna in some such way can alone make the sense whole, continuous and clear.

[9] It will be seen from n. 3 on RE. V that *nijhati* means 'making a matter intelligible by placing facts and reasons.' This may be done with a view to making a man relent (n. 7 on PE. IV) or make him lead a good life (n. 6 on RE. XIII). *Nijhati* thus seems to mean here 'moral exhortation'=*dhaṃmānusathi*.

[10] Hultzsch translates the passage as follows: "Now for the following purposes has this been ordered, that it may last as long as (my) sons and great-grandsons (shall reign and) as long as the moon and the sun (shall shine),

OTHER ROCK INSCRIPTIONS

A.—SEPARATE KALIÑGA EDICTS

Translation

I

By command of the Beloved of the gods, the Mahāmātras of Tosali (or Samāpā) who are the city Judiciaries should be addressed thus: Whatever I perceive (with the mind), I desire—what?—that I may put it into action; and I initiate it through the (proper) means. And I deem this to be the principal means to the end, namely, instructions to you. You have indeed been set over many thousands of lives in order that you may certainly[1] gain the affection of men. All men are my offspring. Just as for (my) offspring I desire that they be united with all welfare and happiness of this world and of the next, precisely do I desire it for all men. But you do not understand as much as this thing indicates. Some individual official[2] regards it, but he is a part only, not the whole. See to this then. The maxim of conduct[3] also is well established. There is just one individual who incurs harassment or imprisonment. There it causelessly develops thereby into imprisonment or death.[4] Many other people more distant also suffer. Consequently you should desire—what?—that you may follow the middle path. No one can act properly with such dispositions as envy, want of perseverance, cruelty, hastiness, want of application, laziness, and weariness. Hence you should desire—what?—that these dispositions may not be yours. And the root of all this is perseverance and avoidance of hastiness. This is the maxim of conduct: namely, 'He who is wearied will not rise. But one ought to move, proceed and advance.' This is the maxim of conduct which you should consider.[5] Say then (unto yourselves, and) look to nothing else:[6] "Thus and thus are the instructions of the Beloved of the gods." Fulfilment of it bears great fruit, non-fulfilment, great harm. If this is not fulfilled, there is neither attainment of heaven, nor propitiation of the king. Why?—because zealousness of mind in this my work has a two-fold consequence.[7] If it is well performed, you will gain heaven and also discharge your debt to me.

And this document should be heard under the constellation of Tishya, and on every festive occasion in between the Tishya days it may be heard even by one (official).[8] And acting thus, you should endeavour to fulfil this duty. For this purpose has this document been here written: in order that the Mahāmātras who are the city Judiciaries may be devoted to the eternal rule of conduct,[9] and that causeless imprisonment or causeless harassment of the townspeople may not take place. And for this purpose, I shall cause a Mahāmātra to go forth on tour every five years,[10] who will be neither harsh nor fiery (but) gentle in action, so that being aware of this object (the city Judiciaries) will act according to my instructions. But from Ujjain the royal prince will send forth this class of officers and will not overstep three years. In like manner from Takshaśilā. When those Mahāmātras go forth on tour, without neglecting their own function, they will mind this also, namely, whether (the city) Judiciaries are acting according to the instructions of the king.

Notes

[1] Lüders is right in separating *su* from *munisānaṃ* and explaining it by the Sk. *svit*. The very next sentence shows that Aśoka is here speaking, not of 'good men,' but of 'men in general.'

[2] *Purusha* signifies both 'an official' and 'a man.' Here in both the versions we have *eka-pulise*. Immediately after this the same word occurs in the Dh. copy of this edict, for which the Jaug. version substitutes *eka-munise*. In the second instance *purusha* obviously means 'a man,' but in the first, 'an official.'

[3] Hult. reads *nītiyaṃ*, whereas Sen. and Büh. read *nitiyaṃ*. The latter reading is more correct. Secondly, he separates this word from *suvihittāpi* and tacks it on to what follows. He wrongly takes *nitiyam* = Sk. *nityaṃ* and with Lüd. rightly understands it as = *daṇḍa-nīti*. This term however denotes 'science of polity,' 'policy' or even 'a maxim of polity,' but not 'the administration (of justice,)' as he has done. Similarly, Hult. reads *dekhata hi tuphe*

etam suvihitā pi as one sentence, and translates it by "now you must pay attention to this, although you are well provided for." Mookerji follows him here also. But as none of them gives any explanation, their translation is anything but intelligible. See n. 5 below.

4 Hult. following Lüd. renders the passage as follows: "In this case (an order) cancelling the imprisonment is (obtained) by him accidentally, while (many) other people continue to suffer." But this whole edict should be compared to RE. V, and this passage in particular to (L) of Hult.'s transcript of the K. recension of this last edict. What Aśoka apparently means is that when an individual is harassed or imprisoned, (1) that harassment may causelessly develop into imprisonment, or (2) imprisonment into death. In the first case which is one of *katābhikāre*, *aparibodha* is required; and in the second which is of *mahālaka*, *mokha* is desirable, as recommended in RE. V (see p. 276). *Daviye*=Sk. *daviyas*, comparative of *dūra*. The more distant people who suffer must be the relatives of the convicts.

5 Jaug. has *nītiyam e ve dakheyā*. *E ve* corresponds of course to *yā vo*. Hult. joins the two together, but does not explain what *eve* stands for. If it stands for *eva*, we should have had *yeva* or *va*, and if for *evaṃ*, *hevaṃ*, as required by the dialect represented in Dh. and Jau. edicts. So the above expression=Sk. *nītir=iyam yā vo drakshavya*. *Nīti* here as above must denote 'a maxim of conduct' laid down by the science of polity. See n. 3 above.

6 Bühler reads *(aṃ) naṃ ne dekhata=anyad no paśyata*, whereas Hult. reads *ānaṃne dekhata*. The latter takes *ānaṃne=ānṛiyam*, and translates the expression by "See that (you) discharge the debt (which you owe to the king)." In this connection he refers us to Section U of his transcript, which has [*a*]*naniyam ehatha*. The equation of *ānaniyaṃ* with *ānṛiṇyaṃ* is intelligible in the case

of the Dh.-Jaug. dialect. The word occurs in that form also in the Dh.-Jaug. versions of RE, VI. But *ānaṃne* cannot be reasonably expected as a form of *ānṛiṇyaṃ* in any one of Dh. or Jaug. edicts. Besides, it is strange that in two almost consecutive sentences *ānṛiṇyaṃ* is written once as *ānaniyaṃ* and another time as *ānaṃne*. It is therefore best to split *ānaṃne* and equate it with *anyad ne*.

7 *Duāhale=dur+āhara=*" imperfect carrying-out" —Franke. Following Franke, Hult. translates the passage thus: " For how could my mind be pleased (*mane atileke*) if one badly fulfils (*duāhale*) this duty?" Woolner however rightly says that in that case we should have had *dulāhale*, not *duāhale*. It is best to take *duāhale* =*dv-āhara*, as done by Sen. and Buh. and in the sense of " procuring two (things)-" *Mane -atileke* I take as meaning 'exuberance of mind,' 'zeal.'

8 *Ekena pi=*' Even by a single (person),' Hult. But if we carefully study the contents of Sār. PE., we find that the king's edict was heard by the officials and the people separately. And as this edict is concerned with officials, *ekena pi* must here be 'even by one (official);' because from Sār. PE. it is clear that on the *uposatha* day there must be at least one official come back to the head-quarters from tour.

9 Following Kern and Lüd., Hult. translates *sasvataṃ samayaṃ yujevu* by " may strive at all times." But in the first place, *yuj* does not signify ' to strive.' Secondly, ' striving at all times ' is vague. On the other hand, as there are two *tis*, one after *yujevu* and the other after *siyā*, two distinct things are indicated by the two clauses. *Samaya* had therefore be better taken in the sense of established rule of conduct ' which here refers to the *nīti* maxim quoted above, *viz.* *e kilamte siyā &c.*

10 *Above*, pp. 62-5.

II

By command of the Beloved of the gods, the Prince Royal and the Mahāmātras at Tosalî should be addressed[1] (as follows): Whatever I perceive (with the mind), I desire—what—that I may put it into action; and I initiate it through the (proper) means. And I deem this to be the principal means to this end, namely, instructions to you. All men are my offspring. Just as for (my) offspring I desire that they may be united with all welfare and happiness of this world and of the next, precisely do I desire it for all men.

It may be[2] (in the mind) of (the people) the unconquered frontier sovereigns: 'what is the will of the king in respect of us?' This much alone is my wish in regard to (the people) of the frontier sovereigns, that they may understand (this), namely, that the beloved of the gods desires: 'they should be unperturbed towards me, they should trust mine, (and) they would receive from me happiness, not misery.' And they should further understand: 'the king will bear with us as far as it is possible to bear,' (but) they should follow Dhaṃma for my sake and gain this world and the next. For this end do I instruct you, namely, that having given you instructions and made known my will, nay, my immovable resolve and vow, may I be free from debt (to them)! So acting accordingly, you must discharge your functions and must inspire them with confidence, so that they might understand: 'the king is to us even as a father; he sympathises with us even as he sympathises with himself; we are to the king even as (his) children.' So having instructed you and intimated the will, my immovable resolve and vow, I shall become a sovereign over all countries [3] for this object; for you are competent to inspire them with confidence and (ensure) their welfare and happiness of this world and the next. By so doing, you will gain heaven and also discharge your debt to me.

And for this purpose has this document been here written: in order that the Mahāmātras may be devoted to the eternal rule of conduct [4] for inspiring (the people of) those frontier sovereigns with confidence and ensuring (their) practice of Dhaṃma. And this document should be heard on the Tishya day every four-monthly season; [5] and, indeed, on every festive occasion in between the Tishya days it may be heard even by one (official). By acting thus, endeavour to fulfil (my instructions).

Notes

[1] The Jaug. edict is addressed to the Mahāmātra Rājavachanikas of Samāpā. The actual wording is: *Samāpāyaṃ Mahamatā L[ā]javachanikā vataviyā*. This might be compared with the words: *Tosaliyaṃ (Samāpā-*

yaṃ) Mahāmātā Nagala-viyohālakā hebaṃ vataviyā with which the Dh. & Jaug. copies of SRE (Separate Rock Edict I) begin. It will be seen that *Mahāmatā Lāja-vachanikā* of the former corresponds to *Mahāmātā Nagala-viyohālakā* of the latter. *Naga-laviyohālaka* has been rightly translated by Hult. as 'the judicial officers of the city.' But *Lājavachanika* which should have denoted similar officers is translated by him as 'at the word of the king.' This is very strange. If *Nagala viyohālakā* represent the Judicial, *Lājavachanikā* had better be taken to represent the Executive Officers of a District town.

2 Hult. rightly follows the construction pointed out by Lüders. *Siyā* should thus be separated from what precedes it and tacked on to *aṃtānaṃ*.

3 *Desāvutike* is a knotty phrase and has exercised scholars. Senart: "I shall possess in you, for this object, persons fit to actively carry out my orders." Bühler: "I shall have superintendents in *all* countries as far as this matter is *concerned*." Hult.: "I shall have (*i.e.*, maintain) officers in all provinces for this object." It is worthy of note that Dh. has *desāvutika* and Jaug. [*saka*]*la-desā-āyutika*. Secondly, *āvuti* occurs in PE. IV in the sense of 'order.' The phrase therefore means: "One whose order (prevails) over all countries." There seems to be here a reference to his *dhaṃmavijaya* by means of which Aśoka aspired to be a Chakravartī Dharmarāja. This inscription apparently fills up the void created by the non-occurrence of RE. XIII at Dh. & Jaug.

4 See n. 9 of the preceding edict.

5 See n. 5 on PE. V.

B.—MINOR ROCK INSCRIPTIONS

Translation

I

BRAHMAGIRI

By command of the Prince Viceregent[1] and the Mahāmātras from Suvarṇagiri the Mahāmātras at Isila should be asked (their) health, and (then) addressed as follows: "The Beloved of gods saith: 'It is more than two years and a half that I am[2] a lay-worshipper. I did not exert myself strenuously for one year: but, indeed, more than one year that I have lived with the Saṃgha, I have exerted myself strenuously. During this period, however, men who were unmixed, were caused to be mixed, with gods throughout Jambudvīpa.[3] [R.—During this period gods, who were unmixed, were caused to be mixed (with men), throughout Jambudvīpa.] For this is the fruit of exertion. This is possible not only for the superior (official)[4] to achieve, but indeed it is possible for even a subordinate one, if he exerts himself, to cause (people) to attain much heavenly bliss. For this purpose this proclamation has been made; in order that the subordinate ones and the superior ones shall exert themselves to this (end), that my neighbours should know this and that this exertion may long endure. And this object shall grow, indeed shall grow profusely, shall grow (at least) one-and-half fold. And this discourse has been caused to be heard when there had elapsed [5] 256 (years)'. "

Sahasram

The discourse (was made) when there had elapsed 256 (years), that is, two hundred (years) increased by fifty-six had elapsed.[5] And have ye this matter engraved on rocks, and have it engraved also where there are stone columns.

Rupnath

Have this matter engraved on rocks. Here and far off where there is any stone column, have it engraved on the stone column. And with this verbal order go ye forth on tour everywhere so far as your jurisdiction extends. The discourse was made when there had elapsed 256 (years) by the passing of centuries.

Notes

1 For *Ayaputa* and Suvarṇagiri, see *above*, p. 49 ff.

2 It is worthy of note, as pointed out by Hultzsch, that the word *sumi* (= Sk. *asmi*) is found in three recensions along with *upāsaka*. This shows that till the time of the promulgation of this edict Aśoka had been a

lay-worshipper for more than two years and a half. Similarly, the word *sumi* occurs along with *sagh* [*a*] *up* [*e*] *te* further on. This also shows that up till the time when this edict was issued Aśoka had been associated with the Saṃgha for more than a year. This record thus distinguishes between two stages in Aśoka's religious life – one a stage of non-enthusiasm and inaction, the other a stage of fervent zeal and strenuous action, the first lasting for one year, the second for more than one year, but both in his career as Upāsaka. It will thus be seen, as correctly maintained by Hultzsch, that the period of two years and a half does not precede but includes the period of one year and more that the king was with the Saṃgha. It is unfortunate that this interpretation of Hultzsch, though it is of such paramount importance for the chronology of the edicts and the early religious history of Aśoka, has not been even so much as considered by either Barua (*Aśoka Edicts in New Light*, p. 89 ff.) or Mookerji (*Aśoka*, p. 108 ff.). For my criticism of their views, see ABORI:, Vol. X, pp. 246-52. For further elucidation of this subject, see *above*, p. 71 ff.

[3] What Aśoka means is that by leading men in the path of Dhaṃma they have become so virtuous that they were commingled with gods. Knowing as we do how people have believed that denizens of worlds other than their own can visit them, it is not unreasonable to suppose that those men of Jambudvīpa who followed Aśoka's Dhaṃma came to be looked upon as saintly souls and that either they believed themselves or people believed them to be waited upon by gods. Instances are not wanting from the Pali literature in support of the belief that gods associated themselves with virtuous men and saints while they lived in this world. This point has been discussed by me in detail in ABORI., Vol. X, pp. 254-8, and elucidated here, *above*, p. 122 f.

This passage bears a close resemblance to the second half of RE. X. Here we have (1) *svargasya ārādhanā* and (2) exhortation to the *mahātman* (=*udāra*) and *khudaka* (=*kshudraka*) to put forth *parākrama*. The first of these phrases has been paraphrased into *apaparisravatva* in RE. X., to achieve which object the same edict also recommends *parākrama* to the *kshudraka* and *usaṭa* (=*uchchrita*) *vargas*. The Separate Dhauli Edict I uses the word *vaga* in l. 23, where it cannot but denote 'the officials.' It thus seems that the *khudaka* and *mahātman* (*udāra* or *usaṭa*) referred to in MRE. I and RE. X must stand for the subordinate and superior classes of officials—and not the small and great people in general. For detailed explanation of this passage, see ABORI., Vol. X, pp. 258-62.

[5] IA., 1908, p. 21 and p. 341 ; 1912, pp. 171-3 JA., Mai-Juin, 1910 ; Jan.-Feb., 1911. JRAS., 1908, p. 817 ; 1910, pp. 142 and 1308 ; 1911, p. 1114 ; 1913, pp. 477 and 1053. *Vyushṭa* signifies generally 'the passing away' or 'elapsing' (of time) and in particular 'office or royal mode of reckoning time' (*Kauṭilīya*, p. 60). The figure 256 thus denotes a year, which, as Aśoka was a Buddhist, has to be reckoned from some event connected with Buddha, most probably the Nirvāṇa of Buddha which came off 21 years prior to his Parinirvāṇa or Death. For this interpretation see ABORI., Vol. X, pp. 262 & ff.

Bibliography

Bühler, G.—IA., 1893, pp. 209-306 ; 1897, p. 334. EI., Vol. III, pp. 135-42.

Sastri, H. Krishna—The New Aśokan Edict of Maski (Hyderabad Archaelogical Series, No. 1).

Hultzsch. E.—ZDMG., Vol. 70, pp. 539-41.

II

Translation

Even thus saith the Beloved of the gods: "Father and mother shall be hearkened to: Likewise, respect for living creatures shall be made firm. Truth should be spoken." These are the qualities of Dhaṃma which ought to be practised. Likewise, the preceptor shall be reverenced by the pupil; and one should behave oneself fittingly towards the blood-relatives. This is primeval nature; and this is long-enduring.[1] Hence it should be acted upon.

Written by Paḍa the scribe.

Note

[1] *Above*, pp. 158-9.

BHABRU INSCRIPTION

Translation

King Priyadarśin of Magadha, having saluted the Saṃgha,[1] wishes them good health and comfortable (bodily) movement. Ye know, Reverend Sirs, how great are my respect and kindliness towards Buddha, Dhaṃma, and Saṃgha. Whatever, Reverend Sirs, has been said by the Blessed Buddha—all that has been well said. But, Reverend Sirs, if I may point out (anything) in order that the sublime Dhaṃma may thus endure long.[2] I deem it proper to speak it out. Reverend Sirs, these are the text of Dhaṃma: (1) *Vinaya-samukasa*, (2) *Āliya-vaṃsas*, (3) *Anāgatabhayas*, (4) *Muni-gāthā*, (5) *Moneya sūta*, (6) *Upatisa-pasina*, and (7) the Sermon to Rāhula delivered by the Blessed Buddha concerning 'falsehood.'[3] These texts of Dhaṃma, Reverend Sirs, I desire the majority of monks and nuns to constantly listen to and meditate upon. The laymen and laywomen (should do) similarly. It is for this reason, Reverend Sirs, that I am causing this to be engraved: in order that they may know my wish.

Notes

[1] For the time when this edict was most probably issued and to what Saṃgha it was addressed, see *above*, p. 89 f.

[2] Hult. follows E. Hardy (JRAS., 1901, p. 341) in taking these words as a quotation from the Buddhist scriptures. This seems hardly likely, because this does not yield any good translation, and, as a matter of fact, the actual words of the edict have not yet been traced in any Buddhist scripture.

[3] *Above*, pp. 79-81; JRAS.. 1889, p. 639; 1898, p. 639 f.; 1901, pp. 311, 577; 1911, p. 1113; 1913, p. 385; 1915, p. 805; IA., 1891, p. 165; 1912, p. 37; 1919, p. 8; JA., (9), 7, p. 475 ff. Max Walieser, *Das Edikt von Bhabra (Materialien zur Kunde des Buddhismus)*; E. Leumann, *Das Bhabra-Edict des Königs Aśoka (Zeit. Indol. Iran.*, Oct. 2, 1923, pp. 316 and ff.)

MINOR PILLAR INSCRIPTIONS

RUMMINDEI (PADERIA INSCRIPTION)

Translation

King Priyadarśin, Beloved of the gods, when he had been consecrated twenty years, came in person and did worship.[1] Because here the Śākya Sage, Buddha, was born, he caused a huge stone wall[2] to be made and a stone pillar to be erected. Because here the Blessed One was born, the village of Lummini was freed from religious cesses and made to contribute one-eighth share (only, as land revenue).[3]

Notes

[1] *Above*, p. 71 and pp. 75 ff. See also the note following.

[2] The letters *silāvigaḍabhīchā* are being divided by scholars into most embarrassing words, but R. G. Bhandarkar was the first to show that this was really one phrase, meaning " an enclosure or railing made of stone " (JBBRAS., Vol. XX, p. 366, n. 14). Fleet substantially agrees with him (JRAS., 1908, pp. 476-7 and p. 823), but proposes the fantastic division of *silāvigaḍa* into *silā* + *avi* (enclosure, fence, wall) + *gaḍa* (screen), and translates the whole by "stone wall which is an enclosure and screen." Hult. divides it into *silā vigaḍabhī chā*, and renders it by 'a stone bearing a horse (?).' Nothing

can be more absurd. Because here *chā* is taken as a conjunction meaning 'and,' in spite of the fact that the correct form *cha* occurs not once, but twice, almost immediately after it. Besides there is a tendency of *ā* being shortened into *a*, in this inscription. Hence *cha* may stand for *chā*, but *chā* can never stand for *cha*. *Chā* after *bhī* cannot therefore be reasonably taken here as equivalent to *cha* 'and,' but must be taken along with the preceding letter to form one word. Personally I take the letter to stand for *silā-vigaḍa-bhīchā* (= *śilā-vikaṭa-or vikṛita-bhittāni*). The equation of *vigaḍa* with *vikaṭa* (or *vikṛita*) defies no phonetic laws, as feared by Michelson (JAOS., 46, 264). The substitution of the first for the fourth, and of the fourth for the first, letter of a class is not unknown to the Aśokan inscriptions. Thus while we have *vracha* for *vraja* (RE. VI and XII) and *kubhā* for *guhā* (Cave Edict), we have *libi* for *lipi* twice at the end of PE. VII, *hidalogika* for *hidalokika* in Sec. F of Jaug. SRE. II, and *aḍhigichya* for *adhikichcha* in the Bhabrū Edict (see also n. 2 on PE. VII). Then again *bhīchā* stands for *bhittāni*, and not necessarily for *bhittikāḥ*. So this procedure does not involve any dropping of consonants, though such a thing is not unknown to Aśoka inscriptions (*cf*. *ilokachasa* (G.) and *ialoka* (S.) with *hidalokikye* (K.) about the end of RE. XI). The change of *bhitti* into *bhitta* however is exactly analogous to that of *bhaṭi* into *bhaṭa* (see *bhaṭimayesu* (D.) and *bhaṭamayesu* (K. S. M.) of RE. V. In this connection attention may also be drawn to a verse occurring about the end of the *Kaliṅgabodhi-Jātaka* (*Jāt*., Vol. IV, p. 236): *mahāyitvāna Sambodhiṃ nānā-turiyehi vajjamānehi, mālāgandhavilepanam = āharitvā pākāra-parikkhepam. kāresi*. What is curious is that here we have not only the word *mahāyitvāna* which corresponds to *mahīyite* of this edict, but also the mention of *pākāraparikkhepa* or erection of walls which corresponds to *bhichā kārāpita.* The birth site of Buddha was almost as holy a place to a Buddhist as Sambodhi where he attained to enlightenment. And if there were *mahāyitatva* and *prākāra-parikshepa* at the latter, there is no reason why the same should not be at the former also. It is but natural if Aśoka also did worship at the birth-place of Buddha by playing musical instruments and offering wreaths and fragrant pigments. Compare the expression *pūjā-śilā-prākāro* occurring in an inscription at Nagarī (MASI., No. 4, pp. 119 and 128ff.) where a huge stone enclosure wall called Hāthi-bāḍā still exists.

For previous explanations, see EI, Vol V., p. 5; S. B. Pr. A. W., 1903, pp. 724 ff.; IA., 1905, pp. 1 ff.; 1914, pp. 19-20. For Barua's interpretation, see *Aśoka Edicts in New Light*, pp. 86 f. He takes *vigaḍa=vikaṭa* (or=*vikṛita*) and quotes the authority of Buddhaghosha to show that *vikṛitika* signifies 'a figure.' And this enables him at once to suggest that here *silā-vigaḍa* represents indefinitely the 'crowning stone-figure' and that *bhī* "is just an expletive particle *hi*"! But if *vigaḍa* stands here for *vikṛita*, surely a better interpretation of the expression would be "sculptured (*vigaḍa*) walls (*bhīchā*) of stone (*silā*)." For a new interpretation, see S. N. Mitra's article in IHQ., 1929, p. 748. According to him, *silā vigaḍa-bhīchā* (=*vikaṇḍa-bhittiyā*) *kālā pita* means 'stone was worked in or upon the post-base', that is, 'stone was caused to be scrapped to smoothness.'

[3] F. W. Thomas was the first to take *bali* rightly in the sense of 'religious cess' (JRAS., 1909, pp. 466-7). For his correct interpretation of *aṭha-bhāgiya*, see JRAS., 1914, pp. 391-2.

Bibliography

Bühler, G.—EI., Vol. V, pp. 4 and ff.

Smith, V. A.—IA., 1905, pp. I and ff.; and Intro. to Mukherji's Report on Antiquities in the Tarai, Nepal, Calcutta, 1901.

Fleet, J. F.—JRAS., 1908, pp. 471 and ff.

Charpentier, J.—IA., 1914, pp. 17 and ff.

NIGLIVA INSCRIPTION

Translation

King Priyadarśin, Beloved of the gods, when he had been consecrated fourteen years, enlarged the *stūpa* of Buddha Konākamana to double its size.[1] And when he had been consecrated (twenty) years, he came in person, did worship, and had (a stone pillar) erected.

Note

[1] Hult., rightly compares *dutiyaṃ vaḍhite* of this inscription to *diyāḍhiyaṃ vaḍhisati* of the Sahasrām Edict.

INSCRIPTION ON THE SARNATH PILLAR

Translation

Thus orders King Priyadaśin, Beloved of the gods : ....Pāṭaliputra..............the Saṃgha may not be divided by any one. But whosoever breaks the Saṃgha, be it a monk or a nun, shall be clad in white raiment, and compelled to live in what is not a residence[1] (of the mendicants). Thus should this order be respectfully communicated to the Saṃgha of the monks and the Saṃgha of the nuns.

Thus saith beloved of the gods: One such document has been deposited in (your) office in order that it may be accessible to you.[2] And deposit just another such document so as to be accessible to the laity. And these laity should come every fast-day, in order to assure themselves of that same order. And certainly on all fast-days as each[3] Mahāmātra comes in his turn (to the headquarters) for fast, he should assure himself of that same order and understand it. And so far as your jurisdiction[4] goes, you must set out on tour with this specification (of order). So too in all fortified towns and (the) district sub-divisions,[5] you must cause (subordinates) to go out on tours with this specification (of order).

Notes.

[1] The robes of a Buddhist Monk are yellow-coloured, and when he is given white robes, it means that he is unfrocked (Oldenburg's *Vinayapiṭaka*, Vol. III, p. 312, l. 18; also JPASB., 1908, pp. 7-10). As regards *anāvāse*, Venis quotes Buddhaghosha's explanation in SBE., XVII, p. 388, n. 1. But here *anāvāsa* is distinguished from *a-bhikshuka-āvāsa* and taken in the sense of 'a residence unworthy of a mendicant' such as a cemetery, privy and so forth. Aśoka, however, cannot mean this. His

object is only to remove a schismatic from where Bhikshus stay and unfrock him.

[2] The king is, of course, addressing himself to the Mahāmātras; and not to the Bhikshus as supposed by some. The dictionary meanings of *saṃsaraṇa* are 'highway,' 'meeting of junction' and so on, and the word in the present case most probably denotes the *Kacheri* of the district town, which is both on the highway and a common place of meeting. F. W. Thomas' reference to the word in the *Chullavagga* (JRAS., 1915, pp. 109-111) may also denote the standardised type of the *Kacheri* structure.

[3] Hult.: "and invariably on every fast-day, every *Mahāmātra* (will) come to the fast-day service in order to be inspired with confidence in this very edict and to understand (it)." This does not however bring out fully and properly the sense of *ikike*=Sk. *ekaiko*, which means 'one by one, one taken singly, a single one.' According to Hult., all Mahāmātras came on all fast-days. What Aśoka however seems to mean is that one Mahāmātra came on one fast-day, another on another fast-day, and so on. This agrees with *kāmaṃ chu khanasi khanasi aṃtalā pi Tisena ekena pi sotaviya* which occurs about the end of SRE, II. (Dh. ll. 10-11 and Jaug. ll. 15-16).

[4] *Āhāra* means 'a district,' and is frequently found used in this sense in early inscriptions. For *vivasayātha* and general interpretation of this passage, see IA., 1912, p. 172.

[5] Every district (*āhāra*) has more than one subdivision (*vishaya*) or Taluk as it is now called. The principal town of each sub-division must have been a fortified place (*koṭṭa*) (see EI., VIII. 171). Notice the difference between *vivāsayātha* and *vivāsāpayāthā*. The latter is the causal form of the former. If in the first case the Mahāmātras are asked to set out on tour (*vivāsayātha*),

in the second case they are asked to cause others to set out on tour (*vivāsāpayāthā*). These 'others' must be the subordinates of the Mahāmātras; and if *āhāra* or district is the more extensive jurisdiction of the latter, the *vishaya* or Taluk must be the less extensive jurisdiction of the subordinates.

Bibliography

Vogel, J. Ph.—EI., Vol. VIII, pp. 166 and ff.

Venis, Arthur—JASB., 1907, pp. 1 and ff.

Senart, E.—Comptes rendus de l'Academie Inscriptions, 1907, p. 25.

Boyer—JA., Tome X (1907), p. 119.

Inscription on the Sanchi Pillar

[Facsimile of this epigraph may be seen in EI. II. on plate facing p. 369. It is accompanied by a transcript of Bühler, which was afterwards considerably corrected by Hultzsch with the help of excellent *estampages* supplied by the Archaeological Department. His amended reading is contained in JRAS., 1911, pp. 167-9 and in CII. Vol. I.]

Translation

The Saṃgha of monks and of nuns has been made whole and entire, my sons and grandsons (continuing as long as the sun and the moon endure). Whosoever breaks the Saṃgha, be he a monk or a nun, shall be clad in white raiment and compelled to live in what is not a residence (of the mendicants). For my desire is—what is it?—that the Saṃgha may remain whole and entire and may be of long duration.

Inscriptions on the Allahabad Pillar

A. [This also specifies the penalty of schism and is a replica of the preceding two. Very little of this epigraph has been preserved and the only new and important fact revealed by it is that it contains an order of Aśoka addressed to his Mahāmātras in Kauśambī, showing clearly where the pillar was originally put up.]

B. The Queen's Edict

Translation

By command of the Beloved of the gods the Mahāmātras should everywhere be addressed. "Whatever gift there be here of the Second Queen, be it a mango-grove, an orchard, an alms-house, or aught else, register ye all that as 'of the Second Queen, that is, of Kāruvākī, mother of Tīvara.' "[1]

Notes

[1] By notifying the charities of his Second Queen, Aśoka is apparently holding up her example for imitation by the other members of the royal household (*Above*, pp. 133 and ff). Compare with this also the last sentence of R E. III. and its interpretation given on p. 267 above. What Aśoka means is that the charities of this queen are not to be registered merely and vaguely as those of 'the Second Queen' but more specifically by name (*vyañjana*) as those of Kāruvākī, Mother of Tīvara. Kāruvākī reminds us of names like Gautamī, Vāsisthī and such others as occur in Inscriptions of the early centuries of the Christian Era. There are many Gotra names

corresponding to it, namely, Kārāvaya, Kāravacha and so forth, which are perhaps corrupt forms of the original Kāruvāka.

Bibliography

Bühler, G.—IA., Vol. XIX, pp. 124-6.
Hultzsch, E.—JRAS., 1911, pp. 1113-4.
Mitra, S. N.—IHQ, Vol. VII, pp. 458-463.

Barabar Hill Cave Inscriptions

Translation

A.—This Banyan cave was given to the Ājīvikas by King Priyadarśin when he had been anointed twelve years.

B.—This cave in the Khalatika Hill was given to the Ājīvikas, when he had been anointed twelve years.

C.—King Priyadarśin, when he had been anointed nineteen years......in the Kha latika Hill].

Bibliography

Bühler, G.—IA., Vol. XX, p. 364.

INDEX

PAGE

PAGE